RESISTANCE

The LGBT Fight Against Fascism in WWII

Written by Avery Cassell

Edited by Diane Kanzler

Foreword by Laura Antoniou

Stacked Deck Press
Dana Point, California

To my parents, Frances Morton and Bill Sumner,
who raised me to be a troublemaker.

—Avery Cassell

RESISTANCE: The LGBT Fight Against Fascism in WWII
Written by Avery Cassell
Edited by Diane Kanzler
Foreword by Laura Antoniou

184 pages, softcover

Stacked Deck Press
PO Box 922
Dana Point, CA 92629
www.stackeddeckpress.com

Front cover art by Jon Macy. Back cover art drawn by Jon Macy, colored by Avery Cassell.
Book design and layout by Diane Kanzler.

Title font: Day Poster Black NF, designed by Nick Curtis, www.nicksfonts.com
Subtitle font: Berlin Sans FB Demi Bold, designed by David Berlow
All other fonts: Adobe Garamond Pro Family

Stacked Deck Press logo by Gillian Cameron and Tara Madison Avery.
Images are credited where possible, and all efforts have been made to identify the sources of all images.

ISBN: 978-0-9996472-2-6
SDP00011
Printed in the United States

INTRODUCTION
by Avery Cassell and Diane Kanzler

Welcome to *Resistance: The LGBT Fight Against Fascism in WWII*. Inside these pages, you will discover the lives and loves of brave LGBT individuals during WWII. The book started out as a conversation between two people around the question: what can one do in the face of growing fascism and bigotry in one's own country? What can we learn from the past? Raising awareness seemed vital, looking to the past was important, and taking action became a moral necessity.

The natural answer to these questions was, for us, to create this book. The creation of books is, itself, an act of resistance, and we tapped into the creativity of brave and outraged artists and friends in the LGBTQ+ community of 2018 to connect to the past, full circle. Twenty-two artists and writers from around the world became resistors in our own way in bringing this book to you. *Resistance: The LGBT Fight Against Fascism in WWII* started out as a coloring book, much like its predecessors, the historical *Butch Lesbians Coloring Books* series, but quickly transformed into so much more.

The people documented in this book prove that resistance can take many shapes, from forging identity documents, writing anti-fascist poetry, and providing shelter to refugees, to flummoxing Nazis with anti-fascist leaflets. The act of resistance is not a one-size-fits-all political activity; we must utilize our unique individual talents to resist in creative and timely ways. We hope the stories of the activists' personal lives, their activities both heroic and intimate, and—in some cases—their tragic, too-soon deaths will inspire you to find your voice. Become a resistor in your own way, in your own life, in your own town, during these trying and anxiety-ridden times for so many of us—all power to the people!

Despair into action.

Plowshares into swords.

Long live the Resistance.

Avery Cassell, author
Diane Kanzler, editor and designer
2018

Acknowledgements

Many thanks to the artists who illustrated this book and brought brave, beloved faces from the past into the present. Our love, our tears, and our thanks go to every activist featured, and to all the resistance fighters from that era right into the present. Thank you to Tara Madison Avery of Stacked Deck Press for nurturing and publishing this project, to Laura Antoniou for writing a heartfelt Foreword, and to Jon Macy for creating the inspiring cover art. We would like to thank the following organizations and individuals who assisted in the creation of this book, giving freely of time, resources, information, and enthusiastic support: The San Francisco Public Library, particularly the staff of the James C. Hormel LGBTQIA Center and the staff of the San Francisco History Center and Photograph Collection, The GLBT Historical Society in San Francisco, Gerard Koskovich, Jassy Casella Timberlake, Gabriel Clark, Sasha T. Goldberg, Paul Volkner, Gregory Johnson, and Larry-Bob Roberts. The editor would like to thank author Avery Cassell for diving bravely, with no life-vest, into the world of historical non-fiction and citations, and for being such a pleasure to work alongside. Finally, the author would like to give special thanks to the wonderful staff at the San Francisco Botanical Garden in Golden Gate Park for providing greatly needed respite as they wrote this often heartbreaking book.

Credits:

The drawing of Vera Lachmann is inspired from the photograph owned by Ron Blau, used with permission. Photo taken in dormitory, known as "The Citadel," at Camp Catawba, Blowing Rock, NC, circa 1967. The unicorn in the "Feed Your Queer Brain" icon on the title page is from an illustrated book by Edward Topsell, c. 1607, image courtesy of the Wellcome Collection and reproduced under the Creative Commons license (https://creativecommons.org/licenses/by/4.0/). The illustration on page i was drawn by Avery Cassell. The illustration on page iii was drawn by Diane Kanzler. The illustrations on pages 34, 62, 78, 86 and 126 were drawn by Jon Macy. The illustrations on the copyright page and page 167 were drawn by Rachael House. The illustration on page 177 was drawn by Burton Clarke.

TABLE OF CONTENTS

FOREWORD
by Laura Antoniou

When they asked me to do the Foreword to this book, my immediate answer was "no." I'm not an academician, I'm not a historian, I didn't even know most of the names of the people being highlighted in this amazing collection of chiaroscuros. When they asked me to reconsider, I was still hesitant. Right now, the world feels like an awful place: there is a hateful dictator wanna-be in the White House, and a man accused of raping at least one woman has been sworn into the Supreme Court. Immigrant families are being separated, and hundreds of their children have disappeared in the process. More and more women are speaking up about sexual abuse, and more and more acts of violent racism and homophobia are splashed across the headlines. Every day feels like we are facing another wave of attacks on civil liberties, democracy, justice, and common decency. To be honest, I can't even do my own writing, much less write introductions for other people, because I feel lost in despair and existential dread.

Still, they persisted. One must respect the persistence of righteous voices.

So I read the bios of some of the activists highlighted in this book. As I did, I realized I knew more than I had guessed I would—but not *enough* about any except a very few.

Here's the thing: when historians write biographies, they can choose to emphasize or remove parts of the story that help drive the narrative of the person they're talking about. As a novelist, I do the same—why tell you the parts that don't drive the story forward?

But these aren't fictional people. They were real. When you read a phrase like "they joined the French Resistance," it doesn't tell you what finally drove them to do it. Did fear of losing everything compel him? Did a lover entice them to go to a meeting? Was she brave, or in the grasp of such horrible tragedy all she could think of was vengeance?

Why would Alberta Hunter, who headed the first all-black USO show and had a thirty-year singing career, suddenly leave at the height of her fame and become a nurse? The biographies simply state "when her mother died, Hunter left singing and went to nursing school." It must have been a terrible loss for her—a mother who was likely born into slavery and remained by her daughter's side all her life. But Hunter also hid her singing career from her fellow nurses for decades. Was she suffering from emotional fatigue? From the persistent toxin of systemic racism/sexism that faces independent black women? Or was it an act of freedom?

Then there's Sjoerd Bakker, Frieda Belinfante, Willem Arondeus, and their friends who bombed the Amsterdam Public Records Office, so that the Jewish population of that city could not be identified and sent to concentration camps. It does not take away from this righteous act that the actual design and implementation of this event sounds like a badly plotted caper movie. I imagine them bolstering each other's misgivings with schnapps-enhanced bravado and songs of resistance, leaning on each other's love even as they planned an action that could only end with death.

So many stories end in death that came too soon.

I was particularly struck by the inclusion of bar owners in this collection, and thinking of the queer bar owners I've known in my life. Did they go into the business to create a place for radical activists to meet? Not likely—they went into the business because they thought they could make a dollar or two, and to give folks like them a place to feel safe while they had a drink. I remember talking to my friend Chuck Renslow (of blessed memory), who owned Chicago's Gold Coast Bar, where the International Mr. Leather contest was born. He wasn't planning to create a world-wide event celebrating BDSM, Chuck told me. He started the contest to inspire men to stay in the bar longer to admire the sexy contestants.

This doesn't take away from Chuck, or from Lotte Hahm, or Bet van Beeren, in this book. What it does is *humanize* them for me. We may now think of them as being very brave—opening such radical places that became community centers for the queers and outcasts and shady cultural subversives of their time. But I also think it's equally likely that they opened and ran these businesses for the simple reason that *no other bars would have wanted them as patrons*. And when they saw dangers coming to their community, they did their best to warn others—but as business owners, it wasn't likely that they could leave themselves.

Lotte and Bet are reminders that most of us don't decide as children to grow up to be activists. Activism is often thrust upon us because of how we look, the spaces we take, the lovers and stories we shared. Activism—whether in the corporate world of lobbyists and boardrooms or the scrappy resistance grown out of frustration and anguish in the face of unbearable loss or because our backs are up against the wall and we reach out to clasp the hands of the people near us for comfort and a sense of solidarity—is all one story.

The story of people who, nevertheless, persisted.

That doesn't make these people any less revolutionary. It allows for us to see them as human. In the cracks of the stories the biographer has dug up about these amazing radicals and visionaries, there must have been moments of rage, grief, betrayal, despair, fear, and dread—all those emotions I am currently feeling.

Like Tatamkhulu Afrika, who learned at the age of 17 from his South African parents that he was adopted and oh, yes, he was not white.

Or Nadine Hwang, a successful attorney and daughter of diplomats, surviving in the Ravensbrück death camp.

And like Alan Turing, who helped win World War II, but could never be publicly thanked for it; Alan was, instead, arrested, tortured by his own government, and driven to suicide.

Good historians do their best to stick to facts: written documents, recollections of those who lived in the time, comparisons of times and dates. Of course, if family, friends, or editors and other gatekeepers work to obscure those facts because of homophobia, sexism or racism, that life is even harder to uncover.

No, I'm not an academician, nor a historian. I am a fiction writer. But fiction is just the distillation of the real stories we live, bound together in pleasing shape much like the array of drawings you will soon be bringing to life in glorious colors. Just don't mistake "pleasing shape" for "easy," or "ending happily." The tragedies and dramas of fiction come from the worst things we have ever done to each other in real life.

These are activists who faced dark, fearful times. Their written histories may only include the actions they took, but my curious mind fills in the *feelings* they may have experienced as well. I *want* to know that my feelings of rage and despair were felt by other queer people at other times in history. I want to read what they did, even while feeling those moments now. I want to feel a camaraderie, a continuum of progress in the great struggles that span generations. I want to draw strength from our commonalities while honoring their heroism and seeing it reflected now in the faces of teenagers crying out for their lives, in fists held up in staunch unity sweeping through the streets past scenes of modern martyrdom, in the suburban moms discovering their voices while the urban punks exhaust their own, in the subversive "secret" online groups and the furious shouts making red-faced white men seek refuge in their private elevators and toilets, away from howls of wounded women.

May we all draw strength as we paint in the colors. May we all continue the work in comforting the afflicted and afflicting the comfortable. Because as we see from the people in this collection you hold, the foundations have been laid for us over generations. We are not required to complete the repair of the world, the rabbis remind us, but we are not excused from these labors.

Use all the colors you have.

Laura Antoniou
New York City
2018

Laura Antoniou's rambling publishing career started with creating and editing the groundbreaking gaming/media magazine Gateways *back in the 80s, followed by her work on the* People With AIDS Newsline *for several years during those dark days. Now, she's better known for her kinky erotica, especially for the* Marketplace *books, a BDSM-themed series well outside the tropes of romance novels.* The Killer Wore Leather*, her first mystery, lampooned a kinky gathering of leather enthusiasts. 2018-19 will see the release of a second* Marketplace *fan-fiction collection and* Silk Threads*, her unique collaboration with Cecilia Tan and Midori. Laura's been teaching human sexuality topics for decades; lately, she's combined her passions into a series of workshops themed "Get Your Freak On With Your Geek On," because compartmentalism is annoying, and geeky sex is fun sex. She's a knee-jerk, bleeding-heart, tax-and-spend, queer-as-possible Jewish feminist. Keep up with her or hit block/ignore at: https://www.facebook.com/laura.antoniou, https://twitter.com/LAntoniou, https://www.patreon.com/Kvetch, http://lauraantoniou.tumblr.com/*

Nadine Hwang, a.k.a. *la Amazona del Norte*
1902–1970s, Spain/China/France/Venezuela/Belgium
drawn by Anne Williams

Nadine Hwang was a debonair butch, a sword-dancing lawyer, a linguist who was fluent in Chinese, French, Spanish, English, and Italian, an airplane pilot, an officer in the Chinese National Revolutionary Army, and likely a spy for the French Resistance. Natalie Barney, the notorious owner of the *L'Académie des Femmes* (Women's Academy), novelist, and Parisian lesbian Casanova, employed Nadine as her assistant and shared her bed with her. Dolly Wilde, Oscar's boyish and debauched niece and one of Natalie's closest lovers, detested her.

Nadine was born to an upper class Chinese-Belgian family in Spain. Her father was the Chinese Minister to Spain and her mother was Belgian. In 1912, the last emperor of China, Hsian-T'ung, abdicated, ending 2,000 years of imperial rule in China. When the government in China changed, the Hwang family then moved from Spain back to China, where she was raised. In 1926, she served in the *Guómín Gémìng Jūn* (the Chinese National Revolutionary Army) as a liaison officer, possibly under General Lo Jui-ch'ing. Nadine was then given the honorary title of colonel.[1] While living in China, she took correspondence courses with Hamilton College in Chicago and graduated with a law degree. In 1927, Nadine worked as Premiere Pan Fu's press secretary in the Bureau of Economic Information of China.[2] Nadine was glamorous, elegant, hard working, hard playing, and brilliant. She was given the nickname *la Amazona del Norte* by her admirers, played cricket or polo in the spring and summer and ice hockey in the winter, and cavorted every night, dancing the foxtrot and the Charleston.[3]

In 1933, Nadine moved to Paris, France, where she told newspaper reporters that she studied "economic conditions with a view to extending Sino-French intellectual and commercial relations."[4] In 1934, Nadine met her match and sister namesake, *l'amazone*, Natalie Barney.[5] Natalie was in her late 50s, generously polyamorous, and had been hosting the lesbian artist's salon *L'Académie des Femmes* at her home at 20 rue de Jacob since 1927. By the time *l'amazone* and *Amazona del Norte* crossed paths, they both were legendary Parisian power lesbians. The literary soirée was held each Friday between 4:30 and 8:00 p.m., often spilling into the garden where there was a Doric temple with the words *à l'amité* (to friendship) carved over its entrance.[6] The famed spy Mata Hari rode through one party on a white horse and nude except for jewels, Pulitzer Prize winning feminist poet Edna St. Vincent Millay read at the salon, as did the author of *The Well of Loneliness*, Radclyffe Hall.

By 1934, Nadine was a comely butch, elegant and mysterious. She and Natalie quickly became lovers, with Nadine acting as Natalie's chauffeur, secretary, and errand boy. Nadine was an honored guest at Natalie's *L'Académie des Femmes*, performing a ravishing sword dance and presenting alternatively as a "piratical"[7] or as a handsome young gay man. Natalie had several serious long-term lovers, including the famed painter of lesbians, Romaine Brooks, and the divine raconteur, Dolly Wilde. Dolly started using opioids after serving in WWI and was suffering from addiction, depression, the beginnings of what turned out to be fatal breast cancer, and possibly war-induced PTSD. Dolly and Nadine locked horns over Natalie. Dolly had returned to London from Paris, and in her absence Nadine was cavorting with her beloved Natalie.

Dolly was vicious in her jealousy of Nadine, writing cattily to Natalie, "Darling, don't have N. [Nadine] back again. Nothing to do with me as I shan't be in your house but for *yourself*. She is *so* shallow. Has been in high spirits after two days from your departure– boasting of her many conquests & her power over you!"[8]

Not to be outdone, Nadine wrote to Natalie about Dolly in March, 1935: "Darlingest Own, It is absolutely imperative the D. [Dolly] leaved the house at once….Apart from daily drugging and small packets of stuff being found in D.'s hand-bag, a letter from M.F.D. who had gone to Fontainebleau at D.'s instigation to fetch *150 kilograms of opium*, was also found in the same hand-bag….The proof of the abominable traffic in which these two are indulging is enough, it seems, for you to act *immediately*….My ultimatum is: either you make D. evacuate your house *at once* or I will do it myself, and my arguments will be persuasive you can be assured of that…"[9]

The years prior to the start of WWII were tumultuous. Certainly, the unease that was affecting the continent also affected Dolly, Nadine, Natalie, and their compatriots. By March 1933, fascism was spreading across the continent. Next door in Germany, Hitler was appointed Chancellor and the *Gesetz zur Behebung der Not von Volk und Reich* (Enabling Act of 1933, or the Law to Remedy the Distress of People and Reich) was passed. The Enabling Act of 1933 was the beginning of institutionalized anti-Semitic, anti-homosexual, and anti-Romani legislation in Germany. Benito Mussolini, the founder of Italian Fascism, had been lording over Italy since 1919. The Spanish Civil War would commence in 1936. When WWII started with Hitler's invasion of Poland in September of 1939, France joined the war against Hitler and Germany within days.

By 1940, Dolly, perhaps remembering her years during WWI in Paris driving ambulances and rescuing the wounded and dying, had fled the approaching Germans to return to England to die of breast cancer and drug addiction. Natalie fled to Italy and Nadine stayed in Paris. On June 14, 1940 the first German Nazi troops entered the City of Light, starting an occupation that lasted until August of 1944.

In 1944, shortly before the liberation of Paris from the Nazi occupation, Nadine was arrested and sent to the Ravensbrück concentration camp for women. Although we don't know why she was arrested, there are rumors that she worked underground in the French Resistance while disguised in a German Gestapo uniform.[10] A woman who Nadine babysat for after the war in the 1960s reminisced, "When I was a teen I found a box with some of her belongings (letters, photos etc). At the time it was taboo to talk of her sexuality so most unfortunately my parents got rid of the box. I managed to read some of the letters, the ones in English and French. The others were in German. I remember there was one picture of her with a young man, both of them in what seemed German military attire."[11] With Nadine's background in the Chinese military and her love of risk, this seems plausible. Nadine was arrested in Paris around the same time as documented member of the French Resistance, Geneviève de Gaulle,[12] then they were transferred to Ravensbrück. Nadine spent approximately one year in Ravensbrück.

Women in Ravensbrück were divided into categories, made to wear a color-coded cloth triangle sewn onto their clothing, and assigned to a block; Polish women wore red, criminals wore green, Jehovah's Witnesses wore lavender, and Jewish women wore yellow. Prostitutes, Romani, lesbians, and spinsters were in one category, and assigned to wear black triangles. Within Ravensbrück, lesbians were considered the lowest of the low among the prisoners and looked upon with horror. Women who were interviewed after the war said that there were, "ugly and inhumane acts of lesbian love"[13] and described the women wearing black triangles as being "from Sodom and Gomorrah"[14] possessing horrifying "moral filth."[15] We can only guess that Nadine may have been placed in the asocials or lesbian block. Ravensbrück was known for its propensity for medical experimentation upon its prisoners. In January of 1945, a gas chamber was constructed for mass killings. When it was obvious that the Germans were losing the war, there was a concerted effort to kill as many prisoners as possible. Of the total of 130,000–132,000 prisoners in Ravensbrück between 1939 and 1945, only 15,000 survived to be freed.

While in Ravensbrück, Nadine became close friends with a Jewish woman named Rachel Krausz and her nine-year-old daughter Irène. In 1945, the Swedish Red Cross negotiated with the Nazis to rescue approved prisoners from Ravensbrück. The Swedish Red Cross painted the buses white with red crosses to mark them as rescue vehicles, and the operation was called *Vita bussarna* (White Buses). Thousands of women and children from Ravensbrück were rescued by the White Buses during April of 1945. On April 25, 1945, Nadine, Rachel, and Irene were three of the fortunate people to leave Ravensbrück in a White Bus. The three of them arrived in Malmö, Sweden on April 28, 1945. Many years later, Irene named her own daughter "Nadine."[15]

After Malmö, Nadine moved to Brussels where she met a former resistance fighter named Claire Mousset, a.k.a. Nelly Voss. Claire worked at the Embassy of Venezuela and, impressed with the pacifist nature of the country, the couple moved to Venezuela. They were happy in their new country, often entertaining their friends and socializing. A friend, Jose Rafael Lovera, recollected: "When I met Nadine she was already settled in Venezuela. She and Claire often invited groups of friends, amongst others my wife and I. The Consul General of France and his wife, and the fashion designer Guy Meliet, were also part of this group....Nadine was an excellent cook and she had a special grace; I remember a Chinese dance which she performed on one occasion with such delicate movements. Her outstanding intelligence and impressive talents were other powerful characteristics of her personality."[16] Sometime in the late 1960s, Nadine started suffering from health issues, so she and Claire moved back to Brussels. It is believed that Nadine Hwang died in the 1970s.

Resources

Gertten, Magnus, dir. *Every Face Has a Name*. By Jesper Osmund. Sweden: Auto Images, 2015. December 4, 2015. Accessed September 23, 2018. https://vimeo.com/ondemand/everyfacehasaname/119082619.

Gertten, Magnus, dir. *Harbour of Hope*. By Lars Åberg. Sweden: Auto Images. DVD.

Nadine Hwang, drawn by Anne Williams

This page is intentionally blank to facilitate coloring the reverse side.

Josephine Baker
1906–1975, United States/France
drawn by Margo Rivera-Weiss

Josephine Baker was a glamorous and sophisticated comedic dancer, singer, French Resistance fighter, civil rights activist, mother, and bisexual. A tender-hearted lover of animals and children, she adopted twelve children ("The Rainbow Tribe"), a cheetah named Chiquita, a pig, goats, dogs, a zebra, and several monkeys.

Josephine was born in Missouri to a husband and wife vaudeville team, sometimes appearing with them as a child performer. Her family was poor, and when she was only eight years old, she started working as a live-in domestic maid to help out. As a child, Josephine was periodically homeless on the streets of St. Louis and busked to earn money to eat. At age 13, she got a job as a waitress, married Willie Wells, and quickly divorced him. In 1920 and at age 14, she joined the Jones Family Band, began appearing in vaudeville theater, and started seeing the singer Clara Smith. The same year, she met a pretty boy Pullman porter named Willie Baker[1] while touring with the troupe and married him, keeping the surname "Baker" as her working name for the rest of her life.

In 1921, Josephine moved to New York City and immersed herself in the rich culture of the Harlem Renaissance where lesbian, gay, and bisexual artists flourished. Scholar and literary critic Henry Gates, in the foreword of *Gay Rebel of the Harlem Renaissance* noted, "The movement that enabled outsider Negro artists to emerge as a group for the first time was also the movement that enabled gay and lesbian artists to express their sexuality with a greater degree of freedom than at any other period in American history."[2]

Josephine was in her element in New York's glamorous, sexually permissive Harlem Renaissance. Fellow entertainer Maude Russell talked about lesbian and bisexual women during that era: "We had girl friendships, the famous lady lovers, but lesbians weren't well accepted in show business, they were called bull dykers. I guess we were bisexual, is what you'd call it today."[3] Between 1921 and 1923, Josephine acted and danced in the touring hit musical *Shuffle Along* to comedic success. Josephine was sleeping with a doe-eyed dancer named Little Shep while touring with *Shuffle Along*. When performing in Chicago, Josephine befriended Alberta Hunter, who subsequently followed Josephine to Paris. Josephine was nicknamed "Tumpy," and was comedic genius, copying a fellow dancer named Mama Dinks: "Dinks was nothing but a chorus girl….She was an ugly little thing, but she was funny…she had funny legs, she could bend them way back, and she did these antics, walkin' like a chicken, lookin' cross-eyed, and then she'd go offstage bowlegged with her butt stuck out."[4]

In 1925, Josephine sailed to Paris, France to seek her fortune. Like so many black Americans in that era, Josephine moved to Paris to join her compatriots and escape racism in the U.S. She said, "I just couldn't stand America and I was one of the first coloured Americans to move to Paris."[5] She appeared in *La Revue Nègre* at the grand Art Deco *Théâtre des Champs-Élysées*. Josephine became a hit; her erotic dancing, sense of humor, and skimpy costumes drew wildly enthusiastic crowds, and she went on to tour Europe. After her tour, she returned to Paris to perform as a star entertainer at the renowned *Folies Bergère*. It was during this period that she became notorious for her *danse sauvage* while wearing her golden banana skirt, becoming a cultural icon.

Josephine was larger-than-life. Cabaret singer and choreographer Brian Bagley talked about her: "Everybody imagines something different when they come to Paris, but it's the Harlem of Paris that not everyone knows about but should, because that's where the energy is still so potent. Josephine was the center of it. She came here and—boom—she could live in a world without segregation. Boom, she was a major star. She lived that European dream we all want, of liberation and sexual freedom."[6]

It was during the 1930s that Josephine was gifted a cheetah by Henri Varna, the owner of the nightclub *Casino de Paris*. Josephine adored the cheetah, named the wild cat Chiquita, and bought it a diamond collar. A tale that *Vogue* magazine editor Diana Vreeland related about Josephine and Chiquita described them attending a screening of the film, *L'Atlantique* so that Chiquita could see the cheetahs in the movie, driving off in a white and silver Rolls Royce when the movie ended, then "Diana Vreeland describes how the driver opened the car door, Josephine let go of the cheetah's lead, Chiquita whooped and took one elongated leap into the back of the Rolls Royce, with Josephine Baker in her couture Vionnet dress leaping in behind. And then they were off with such speed and style."[7]

For such a forward and dramatic woman, Josephine was remarkably close-lipped about her female lovers. She continued to see women, including Ida "Bricktop" Smith, the legendary American singer and Paris nightclub owner; Colette, the French feminist novelist; and the brilliant Mexican painter, Frida Kahlo.

In 1937, Josephine married Jean Lion (a.k.a. Levy), a Jewish industrialist, and became a French citizen. When WWII started in 1939, Josephine joined the French Resistance. Her cover as an eccentric, glamorous performer served her well. Josephine's Resistance work was multifaceted; she ran a refugee center in Gare du Nord, sheltered refugees and hid weapons in her home, and wrote letters to soldiers who were fighting on the front. She surreptitiously gathered information at embassy cocktail parties to pass along to French Intelligence, including details about the movements of German troops and the intentions of Mussolini gleaned during receptions at the Italian and Portuguese embassies. Josephine famously "employed" French Resistance member Jaques Abtey as his cover in order to transmit information about German positions in the occupied zone. The valuable information was encrypted and written in disappearing ink on musical scores. She traveled to Spain and brought back missives pinned to her brassiere. Josephine said about her Spanish undercover trip, "It's very convenient to be Josephine Baker. As soon as I'm announced in a city, the invitations shower upon the hotel. In Seville, Madrid, Barcelona, the scenario is the same. I am fond of embassies and consulates that are teeming with interesting people. I take careful notes when I get home, and those papers would probably be compromising if they were found. But who would dare to search Josephine Baker down to bare skin? They are well hidden, fastened by a safety pin. Anyway, my passage through customs is always easy….The customs officials give me big smiles, and they do take papers from me, but those are autographs!"[8]

After the war, Josephine was awarded the *Croix de guerre* and was named a *Chevalier* of the *Légion d'honneur* for her work in the French Resistance. Josephine married again, this time to French orchestra leader Jo Bouillon. Josephine and Jo started adopting children, forming a Rainbow Tribe of twelve children of different nationalities and ethnicities. In 1949, Josephine successfully returned to the stage at the *Folies Bergère*.

In the 1950s and the 1960s, Josephine begin to tour in the U.S. again. She quickly became a spokesperson against the pervading racism in the States, writing newspaper articles and lecturing at colleges. In 1951, when Josephine was refused service at the popular Manhattan restaurant, the Stork Club, she got into a heated public tiff with news columnist Walter Winchell. Walter accused her of being a Communist, so she became blacklisted and her work visa was revoked. In 1963, she spoke at the March on Washington, standing at the side of Rev. Martin Luther King, Jr. She stood in front of 250,000 marchers in her Free French uniform emblazoned with her medal of the *Légion d'honneur* and said, "You know, friends, that I do not lie to you when I tell you I have walked into the palaces of kings and queens and into the houses of presidents. And much more. But I could not walk into a hotel in America and get a cup of coffee, and that made me mad. And when I get mad, you know that I open my big mouth. And then look out, 'cause when Josephine opens her mouth, they hear it all over the world."[9]

Josephine was singing in renowned international venues such as Carnegie Hall, *Gala du Cirque*, and The London Palladium in the decade before her death. On April 8, 1975, Josephine gave a command performance at the Bobino in Paris, *Joséphine à Bobino 1975*. Sometime the next day, she suffered a fatal cerebral hemorrhage while in her bed, surrounded by newspapers filled with rave reviews of her performance.

Resources

Abtey, Jacques. *La Guerre Secrète De Joséphine Baker*. Périgueux: La Lauze, 2002.

Baker, Jean-Claude, and Chris Chase. *Josephine: The Hungry Heart*. New York: Cooper Square Press, 2001.

Gibson, Brian, dir. T*he Josephine Baker Story*. Performed by Lynn Whitfield. United States: HBO Films, 1991. DVD. March 16, 1991.

Haney, Lynn. *Naked at the Feast: A Biography of Josephine Baker*. London: Robson Books, 2002.

Jules-Rosette, Bennetta, and Josephine Baker. *Josephine Baker in Art and Life: The Icon and the Image*. Urbana, IL: University of Illinois Press, 2007.

Jules-Rosette, Bennetta. *Josephine Baker in Art and Life: The Icon and the Image*. Urbana: University of Illinois Press, 2007.

Papich, Stephen. *Remembering Josephine Baker*. Indianapolis: Bobbs-Merrill, 1976.

Ross, Phyliss, *Jazz Cleopatra: Josephine Baker in Her Time*. New York: Vintage Books, 1991.

Archive

Harvard Library, HOLLIS for Archival Discovery, Josephine Baker papers, COLLECTION Identifier: MS Thr 497

Josephine Baker, drawn by Margo Rivera-Weiss

This page is intentionally blank to facilitate coloring the reverse side.

Claude Cahun, a.k.a. Lucy Renee Mathilde Schwob, Claude Courlis, Daniel Douglas
1894–1954, France/England
Marcel Moore, a.k.a. Suzanne Alberte Malherbe, a.k.a Bertie
1892–1972, France/England
drawn by Dorian Katz

Claude Cahun and Marcel Moore were lovers, collaborators, surrealist artists, anti-Nazi activists, and step-sisters. Claude was gender neutral before there was a word for this identity. She stated, "Masculine? Feminine? But it depends on the situation. Neuter is the only gender that always suits me."[1]

Claude Cahun was born in Nantes, France to a well-to-do, intellectual Jewish family. Her father, Maurice Schwob, owned and ran the family business, a Loire newspaper called *Le Phare de la Loire* (*The Lighthouse of the Loire*), and she had family members that were distinguished published writers, whose topics included pieces about Jewish customs and political treatises. In 1898, her mother was permanently confined to a mental institution and her paternal grandmother took over her care. Claude went to an English boarding school after being bullied for being Jewish in her local school, then attended the University of Paris, Sorbonne.

Marcel Moore was also born in Nantes, France to an educated family, and named Suzanne Alberte Malherbe at birth. Her father was a professor of histopathology at the School of Medicine, and Marcel studied at the town Fine Arts Academy.[2] In 1909 and at the age of 17, Marcel met Claude and they fell in love, becoming lifelong partners. After the couple met, Marcel's creativity went in the direction of illustration, while Claude experimented with photography and self-portraiture.

By 1913, Marcel was selling fashion illustrations to *Le Phare de la Loire* under the nom de plume Marcel Moore. The women she drew wore *la mode garçonne*, feminized menswear, were cheeky, louche, and relaxed, hands in pockets and confident in their physicality. In 1917, Marcel's mother remarried. The object of her second marriage was Maurice Schwob, her lover's father. With this marriage, Marcel and Claude became even more intertwined; step-sisters, lovers, and collaborators. This same year, Claude and Marcel moved in together into a top-floor apartment over the family newspaper offices in Nantes.

In 1917, when she was 25, Claude changed her professional name to from Lucy to Claude Cahun, saying, "I always used a pseudonym to write, the name of my obscure Jewish relatives (Cahun) with whom I felt more affinity."[3] Although she continued to use the name Lucy for some personal dealings, Claude Cahun remained her nom de plume. This is the same year that Claude started shaving her head and wearing men's suits, components of a lifelong fascination with the visual signifiers of gender identity, Jewish identity, femininity, masculinity, and sexuality.[4]

In 1919, the couple published their first collaboration, *Vues et Visions* (*Views and Visions*), with Marcel illustrating and Claude writing the book. Claude's dedication in the book read, "'To Marcel Moore' I dedicate this puerile prose to you so that your designs may redeem my text in our eyes."[5] Their intertwining relationship was apparent even in this simple dedication. In 1922, the couple moved to Paris, and became involved with the growing male-dominated and often sexist Surrealist art movement[6] and with experimental theater. Marcel created theatrical costumes, and Claude continued to take groundbreaking self-portraits; her work was 60 years ahead of its time and a precursor to Cindy Sherman's staged self-portraits, circa 1976–current.

In 1930, the couple published another collaborative book, *Aveux non Avenus* (*Disavowed Confession*). For years, all but one of the book's illustrations was attributed to Claude; however, critics have recently acknowledged that this was another collaborative work between the two artists. Misattribution proved to become a problem that plagued the couple throughout their career and long past their deaths. Although Marcel and Claude were explicit that they had a collaborative and egalitarian artistic relationship, critics have arrogantly insisted upon foisting Western hierarchical values upon their artistic collaborations, making Claude the art top and Marcel her less significant bottom.

As the political scenario in Europe led up to WWII in the early 1930s, Marcel and Claude were appalled by the spread of fascism across the continent. In 1932 they joined the anti-fascist, pacifist organization *Association des Ecrivains et Artistes Révoltionnaires* (Association of Revolutionary Writers and Artists), joining such luminaries as Henri Cartier-Bresson, Man Ray, and André Breton.

In 1937, the couple fled Paris for St. Brelade's Bay, Jersey, a small coastal resort town on an island located off the coast of Normandy, France. In addition to the bleak political climate and its divisive effects on the Paris avant-garde art community, were they also fleeing the difficulties of being lesbian feminist artists in the overtly sexist world of surrealism?

Once in St. Brelade's Bay, Claude and Marcel bought a home across the street from the St Brelade's Bay Hotel, where they had both vacationed when they were younger, and next to St Brelade's Church and cemetery. Their home was named *La Rocquaise*. They quickly established a reputation for eccentric behavior that was partially forgiven because they were artists. They were out as a lesbian couple when it wasn't especially common, were known for immodestly sunbathing in the nude, promenaded their cat on a leash, and scandalously sported men's clothing when such a thing was considered cross-dressing. Marcel started calling herself "Bertie," a diminutive of her middle name Alberte, and Claude reverted to Lucy, her middle name.

In 1939, WWII started and, in 1940, the German Nazis invaded and occupied Jersey and France. The couple quite deliberately decided to stay put in their new home rather than flee to safety and, really, there was very little safely to be had in Europe. They had been active anti-fascists in Paris, and would continue their activism in St. Brelade's Bay.

The lovers were inspired by "Colonel Britton" on the BBC, the pseudonym of Douglas Ritchie, who expanded the "V for Victory" campaign in 1941 and 1942, encouraging active and specific methods of subversion. With a burning love of their country and a deep hatred of the German Nazi soldiers, Marcel and Claude begun their two-person, anti-Nazi crusade. Marcel explained, they "used to take the salient points, translate them into German on small pieces of paper which were typed by my sister, and sign them 'The nameless German soldier'. We distributed them by placing them in cigarette paper cartons, matchboxes, and so on and placed them in German cars when and where we could. We used to make special trips to St Helier for this purpose."[7] Marcel and Claude's mission was to undermine the Nazis by targeting occupying German soldiers with their hand-typed anti-Nazi propaganda.

One of their anti-Nazi notes, typed on fragile cigarette wrapping paper, reads, "Which man has the people to sacrifice to save a government?—Is there a revolution in Germany? Certainly. And the longer the war, the longer and more confused the inevitable revolution, the worse the songs of our wives and children. So spoke the soldier without a name." [translated from German][8]

Their home was next to the cemetery where the Nazis buried their dead, so the couple would silently drop the notes into Nazi German staff cars during funerals, hoping to awaken their consciences. In 1944, the cigarette paper seller snitched out Claude and Marcel to the Nazis, and they were arrested and thrown into prison. Once on trial, they were sentenced to execution, with the judge stating, "...even though you used spiritual arms instead of firearms. It is indeed a more serious crime. With firearms, one knows at once what damage had been done, but with spiritual arms, one cannot tell how far-reaching it may be."[9]

On May 8, 1945, the last day of the German Occupation, they were released from prison; their home and much of their artwork had been destroyed by Nazi soldiers, and Claude's health suffered from the time spent in prison. Claude died in 1954, and Marcel committed suicide in 1972. Marcel and Claude are buried together in the St. Brelade's Church cemetery.

"If there is horror, it is for those who speak indifferently of the next war. If there is hate, it is for hateful qualities, not nations. If there is love, it is because this alone kept me alive."[10] –Claude Cahun

Resources

Cahun, Claude, and Marcel Moore. *Don't Kiss Me: The Art of Claude Cahun & Marcel Moore.* New York: Aperture/Tate, 2006.

Hammer, Barbara, dir. *Lover Other: The Story of Claude Cahun and Marcel Moore.* New York: An Outcast Films, Barbara Hammer Films Production, 2006. DVD.

Shaw, Jennifer L. *Exist Otherwise: The Life and Works of Claude Cahun.* London: Reaktion Books, 2017.

Archive

Claude Cahun, Jersey Heritage, https://www.jerseyheritage.org/collection-items/claude-cahun

Claude Cahun and Marcel Moore, drawn by Dorian Katz

This page is intentionally blank to facilitate coloring the reverse side.

Thérèse Pierre
1908–1943, France
drawn by M Rocket

Thérèse Pierre was a feminist, a teacher, a Communist, and a member of the French Resistance. Although she is a well-known hero of the French Resistance in France, there is little written about her life in English, aside from the circumstances of her imprisonment and death in a French prison cell.

Thérèse was born in Épernay, France, a town renowned for its champagne and situated around 80 miles northeast of Paris. She came from a family of teachers; both Thérèse and her younger sister followed in their parents' footsteps. In 1929, Thérèse earned her partial professorship. She taught in schools in several towns throughout France. In the late 1920s and early 1930s, Thérèse became politically aware of class issues and joined the Communist party.[1] In 1929, Thérèse met another aspiring teacher named Emma Pitoizet while taking a preparatory class for the entrance examination at *L'École Normale Supérieure des filles de Fontenay-aux-Roses* (Higher School for Girls at Fontenay-aux-Roses) a primary teacher's training school. Although both women failed the exam, they developed a friendship. Thérèse and Emma were opposites; Thérèse was sensitive and serious, whereas Emma was unconventional and lively.

In September of 1930, Thérèse and Emma moved to Paris together for a year to study for the teacher's exam that they'd failed earlier. In Paris, the couple met Karl, a Jewish German Communist who'd fled Germany. Emma became Karl's lover, then Karl moved back to Germany. Thérèse and Emma got new jobs in different towns, Emma in Mende in southern France, and Thérèse in Creus in central France. As Thérèse and Emma wrote to one another, their friendship deepened until they became long distant lovers in an open relationship, with Emma continuing to write love letters to Karl. By 1931, Emma was declaring her love to Thérèse, "Therese, I'm so discreet that I am noisy; so light that I'm heavy; who buries her mystery deep inside herself when I shout at the rooftops. I love you."[2] and was concurrently smitten with Kurt in Germany: "In reviewing Karl. At times he attracts me violently, at times he exasperates me. He suddenly fell into a sea of desire, unleashed, nostalgic. I saw how he looked like a young wolf, too sure of himself, with his head wide, his chin split, his jaws hungry."[3]

In 1932, Emma, eager to be with both of her lovers, hatched a scheme to go to Germany, get impregnated by Karl, come back to France, and raise the resulting child with Thérèse. She wanted to name the baby girl Manuela, and suggested that they move to Dalmatia, Croatia, or Syria to raise her. She pointed out that Karl would not likely want to become involved with parenting. Before Emma could visit Karl in Germany, she met a businessman man named François and started seeing him. Emma sought to reassure her long distance girlfriend, the lovelorn Thérèse, "I'm guilty only of momentary betrayals. My little Jansenist with a bulging forehead, do not worry. As one can have desires to walk, to run, to swim, I have an obscure desire to love. This adventurous affair is just an experience and an emancipation." Karl confided to Thérèse that he was jealous of François, Thérèse encouraged Karl to be open and unpossessive, and Emma reassured Thérèse that she was her primary partner. Between October of 1933 until May of 1934, Thérèse and Emma lived together. Karl, heartbroken and bitter, decided to move on and started seeing another woman.

In 1934, with fascism blooming in Italy, the conservative Republicans gearing up for war in Spain, and the Nazis gaining power in Germany, Thérèse renewed her activism and encouraged Emma to join her in the Communist Party. The two of them begin reading the *Commune*, the official Communist Party newspaper, and attending anti-fascist meetings. Emma was enthusiastic, the idea of revolution acting upon her like an aphrodisiac; she wrote in her diary, "Read Lenin and sexual questions. Luminous happiness." Aware that Europe was on the verge of war, Emma wrote to Thérèse, "The war is hovering. We have to prepare for the future. I want to gather my strength to meet this upheaval….Try to work my little friend. My best friend, the strongest, the most tender and the most severe, I kiss you."

In the summer of 1935, Thérèse and Emma traveled to Russia, looking for feminist sisterhood and inspiration. They were enthralled with a vision of the future and returned to France revived and energetic. This was to come to a fast end, though. Emma had continued to brood about having a child, so when she met Marcel, a widower with two children, at a teachers conference that she attended with Thérèse in December, she was ripe for change. Marcel immediately pursued Emma, and the die was cast. In June of 1936, Emma married Marcel, turned her back on her past and her activism, returned the bundle of Thérèse's love letters to her, and settled into a middle class life of babies, domesticity, and a husband. Between 1936 and 1940, Emma had three children with Marcel. Marcel turned out to be a brute, a member of the National Socialist Party, and a Nazi. Emma docilely followed her husband, joining the women's Nazi groups, leaving Thérèse and their revolutionary aspirations behind.

Heartbroken about the breakup and the duplicitous Emma's drastic changes, Thérèse threw herself into activism. When the Spanish Civil War started in 1936, Thérèse worked with the refugees that sought safety in France from neighboring Spain. Around 500,000 Spaniards fled persecution and death, crossing the border into France, but France was hostile and disinterested in helping the refugees. WWII broke out in September of 1939, and France was quickly occupied by German Nazi forces. In September of 1942, Thérèse got a job teaching mathematics and science at *L'École Normale Supérieure des filles* (Higher School for Girls) in Fougères. She met up with Lieutenant-Colonel Pascal and join the *Francs-Tireurs et Partisans* (FTP), the armed resistance organization founded by the French Communist Party. A small, frail-looking but strong woman, Thérèse proved herself to be cool-headed, reserved, uncompromising, organized, demanding, cautious, and a natural leader. For the next year, Thérèse was the leader of the Fougères branch of the *Francs-Tireurs et Partisans* and managed over one hundred local resistance members. She also wrote pamphlets and newspapers for the FTP, was a courier of documents and of weapons such as explosives and grenades between French Resistance groups, sheltered people in her home, and provided people with false identification papers. Thérèse participated in the destruction of Gestapo trucks and an attack upon the *Feldkommandantur* (Field Commandant), the department which oversaw the administration of the occupied territories, the German *Kreiskommandanturen* (District Commandant) and the German occupation forces.

On October 21, 1943 Thérèse was arrested by the *Sicherheitsdienst* (SD, SS Intelligence Service) at her home in Fougères. Thérèse was transferred 32 miles away to Jacques-Cartier Prison in Rennes. Jacques-Cartier Prison was run by the French Gestapo, aided by the German military. Not only was it used to imprison a large number of suspected French Resistance members, but it also had a women's wing. The Gestapo, realizing that Thérèse was the leader of the Fougères branch of the *Francs-Tireurs et Partisans*, brought in the French Gestapo, the SPAC (Anti-Communist Police Bureau), to encourage Thérèse to name the other members in the group. They broke both of Thérèse's legs, tortured, and beat her for two straight days, but she did not talk. Her last words, heard through the central heating channel by another prisoner, Madame Lequeu, were, "They got nothing from me."[4] She was found hung with her stockings in her cell the following day.

Thérèse died at age 33. Thérèse was awarded the *Croix de guerre avec étoile d'argent* (Silver War Cross) and the highest level of the *Chevalier de la Légion d'Honneur* (Knight of the Legion of Honor) for her bravery and service in the French Resistance during WWII. There is a school in Fougères which is named after her, the *Collège Thérèse Pierre de Fougères*.

Resources

Hunzinger, Claudie. *Elles vivaient d'espoir*. Paris: Grasset, 2010.

Hunzinger, Robin, dir. *Où sont nos amoureuses*. Real Productions:France 3. 2007, DVD.

Terrenoire, Élisabeth. *Combattantes Sans Uniforme; Les Femmes Dans La Résistance*. Paris: Bloud Et Gay, 1946.

Thérèse Pierre, drawn by M Rocket

This page is intentionally blank to facilitate coloring the reverse side.

Pierre Seel
1923–2005, France
drawn by Rachael House

Pierre Seel was born in the family castle in historic Haguenau, France, a town close to the French-German border that had been passed back and forth several times between France and Germany over the centuries. Haguenau was declared a town in 1154. Pierre was one of five sons from a prosperous, close-knit, Catholic, working class family. His parents moved to Mulhouse and ran a popular patisserie with the family living in an apartment over the shop. Pierre felt his first attraction to other boys when he was 12 years old, when he became agog at the sight of nude men cavorting on the beach. By the time he was 15, he knew that he was gay and that this was at odds with his family, his friends, and the Catholic religion. He was ashamed of his homosexuality and struggled with confession in the Church. By the time Pierre was 17, he'd lost faith in Catholicism and no longer struggled with the Church.

WWII started in 1939, and Mulhouse was invaded and occupied by the German Nazis in 1940. When the Nazis arrived, Pierre was a 17-year-old gay teenager. Searching for identity, Pierre had started hanging out with the Zazou youth subculture and had found a group of gay friends. The Zazou were heavily influenced by black American jazz; the name of the group may be taken from Cab Calloway's delightful song "Zah Zuh Za." The Zazous were dandies and rebellious, the boys grew their hair long and wore flashy, baggy suits, while the girls wore jackets with exaggerated shoulder pads and wood-soled platform shoes. Pierre noted, "The Zazous were very obviously detested by the Nazis, who on the other side of the Rhine, had [for] a long time decimated the German cultural avant garde, forbidden jazz and all visible signs of... degenerations of Germanic culture…"[1] The Zazous were popular in Paris, but considered immoral and widely reviled. In addition to their interest in fashion and jazz music, the Zazous were anti-fascists. In 1942, French Jews were ordered to sew yellow stars inscribed with *Juif* to signify their Judaism onto their coats. One of the ways the Zazous expressed their solidarity with Jews was to wear yellow stars with "Zazou" instead of *Juif* written on the star. The blue-uniformed French fascist youth organization, *Jeunesse Populaire Française* (French Popular Youth) fought with the Zazous, beating them up and shaving their heads.[2]

Pierre had taken to dressing up in his flashy Zazou clothing and looking for sex at Le square Steinbach in Mulhouse, a popular cruising ground for gay men. Late one night in 1939, Pierre's beloved watch was lifted from him while he was there. The watch had been a communion gift from his godmother, so he reported the theft to the police. By admitting that he was at Le square Steinbach late at night, Pierre was also admitting that he was gay. The police officer bullied young Pierre about being a homosexual and added his name to the town's list of known homosexuals. By the time the Nazis occupied Mulhouse in 1940, Pierre's brothers had been drafted, Pierre had a boyfriend named Jo and a job as a window dresser, Jews were fleeing the province, and Pierre's family was helping their Jewish friends by hiding their possessions for safekeeping.[3] He was involved in the beginnings of the local French Resistance, replacing Nazi posters with resistance posters, carrying messages to other members, and mailing secretive letters. Because he was so young, he often flew under the Gestapo's radar.

All of this changed in May of 1941; the Nazis requisitioned the list of known homosexuals and arrested young Pierre along with several of his gay friends from Le square Steinbach. They called him *schweinehund* (filthy dog) tortured him, and raped him, all in an attempt to discover the names of other homosexuals in Mulhouse. The Gestapo outed Pierre to his family as a homosexual and, ten days later, shipped him 50 miles south to Schirmeck-Vorbrück internment camp. At the camp, his long hair was shorn and his shirt was marked with a blue bar, the sign of the asocial and the homosexual.[4] During Pierre's time at Schirmeck, he was tortured, submitted to medical experimentation, and raped, but the cruelest ordeal was Pierre's witnessing of the brutal killing of his lover, Jo, naked and torn apart by a pack of blood-thirsty, trained dogs.

In November of 1941, six months after his initial arrest, Pierre was called into the commandant's office, forced to sign papers promising silence, given German citizenship, then mysteriously released from Schirmeck for good behavior and sent back home. Pierre was traumatized by his time at Schirmeck. Because of the papers that he signed promising silence and the Catholic church's abhorrence toward homosexuality, Pierre now felt compelled to bury his experiences at Schirmeck and his love of men. In March of 1942, Pierre was drafted into the German *Reichsarbeitsdienst* (RAD or Reich Labor Service.) He was now a *malgré-nous* (despite ourselves), French men from Alsace or Lorraine fighting with their enemies in the Reich Labor Service against their compatriots, often those in the French Resistance. Pierre was sent to several countries during the war, including Yugoslavia, Germany, and, toward the end of the war, the Russian front. In the winter of 1945, and after illicitly listening to a BBC broadcast that foretold of the impending collapse of the German army and end of the war, Pierre deserted with his German commanding officer, the two of them making their way home through enemy territory. His friend was shot down, but Pierre continued onward to France. After a detour through Poland, Pierre arrived in Paris on August 7, 1945. Paris had been liberated from the Nazi occupation since August 24, 1944, but WWII did not end until September 2, 1945.

Pierre suffered from shell shock and nightmares. He stayed with his family, silent and in despair. His old homosexual friends that were still around from Le square Steinbach were nonchalant, pretending that nothing had ever happened. Although the laws against antisemitism were abolished in the French Penal Code, the laws against homosexuality remained. After the war ended in 1945, there was a rise in homophobia and in hate crimes against homosexuals. Cruising in Le square Steinbach became dangerous, his godfather disowned him, and family members made homophobic jokes in front of him. Although his family knew why Pierre had been punished by the Nazis, his homosexuality remained a deep family secret. Pierre wanted his family's love and acceptance, so he continued to suppress his attraction to men. He occupied his time with volunteering with the Society of War Victims and Other Victims in Alsace. Pierre's mother was bed-bound and, as he took care of her, their already close relationship became more intimate and he was able to confide everything: the death of Jo, the time in Schirmeck, and his feelings of shame over his homosexuality. His mother gave him acceptance and love. This renewed closeness was a great relief to them both, but she died soon after in 1949.

Pierre decided that he wanted a heteronormative life, one with a wife and children. In 1950, he married the daughter of a refugee from the Spanish Civil War. They moved from Haguenau and opened a fabric store. Three children later, Pierre's secret remain buried and he became more and more distant and non-communicative from his wife and children. They moved several times, finally staying in Toulouse. Pierre was tormented with shame about his desires for men and his homosexual past, so started medicating himself with tranquilizers and alcohol. In 1978, his wife left him and asked for a divorce. In May of 1981 and at 58 years old, Pierre stumbled upon a bookstore reading of Heinz Heger's *The Men with the Pink Triangle*, a concentration camp memoir.[5] Pierre met the reader the next day and momentously told his story. It was the first time since confiding with his mother 30 years previous that he'd spoken to anyone of his painful past. That chance book reading changed his life.

Newly emboldened and finally coming out as gay, Pierre joined *David et Jonathan*, a French gay and lesbian Christian association. In April 1982, after Léon Elchinger, the Bishop of Strasbourg, called for a last minute cancellation of room reservations in the Catholic dormitory for an International Gay Association (IGA) conference and then proclaimed, "I consider homosexuality as a sickness. I respect homosexuals as I respect sick people. But if they want to transform their sickness into health, I cannot agree."[6] Upon hearing this hate speech against homosexuals, Pierre wrote a public coming out letter, taking care to come out privately to his family first. To Pierre's joy, his wife accepted his proclamation, as did his employer. He applied with the government to have "homosexual" added to his application documents, and applied for reparations. Unfortunately, the government required impossible documentation; two affidavits by eyewitnesses in Schirmeck-Vorbrück internment camp, but most prisoners who survived were dead by then.

Pierre finally found love with another man, Éric Feliu. Pierre and Éric shared their home with two dogs. "For forty years following the atrocious death of my friend Jo I didn't dare touch a dog, but thanks to [Feliu], I have been able to conquer my fear," stated Pierre who called their pets "a daily pleasure."[7]

Pierre became an outspoken rights activist for homosexuals that had been imprisoned during WWII, appearing on television, giving interviews, and writing two memoirs. During this period, he experienced bullying, homophobic behavior from politicians, and was gay bashed. He was involved with *Mémorial de la Déportation Homosexuelle* (Memorial of the Homosexual Deportation), an association founded to honor the memory of homosexuals persecuted by the Nazis in WWII. In 2005, Pierre died of cancer in Toulouse, France. After his death, a street in Toulouse was named in his honor with a plaque stating, "Rue Pierre Seel / Déporté français pour homosexualité / 1923–2005."

Resources

Epstein, Robert P. and Jeffrey Friedman, dir. 2002. *Paragraph 175*. New Yorker Films. DVD.

Seel, Pierre. *I, Pierre Seel, Deported Homosexual: A Memoir of Nazi Terror*. Translated by Joachim Neugroschel. Perseus Books Group, 2011.

Seel, Pierre. *Liberation Was for Others: Memoirs of a Gay Survivor of the Nazi Holocaust*. Translated by Joachim Neugroschel. New York: Da Capo Press, 1997.

Pierre Seel, drawn by Rachael House

STACKED
DECK PRESS

This page is intentionally blank to facilitate coloring the reverse side.

Édith Thomas
1909–1970, France
drawn by Tyler Cohen

Édith Thomas was a French historian, feminist, novelist, journalist, bisexual, and member of the French Resistance during WWII. Édith was born into a happy and progressive family. In 1930 at age 21, she began experiencing intense pain in her knees, which was eventually diagnosed as tuberculosis of the bone. She convalesced in bed at her parents' home for over a year, after which she emerged with a pronounced limp, along with acute depression and feelings of low self-worth due to her illness; she believed her fate was to be alone and worried about becoming one of the "horizontals" or helpless people.[1] During this period, she wrote her first novel, *La Mort de Marie* (*Mary's Death*), which was partially self-referential and was awarded the coveted *Prix du Premier Roman*.

In 1933, Hitler had been appointed Chancellor in neighboring Germany, and a grim fascism was sweeping through the continent. Italy, Spain, Austria, Greece, Portugal, Slovakia, and Yugoslavia all had fascist or fascist-influenced movements in the 1930s. On February 6, 1934, a number of fascist, militant, right-wing, anti-parliamentary leagues started an anti-parliamentarian street demonstration in Place de la Concorde, Paris. Thought by some to be an attempted fascist *coup d'état* and others to be merely a disorganized protest, the riot ended with 16 deaths and 2,000 injured, mostly right-wing rioters. Édith was horrified by the riot and the rise of fascism; that year, she became interested in Communism and, despite wondering if she was too bourgeois and sentimental for the left,[2] joined the *Association des Écrivains et Artistes Révolutionnaires* (AEAR), an association of revolutionary artists and writers. In early 1934, she participated in her first demonstration and later that year resigned from the AEAR, citing her reluctance to adhere to orthodoxy and her anarchic beliefs. Édith was searching for her political footing, knowing that she felt compelled to take action, but unsure of her direction. She continued to write novels and started writing political editorials. She traveled to report on the Spanish Civil War in 1936 and 1938, publishing her editorials in political journals.

In 1939 when she was 30, Édith was diagnosed with pulmonary tuberculosis and recovered in the countryside until 1941, when she returned to a vastly different Paris. Between 1939 and 1941, everything had changed in Paris. On June 14th, 1940, the German Nazis marched into Paris, starting the Nazi Occupation of the City of Lights, which did not end until over four long and bloody years later, on August 25 of 1944. On June 25 of 1940, the armistice was signed promising peace between Germany and France, and Édith wrote prophetically, "They are going to teach us now to hate everything we loved and were right to love. They are going to teach us now that reason is wrong and madness and despair are the greatest wisdom. People are ready to believe it and they will believe it….At the bookseller's, at the pharmacist's, we're very happy: 'This time it's going to be okay, you'll see that.' The order they deserve, that of cemeteries and concentration camps, the moral order of the dead."[3]

The changes in the city were incremental, yet brutal. In 1940, rationing of food, dry goods, utilities, and tobacco was put into effect, curfews were imposed, the swastika-emblazoned German flag flew, a large banner was posted on the front of the old French parliament that read *DEUTSCHLAND SIEGT AN ALLEN FRONTEN* (Germany is winning on all fronts), a list of forbidden books called the Otto List was instated by the occupying Nazis. Two years later, in June of 1942, Jewish citizens were commanded to wear the yellow Star of David. In July of 1942, over 13,000 Jewish adults and children were ordered by the Nazis to be rounded up by the French police and sent to the Auschwitz concentration camp.

In 1941, Édith returned, rejuvenated and ready to take action with her sharpest tool, her intellect and her pen. She got a job as an *archiviste paléographe* at the *Archives Nationals* (French Archives) and continued to write, weaving the Occupation into her fiction; "*L'Étoile jaune*" relates a mother sewing a Star of David onto her young daughter's jacket. In the summer of 1942, she intensified her activities with the French Resistance. Édith used her office as a place to hide Resistance materials and pamphlets, and she started writing as a journalist for *les lettres françaises*, the most influential newspaper of intellectual resistance during the Occupation, although she didn't actually join the Communist Party until 1942, three years before the end of the war. One of her first editorials "*Crier la vérité*", was published in the second issue of *les lettres françaises* in October of 1942. In "*Crier la vérité*," she wrote about the Jewish children being deported to the Auschwitz concentration camp: "I saw a train go by. In the first car, there were French policemen and German soldiers. Then came cars sealed with lead. Thin arms of children clenched onto the bars. A hand fluttered like a leaf in the storm. When the train slowed down, voices cried out: 'Maman!' And the only reply was the grinding of the axles…"[4]

In 1943, Édith started hosting secretive undercover meetings for writers of the French Resistance in her apartment to outline actions, plan issues of newsletters, and exchange ideas. In addition to *les lettres françaises*, the underground publishing house, *Les Éditions de Minuit*, was started, which published Édith's politically-themed fiction. *Les Éditions de Minuit* published a stunning total of 33 of their pocket-sized revolutionary books in the two years before the Paris liberation in August of 1944 and, with an archivist's zeal, Édith registered the copyright of each new edition at the *Bibliothèque nationale de France*. In 1944, Paris was liberated and, in 1945, WWII was over. Édith traveled throughout Europe, noting the destruction. As she wrote in a book review of an Auschwitz survivor's memoir, "Tortures did not disappear with Hitlerism, nor did racism. We must be vigilant to what happens around us and within us."[5]

After the liberation of Paris in 1944, Édith became the editor for the women's journal, *Femmes françaises*, where she met a woman who became her lover and life-long confidante. In the 1930s and 40s, Édith developed crushes on various men, but they were never long-lasting or serious. Édith was aloof, cool, and insecure around male romantic partners, but this all changed in 1944 when she was seduced by Dominique Aury. Dominique was also bisexual, but had already had sexual relationships with women, whereas all of Édith's brief sexual experiences had been with men. In November 1946, Édith experienced sexual passion with Dominique for the first time and wrote in her diary, "I'm burning. I'm like a bundle of firewood, like a handful of straw. I'm thirsty. I'm like someone walking in the desert. I'm hungry. Can you be my orchard, my source of water? Or only this devouring fire which, when it withdraws, leaves me mortally unsatisfied?"[6] Less than a year after they started the affair, Dominique started seeing a man, whom she continued to see for the next 20 years. Édith and Dominique remained close friends and possibly lovers, talking daily for the next 23 years; although Dominique was sexually free-spirited, Édith was monogamous.[7] In 1954, Dominique decided to prove to her scoffing male lover that women were quite capable of writing BDSM erotica, and penned the highly successful *The Story of O* under the nom de plume, Pauline Réage. Dominique did not forget Édith in her book; Édith was the inspiration for the coolly sadistic and haughty character of Ann-Marie. In *The Story of O*, Ann-Marie impetuously pierces and brands the protagonist, whose name is O, marking her as forever possessed. *The Story of O* was groundbreaking, bestselling, and scandalous. Dominique described her best friend, confidant, and lover: "Édith was the most noble woman I ever met, in she had a need for truth and authenticity that was fundamental. And a rare generosity, except when politics was involved. She could be intransient. Thank god, she also had a wonderful sense of humor."[8]

In 1952, Édith wrote *Le Témoin Compromis*, her account of the French Resistance and Occupation during WWII. Édith continued to write prolifically until her death, with a concentration on French female icons and feminist history. In 1970, at age 61, Édith died suddenly of viral hepatitis.

Resources

Kaufmann, Dorothy. *Édith Thomas: A Passion for Resistance*. Ithaca, NY: Cornell University Press. 2004.

Réage, Pauline. *The Story of O*. New York: Eurotica, 1991.

Thomas, Édith. *La Mort de Marie*. France: Gallimard, 1934.

Thomas, Édith. *Le Témoin Compromis*. France: Viviane Hamy. 1995.

Thomas, Édith. *The Women Incendiaries*. Translated by James Atkinson and Starr Atkinson. Chicago: Haymarket Books. 2007.

Archive

National Archives of France, Pierrefitte-sur-Seine, Inventaire d'archives : Papiers d'Édith Thomas (XIXe-XXe siècles), https://francearchives.fr/findingaid/cc24810a86fac29fde3a0712c7d4a6836c7ccf78

Édith Thomas, drawn by Tyler Cohen

This page is intentionally blank to facilitate coloring the reverse side.

Rose Valland
1898–1980, France
drawn by Margo Rivera-Weiss

Rose Valland was born into a working class family in rural France. Her father was a blacksmith and her mother was a housewife. Rose was extremely bright and decided to become an art teacher. Quiet and studious, she was awarded a scholarship, and earned her first degree in 1918 from a teacher's school, attended *L'École nationale supérieure des Beaux-Arts de Lyon*, eventually moved to Paris, and studied art history in *L'École du Louvre* and the University of Paris. In 1931, she graduated with a special diploma from *L'École du Louvre* then went on to attend graduate school at the *Collège de France*.[1]

In 1932, Rose begin volunteering at the modern, progressive Jeu de Paume Museum by setting up art exhibits, and writing museum catalog descriptions and art reviews. She developed her writing and shorthand skills, which would prove useful during the years of the Nazi occupation in Paris.[2] Rose loved artwork, and collected paintings and prints. She was particularly fond of the cool linearity of modern Cubist art; the grey and tan marvel by Juan Gris, *Le moulin à café* (The Coffee Grinder, circa 1916), and Fernand Léger's masterpiece *La Gare* (The Train Station, circa 1918) were both added to her private collection.[3] Rose took note of the spread of fascism across the continent of Europe in the early 1930s, and the strange Nazi obsession and derision of *Entartete Kunst* (Degenerate Art). She was horrified by the Nuremberg Laws of 1935 that removed citizenship status and civil rights from German Jews. It was obvious that the machinery of war was slowly heaving to a start, and French art museums began wartime preparations. In 1936, all public art museums in France, including the Jeu de Paume Museum, developed evacuation plans to protect their art collections. Rose assisted the museum in updating the inventory, researching methods of transportation, identifying potential hiding places for the artwork, and prioritizing the collection.[4] In fall of 1938, the first deployment of art was sent to *Château de Chambord* (Chambord castle) in Chambord. *Château de Chambord*, a sprawling 440-room French Renaissance castle that was constructed between 1519 and 1547, ended up being used extensively as storage for artwork during the occupation of France. In 1939, over 40 trucks laden with artwork from public and private collections traveled to storage areas around France for protection from war, and the Jeu de Paume Museum closed its doors to the public.

Hitler was appointed Chancellor of Germany in 1933. A failed artist, Hitler had applied to Vienna Academy of Fine Arts when he was 18, but his portfolio was deemed unsatisfactory and he was not admitted. The Nazi regime and Hitler were highly critical of modernist or "cosmopolitan" art, preferring traditional, pre-Impressionist artwork. They called modern artwork *Entartete Kunst* and were obsessed with eradicating it. In a political rally in Nuremberg on September 1, 1933, Hitler railed against *Entartete Kunst*, calling for "a new artistic renaissance of the Aryan human being," and dismissed Jewish and modernist art such as Cubism, Dadaism, and Surrealism.[5] Modern artists, including Pablo Picasso, Salvador Dalí, Max Ernst, Paul Klee, Fernand Léger, Joan Miró, Otto Dix, and Max Beckmann, had their work destroyed. As the Nazi party began regulating, persecuting, and imprisoning Jews and other undesirables, Nazis systematically plundered art from museums and private art collections with the goal of establishing a *Führermuseum* (Leader's Museum) in Linz. In 1933, the *Reichskulturkammer* (Reich Culture Chamber) formed in order to promote virtuous art and culture. Goebbels was made head of the newly established *Reichskulturkammer* and said, "In future only those who are members of [the] chamber are allowed to be productive in our cultural life. Membership is open only to those who fulfill the entrance condition. In this way all unwanted and damaging elements have been excluded."[6] While degenerate artwork was being looted and destroyed, traditional approved art was being looted and stored. In 1937, the Nazi government produced an exhibit in Munich of degenerate art, the infamous traveling *Entartete Kunst* show. This show consisted of a deliberately badly hung jumble of over 600 pieces of art, interspersed with reactionary slogans painted on the walls, such as "An insult to German womanhood," "Revelation of the Jewish racial soul," and "Deliberate sabotage of national defense."[7]

In 1940, Nazis overtook Paris, causing many Parisians to flee to the countryside for the duration of the war. Rose stayed in Paris during the occupation and, at age 42, became the sole French citizen overseer at the Jeu de Paume Museum. A third of the museum's art collection had been removed from Paris for safekeeping, and now the invading Nazis took over the museum to use as a sorting depot for their plundered artwork. They used the Jeu de Paume Museum as their holding grounds for four years, between 1940 and 1944.[8] Rose was a woman, meek and unassuming, slyly hiding the fact that she knew some German, and began her mission of surreptitiously recording the provenance of the purloined artwork and the intended German destinations so that it could be retrieved after the war. Her extensive art education, calm demeanor, writing skills, and ability to write in shorthand served her well. Rose reported to and worked closely with Jacques Jaujard, the director of the French National Museums. Jacques, in turn, worked with the French Resistance. Rose recorded information about the artwork in small notebooks, hiding them when the Germans came into the room.

Being a studious, middle-aged lesbian proved an ideal cover for French Resistance work: "Her dowdy looks certainly did not invite the advances from the Germans, and she was regarded by all as an insignificant administrative functionary. Her presence at the heart of this undertaking, which the Germans wished to conceal from the French, was an anomaly."[9] She was nearly busted several times while recording information in the Jeu de Paume Museum, a charge that could have resulted in her death by execution, but diplomatic fast talking and her meek demeanor convinced the German Nazi Gestapo that she was harmless. Although she was naturally introverted and quiet, Rose cleverly chatted up the guards and other workers in order to gather intelligence information to relay to Jacque. She said, "Without revealing my activities, I had also befriended the person in charge of packing, Alexandre, a very intelligent man who liked to gossip. I was striving to show the same inclination, since when you extensively discuss current events, you are often able to pick up some valuable tidbits that can lead to real information."[10] In May or July 1943, the Nazis burnt hundreds of degenerate artworks in the Paris Louvre courtyard, and in July 1943 more art was burned in the Jeu de Paume Museum gardens while Rose was forced to watch the destruction.[11]

The occupation in Paris was winding down and, in 1944, Paris was liberated by American soldiers. Rose worked with the Monuments Men to retrieve the scattered, stolen artwork and return it to its rightful owners. In 1945 and at nearly 50, Rose received a commission into the French First Army and traveled to Germany to assist in artwork recovery activities. In 1946, Rose testified at the Nuremberg trials, confronting art collector *Reichsmarschall* Hermann Göring for his war crimes.[12] In 1954, Rose returned to Paris and became Chair of *Le Service de protection des oeuvres d'art* (Commission for the Protection of Works of Art). In 1947, Rose met her life partner for the next 30 years,[13] Joyce Heer, an English interpreter employed at the United States Embassy in Paris. Joyce and Rose shared an apartment in Paris, and when Joyce retired, Joyce studied philosophy at the Sorbonne.[14] Joyce died at age 60 in 1977, and Rose died two years later at age 81, in 1980. They are buried together in Rose's hometown, Saint-Etienne-de-Saint-Geoirs.

Rose was granted several distinctions for her resistance work, including being bestowed the title of Fine Arts officer in the French Armed Forces, the non-combatant rank of Lieutenant Colonel of the U.S. Armed Forces, Officer of the French Legion of Honor, Commander of Arts and Letters, the French Resistance Medal, the U.S. Medal of Freedom, and the Confluence German Order of Merit.

Resources

Bouchoux, Corinne. *Rose Valland: Resistance at the Museum.* Translated by Robert M. Edsel. S.I.: Laurel Publishing, LLC, 2013.

Nicholas, Lynn H. *The Rape of Europa: The Fate of Europe's Treasures in the Third Reich and the Second World War.* New York: Viking Press, 1980.

Valland, Rose. *Le Front De L'art: Défense Des Collections Françaises: 1939-1945.* Paris: Réunion Des Musées Nationaux, 2016.

Archive

Rose Valland Archives, Looted*art*: The Central Registry of Information on Looted Cultural Property 1933-1943, https://www.lootedart.com/MFEU4B10227

Rose Valland, drawn by Margo Rivera-Weiss

This page is intentionally blank to facilitate coloring the reverse side.

Gad Beck, a.k.a. Gerhard Beck
1923–2012, Germany
drawn by Ashley Guillory

Gad and his twin sister, Margot, were born in Berlin to a Jewish immigrant father from Austria and a mother who'd converted from Christianity to Judaism. His family was poor, and Gad was only 10 years old when Hitler was appointed Chancellor in 1933. Gad was affected by the rise in antisemitism and remembered being bullied in school by his classmates: "Can I sit somewhere else, not next to Gad? He has such stinking Jewish feet."[1] In 1934, his parents transferred him to a private Jewish school, but when they found they couldn't afford the tuition fees, Gad dropped out of school and got his first job. Gad was close to his family and came out as gay when he was a teenager. His family was immediately accepting, his aunts teasing him about whether he had a "handsome friend" yet and mentioning that the last one wasn't so handsome.[2]

Because Gad's mother was a convert to Judaism, Gad was considered by the German Nazis to be a *mischling* (mixed-blood), therefore was not rounded up with other Jews after the *Gesetz zur Behebung der Not von Volk und Reich* (Law to Remedy the Distress of People and Reich, or the Enabling Act of 1933) was passed. Nazi Germany developed a complex system of categorizing people by their ethnic make-up called the Reich Citizenship Law. In fall of 1935, the Nuremberg Laws were passed in which grossly anti-Semitic and racial laws were instituted; the first was the Law for the Protection of German Blood and German Honour which forbade gentile German women under age 45 from working in Jews' homes, sexual relations between Jews and gentiles, and marriage between Jews and gentiles, and the second was the Reich Citizenship Law which defined who was a Jew. The Reich Citizenship Law was later expanded to include black people and Romani people (gypsies). The goal was to ensure the mythical purity of German bloodlines. There were six classifications under the law, and there was an elaborate legal system of subcategorizing mischlinge which was determined by the *Mischling Test*. Factors in the first part of the test included the number of Jewish grandparents a person possessed. Factors in the second part of the test were more convoluted and included whether a person was a Jewish community member and when they joined, whether they married a Jew and when, whether they were born out of wedlock and when, and whether one of their parents was a Jew and when their parents were married.[3]

As of November 14, 1935, Jews were no longer German citizens and did not have the right to vote. In spring of 1935, the Interior Ministry estimated there were 750,000 *mischlinge*, but after the war that number decreased to around 200,000; 550,000 people were either killed or emigrated from Germany within ten years. In November of 1938, *Kristallnacht* (Night of Broken Glass) occurred; a two-day violent, bloody rampage that was covertly sanctioned by the government and whose sole purpose was to vandalize and annihilate Jewish businesses, synagogues, and cemeteries. Rapes and suicides followed, then a spate of anti-Jewish legislation.[4] By then the Holocaust was well underway.

In 1940, Gad was 18 and, like many young people during that time, joined a Zionist youth group, the *He-halutz*. Religious and secular youth groups for young Jewish folks were more important than ever during the early years of the Holocaust, but in 1936 the Nazis banned non-religious youth groups for Jews. They were willing to tolerate the Zionist youth groups because those groups encouraged emigration to Palestine. Not only did they provide a place to socialize safely and form community, they also became places to learn how to exist under the new repressive regime and were forerunners to the more politicized resistance groups that formed in the early 1940s. Zionist youth groups such as *He-halutz* even prepared their members for possible emigration to Palestine.

Most of the members in *He-halutz* were sporty, but Gad was more citified with sophisticated tastes. Gad said, "For them I was a boy from outside. Why? I was visiting theaters, I was dancing, even ballet dancing. For such a group of pioneers it was impossible to believe this. Just in such a situation, political situation...I had never been in such a group, if there was not Hitler, this is clear. But I had no other way, I had to come with other people together, with these Jewish people together and the Zionist Jewish people together....I was coming from another world, I was coming more from the world from theater, from culture, from [sigh]."[5] Although they saw Gad as too "bourgeois" at first, he quickly fit in and made friends. He soon became closer to one particular group member, a sweet, working class boy named Manfred Lewin, and they became lovers.

As a token of love, Manfred gave Gad a tiny handmade book with a green and yellow bookmark; the book was a mash note, including poems, whimsical sketches, and descriptions of their intertwined life in Berlin as comrades and lovers. Page eight has a sketch of a bed and reads, "Night exists for more than sleep which is why, my love, we stayed awake so often."[6] The book talks about the start of the deportations in Berlin, the restrictions, and what it was like to live in such a charged and dangerous time. Manfred said of the love token, "I did that for you so that you will never forget me."[7] By September 15, 1941, the Nazis ordered all German Jews to wear a yellow star or face arrest and deportation. In fall of 1942, Manfred, along with the rest of his family, was arrested and sent to the pre-deportation camp, Grosse Hamburger Strasse 26. Gad was heartbroken. He borrowed a Hitler Youth uniform as a disguise and went to Grosse Hamburger Strasse 26 to spring Manfred. The ruse worked, but Manfred refused to leave his beloved family behind and rejoined them in Grosse Hamburger Strasse 26. Manfred and his entire family were killed at the Auschwitz concentration camp.[8]

In 1943, with Manfred gone and the Holocaust in full bloody swing, Gad joined the newly formed *Chug Chaluzi* (Pioneer Circle) German Resistance youth group. This underground, illegal group founded by Jizchak Schwersenz and Edith Wolff had between 11 and 40 members, and many of the members had been in Zionist youth groups together before the deportations had splintered the groups. *Chug Chaluzi* group members helped one another get food, distribute ration cards, obtain false identity cards, seek escape routes, and find places to hide. In 1944, the group founder successfully escaped the genocide to Switzerland and Gad became the group leader. Of the 73,842 Berliner Jews in 1941, only 8,700—or fewer than 12%—were still alive after the war ended in 1945.[9]

After the war ended in 1945, Gad worked for a while in a displaced peoples camp in Germany. In 1947, he emigrated to Palestine with Zwie, a lover that he'd met in prison. In 1978, Gad returned to Berlin to work as director of the Jewish Adult Education Center. Gad was interviewed for *Paragraph 175*, the documentary about gay people that were persecuted by the Nazis during WWII. In 2012, Gad died in Berlin at the age of 88.

Resources

Beck, Gad. *An Underground Life: Memoirs of a Gay Jew in Nazi Berlin.* Translated by Allison Brown. Vancouver: Access and Diversity, Crane Library, University of British Columbia, 2014.

Beck, Gad. "Oral History Interview with Gad Beck." Interview by Klaus Müller. United States Holocaust Memorial Museum. Accessed August 28, 2018. https://collections.ushmm.org/search/catalog/irn504854.

Epstein, Robert P. and Jeffrey Friedman, dir. 2002. *Paragraph 175*. New Yorker Films. DVD.

Gad Beck, drawn by Ashley Guillory

This page is intentionally blank to facilitate coloring the reverse side.

Annette Eick
1909–2010, Germany
drawn by Tara Madison Avery

Annette Eick grew up the well-loved, protected child of an upper-class Jewish family of merchants in the metropolis of Berlin. She attended a private girls' school and realized that she was attracted to girls at a young age. When she was ten she wrote this description of her imagined adult life: "I want to live in the country with an elderly girlfriend and have a lot of animals. I don't want to get married and I don't want to have children, but I'll write."[1] Her attraction to girls was clinched when she developed a massive first crush on one of her teachers, Erika von Hörsten. Annette was already interested in poetry when Erika turned her onto the Greek poet, Sappho, during class. Did Annette lie in bed at night imagining her teacher embracing her while whispering Sappho's words into her ears? It seems likely. "The moon has set, and the Pleiades as well; in the deep middle of the night, the time is passing, and I lie alone."[2] Annette was bold and made her feelings clear to her teacher; she said, "Once I gave Erika a record with a song which was popular at the time, 'Your mouth says no, but your eyes say yes. Beloved woman, I will kiss you today.' She laughed and asked if I meant her."[3]

In 1928, Annette turned 19 and gathered her courage to seek out other lesbians in the city. It was the heyday of the Weimar Republic, and Berlin was world famous for its flourishing, vibrant lesbian and gay culture. She immediately went to her first lesbian bar, the Damenclub Violetta, run by the young, handsome accordion-playing, gay rights activist and bar-owner, Lotte Hahm.[4] Annette loved writing, so she decided to become a journalist. She wrote articles, short stories, and poetry for the popular lesbian magazine, *Die Freundin* (The Girlfriend), including an article on coming out and meeting women or, as she put it, "how women find their way to their own sex."[5]

In 1933, Hitler was appointed Chancellor, and the viciously conservative and homophobic *Gesetz zur Behebung der Not von Volk und Reich* (Law to Remedy the Distress of People and Reich, or Enabling Act of 1933) was made into law, quickly shutting down over 100 gay bars in Berlin and forcing *Die Freundin* to cease publication. Annette had five years of freedom in Berlin before Hitler and his band of Nazis cut it short. The situation under Nazi reign became intolerable for Jews, homosexuals, and other undesirables. The Holocaust was underway. In the mid-1930s, Annette fell in love with an American butch woman named Frances and got an apartment with her. Frances was going to bring her to America, but she turned out to be physically abusive, schizophrenic, and unfaithful. Frances returned to America with another German woman as the situation intensified in Germany. America had a low quota for German Jewish refugees and a several year waiting list and, without Frances' assistance, emigrating to America was out of the question.[6] Annette looked for another way out of Germany. She wrote to a friend who'd successfully moved to London asking for assistance in getting a British entry permit.

Because Annette's family was Jewish, her parents were gradually destroyed by the Nazi regime; their furniture store was boycotted, then in 1938, the government requisitioned their store.[7] In November of that same year, *Kristallnacht* (Night of Broken Glass) occurred; a violent, bloody rampage that was covertly sanctioned by the government, and whose sole purpose was to vandalize and annihilate Jewish businesses, synagogues, and cemeteries. Rapes and suicides followed, then a spate of anti-Jewish legislation.[8] Annette's family's farm was torched by anti-Semites and burnt completely down,[9] and Annette's relatives were starting to be imprisoned in concentration camps. Annette's dreams of journalism were dashed because Jews were banned from writing for newspapers and magazines, so she got work as a nanny.

Annette became a member of a Jewish youth organization, and persistently sought another way leave the country. She had not heard back from her friend in London and Frances had left for America without her, so she decided to join her aunt in British controlled Palestine as mandated by the League of Nations, one of the few countries that accepted refugee Jews, although this changed in 1939. On the first day of *Kristallnacht*, Annette was arrested and thrown in jail, which the Nazi government called "protective custody." A police officer's wife gave her blankets and food, and then left the door to the jail open for her. Annette escaped. She was on her bicycle heading back to her parent's home when she was stopped by the postman, who said that he had a love letter to deliver to her. The love letter turned out to be that valued rarity, an immigration permit for England! Her friend in London had advocated for Annette and gotten her the paperwork needed to leave Germany. She left by railway that year, waving good-bye to her parents as she left them forever, "But the people that were older didn't think it would get so bad. So I took my few things and left from the Bahnhof Zoo train station. I couldn't take much with me. The worse thing, of course, that I saw my parents waving on the platform when the train pulled out and I knew that I'd never see them again."[10] In the end, her parents and most of her relatives were arrested by the Gestapo and sent to Auschwitz concentration camp, where they died.

Annette arrived in the chilly wintertime in London with ten marks (current value, $69.00 U.S.), all the money that Germany allowed her to bring. Annette's friend had gotten her a work permit as a domestic. She spent the first night in a Salvation Army shelter run by Nazi-admiring anti-Semites, and the following night slept rough in a park, but finally found her friend, got a job that she enjoyed, made friends with other immigrants, and joined the Free German Cultural Association. These were happy times for Annette. She continued to write poetry and started to read it publicly. In 1949, she met a new friend, Trud, and although they were not one another's type to start with, they changed from just friends to lovers, and this eventually blossomed into a 40-year partnership. In 1964, Trud retired; Annette and Trud moved to a small English town, and Annette opened a nursery for children. In 1984, her book of poetry, *Immortal Muse*, was published. In 2010, Annette died at age 100.

Resources

Eick, Annette. *Immortal Muse*. Braunton: Merlin, 1984.

Epstein, Robert P. and Jeffrey Friedman, dir. 2002. *Paragraph 175*. New Yorker Films. DVD.

Giovanni, Sue, dir. Immortal Muse. 2005. Accessed August 17, 2018. http://www.cultureunplugged.com/play/3795/Immortal-Muse.

Schoppmann, Claudia. *Days of Masquerade: Life Stories of Lesbians During the Third Reich*. New York: Columbia University Press, 1996.

ANNETTE EICK

Annette Eick, drawn by Tara Madison Avery

35

STACKED
DECK PRESS

This page is intentionally blank to facilitate coloring the reverse side.

Lotte Hahm
1890–1967, Germany
drawn by Dorian Katz

Lotte Hahm was not only the flamboyant, accordion playing, tuxedo-clad butch owner of the popular Berlin lesbian club, Damenclub Violetta, but she was also a prominent gay and transvestites' rights activist in Berlin. The word "transgender" was not commonly used during this era, but "transvestite" was the term of choice. Lotte identified both as butch and as a transvestite, and worked tirelessly in both communities, advocating and crossing lines as queer long before the modern definition of queer existed. The demarcation between butch and transvestite identities in Berlin in the early part of the twentieth century was nebulous by our modern multifaceted definitions of gender identities. Lotte's playful, erotic female masculinity was a forebearer of today's genderfluid queer identity; the more conventional, hegemonic lesbian movement in Germany was chock full of drama, rivalry, and backstabbing, and Lotte's world was full of sexy, rambunctious, gender diverse activism.[1]

Berlin had a flourishing lesbian scene, with over 60 gathering places for lesbians.[2] Lotte was an energetic and charismatic leader in the LGBT community in Berlin's flourishing Weimar Republic, a time of artistic creativity and sexual freedom that lasted from 1919 to 1933. She was instrumental in community-building between the lesbian and the transexual communities in Berlin.[3] In 1926 Lotte opened her first nightclub, the Damenclub Violetta at Bulowstrasse 37,[4] a wildly popular women-only club with over 400 members.[5] She hosted such shindigs as *Damenball mit Saalpost* (Calling-Card Ladies' Ball), *Roulette-Tan* (Dance Roulette), steamboat trips, and fashion shows for butches and transvestites. Two years later, in 1928, Lotte became head of the women's division of the largest gay rights organization in the Weimar Republic, the *Bund für Menschenrecht* (BfM; Union for Human Rights).[6] BfM was the first German gay rights organization, having 48,000 members, and it remained in operation until it was banned by the Nazi government in 1933.

In 1929, Lotte founded the first German transvestite organization, a mixed gender transvestite social group called *Transvestitenvereinigung D`Eon* (Transvestite Association), which initially met in Lotte's apartment but needed to move to a larger venue within months because of the degree of interest. Many forms of sexual and gender identities thrived during the Weimar Republic era. In 1910, the identity and terminology *Transvestitismus* (transvestism) was created by Magnus Hirschfeld, a prominent German sexologist. At the same time, Magnus published a paper, *Die Transvestiten* (The Transvestites); in this paper, Magnus delineated gender expression from sexual orientation, which had not been done in the past. There was a thriving transvestite community of male-to-female and female-to-male people in Germany. Although cross-dressing was illegal and people could be arrested and fined for "gross mischief" and "creating a public nuisance", transvestites were recognized by the law. As a result, and in order to protect transvestites from arrest, in 1908 the German police started issuing *Transvestitenscheine* (transvestite certificates) so that transvestites could safely cross-dress in public. After getting a letter from a doctor, the courts also issued transvestite "passports", which allowed the bearer to travel between provinces using their preferred name and dressed as their preferred gender. Although there was incredible progress being made for homosexuals and transvestites during the Weimar Republic, once Hitler was appointed Chancellor, it only took a few months before these rights were obliterated.

Lotte was a regular contributor to *Die Freundin* (The Girlfriend), a popular newspaper for working class lesbians that featured personal dating posts, fiction, and events listings. In 1930, Lotte and Friedrich Radszuweit started a new gay rights group, *Bund für ideale Freundschaft* (Union for Ideal Friendship) whose goal was to encourage activism against the growing conservatism and political unrest in Germany. This call to action and the group's bill of rights was published in *Die Freundin*,[7] and in 1932 Lotte opened the Manuela Bar, where she played her accordion while decked out in a suit and bow tie.

In February of 1933, one month after Hitler was sworn in as Chancellor, the Reichstag fire was set, torching the German Parliament building. The Nazi government blamed the Communists and used this disaster as an excuse to remove German citizen's civil rights, starting with the *Reichstagsbrandverordnung* (Decree of the Reich President for the Protection of People and State), making opposition to the Nazi government grounds for imprisonment. Freedom of the press to criticize the government was also restricted. It read, "Articles 114, 115, 117, 118, 123, 124 and 153 of the Constitution of the German Reich are suspended until further notice. It is therefore permissible to restrict the rights of personal freedom [*habeas corpus*], freedom of (opinion) expression, including the freedom of the press, the freedom to organize and assemble, the privacy of postal, telegraphic and telephonic communications. Warrants for House searches, orders for confiscations as well as restrictions on property, are also permissible beyond the legal limits otherwise prescribed."[8] One month later the *Gesetz zur Behebung der Not von Volk und Reich* (the Law to Remedy the Distress of People and Reich, or Enabling Act of 1933) was passed, thereby taking final steps to further decimate German citizens' civil rights by giving Hitler the power to enact laws without the approval of Parliament. Hitler was now a dictator.

The Weimar Republic was no match for Hitler and his conservative anti-homosexual laws. In 1933, all same-sex dancing was deemed illegal, and *Die Freundin* ended publication. By 1934, the Nazi Party was the only political party in Germany, the government had shut down all of Berlin's over 100 LGBT cafes, bars, and other gathering places, and LGBT newspapers and magazines were burnt and banned. The Holocaust was underway.

The sequence of events leading to Lotte's arrest and imprisonment are sketchy. In 1933, Lotte was set up and charged with the seduction of a minor by her friend's grandfather,[8] then in 1935, she was charged with being a Communist after the Nazis discovered her with political flyers. A stranger in Alexanderplatz public square had asked Lotte to watch over his luggage, then after he took off, she was detained and inspected by the Gestapo.[9]

She was subsequently arrested and tortured by the Nazis between 1933 and 1935, when they sent her to Moringen concentration camp for women. Moringen imprisoned approximately 1,350 women in all, including Jehovah's Witnesses, lesbians, abortionists, prostitutes, and Communists. Often women were imprisoned for multiple infractions. Other infractions which lead to being imprisoned included making derogatory remarks and women who were of the political opposition to Hitler and the Nazis. In Moringen concentration camp, Lotte joined a Communist group.[10] In 1938, Moringen concentration camp closed down and Lotte was released, but she suffered from partial paralysis from her five years in the concentration camp and prison.

Once WWII ended in 1945, Lotte didn't waste any time renewing her efforts to promote gay rights and human rights. In the mid-1940s, she opened another gay nightclub, and in 1958, she was involved with trying to reestablish *Bund für ideale Freundschaft*. Lotte remained active until her death at age 77 in 1967.

Resources

Lybeck, Marti M. *Desiring Emancipation: New Women and Homosexuality in Germany, 1890–1933*. New York: State University of New York Press, 2015.

"Persönlichkeiten in Berlin 1825 - 2006." Persönlichkeiten in Berlin 1825 - 2006 - Digitale Landesbibliothek Berlin - Zentral- Und Landesbibliothek Berlin. 2018. Accessed August 11, 2018. https://digital.zlb.de/viewer/fulltext/15916855/73/.

Sutton, Katie. *Masculine Woman in Weimar Germany*. New York: Berghahn Books, 2011.

Whisnant, Clayton J. *Queer Identities and Politics in Germany: A History, 1880–1945*. Harrington Park Press: New York. 2016.

Lotte Hahm, drawn by Dorian Katz

This page is intentionally blank to facilitate coloring the reverse side.

Wilhelm Heckmann, a.k.a. Willi Heckmann
1897–1995, Germany
drawn by M Rocket

Wilhelm Heckmann was a musician, a singer, an accordionist, and a gay man. He was born in the town of Altena in northwestern Germany in the scenic Lenne river valley, the son of a conservative innkeeper. Willi, his father, and his three brothers often performed together when the brothers were children. By the time Willi was a young adult, WWI had started. In December 1916, the German government issued the Auxiliary Service Law, a law requiring that all men between ages 17 and 60 who were not in the military or farmers to work in the armament industry or another wartime related sector,[1] so Wilhelm joined the service.

After WWI ended in 1918, Willi traveled to the neighboring town of Hagen to study singing and piano under the conductor, Otto Laugs. Willi spent the 1920s and early 1930s touring. Willi was known as the "Rhineland Tenor"[2] as he toured Germany, playing light, popular music in hotels, bars, and restaurants. He was closeted about being gay with his family; he was the family bachelor uncle—dapper, jovial, silly, much beloved, and always sporting a stylish hat and a cigar.

Hitler's rise to power and the fall of the Weimar Republic in the early 1930s deeply affected many German musicians, performers, writers, and artists. Soon after Hitler was appointed as Chancellor in 1933, the process of *Gleichschaltung* (coordination) or Nazification of Germany had started. A series of laws were passed including ones controlling artistic expression. Art was divided into *Entartete Kunst und Musik* (degenerate or modern art and music) or Nazi-approved, traditional, nationalist art. Nazi art stressed the *Blut und Boden* (blood and soil) values of racial purity, militarism, and obedience. Modernist artists and Jewish artists were forbidden from selling, exhibiting, or making their work. The Nazis recognized that art had the potential for becoming a propaganda tool to spread their message.

Hitler had traditional, conservative European tastes, favoring realist art instead of modernist art, and *Schlager* (popular and light music) instead of jazz which he derided because he considered it black American music. In 1934, a German critic expressed his opinions of degenerate music in the magazine *Die Musik*, "Everywhere in Europe, we Germans have released the immediate products of cultural decay, which fall under the name 'New Music'….This 'music' devours our Volk's living and characteristic art music, directly attacking our healthy origins that presently and by all means long to recover the smallest Lebensraum. This 'New Music,' in sprit and essence, is antithetical to the people (*unvolkstümlich*) because it releases every natural dissatisfaction. Worse yet, it both knowingly and unconsciously denigrates the possession of the healthy feelings and desires felt by the strong, self-knowing Volk, whose music is a singular medium of expression, alert and humorous."[3]

Artistically, Willi was fortunate. He did not play so-called degenerate jazz or classical music written by Jewish composers, both outlawed under Nazification. He was an old-fashioned popular musician, playing pleasant background music for special occasions and occasionally playing in a concert hall. Willi's music was Nazi-approved. In 1935, the music magazine, *Das Deutsche Podium, Kampfblatt für deutsche Musik* (*The German Podium, Activist Newspaper for German Music*) praised Willi for his talent: "…over the months he has conquered an ever-growing group of friends and patrons…with a fine and well trained tenor voice…. Willi Heckmann, who does not lose anything musically…his volume fills the hall….piano, a nice chord, a well-trained singing, Heckmann has it all."[4]

Personally, Willi wasn't as fortunate. Although he was apolitical, he was a gay man, and the German Nazis were vehemently anti-homosexual. In 1935, Hitler broadened the already existing anti-homosexuality Paragraph 175 of the German criminal code to include "lewd acts" between men, even ones that did not involve physical contact. The stipulations in Paragraph 175 did not differentiate whether the behavior was consensual or forced. As a result of this revision, the number of men arrested greatly increased between 1935 and 1939. Between 1933 and 1945, approximately 53,000 men were sentenced under Paragraph 175.[5] In addition, the Nazi's disgust regarding homosexuality led to a disregard of legal proceedings, with the goal being to imprison gay men at any cost. The Gestapo and the *Kriminalpolizei* (criminal police or kripo) rounded up gay men into *Vorbeugehaft* (police detention/protective custody) without charging them in a court of law. After they were rounded up, they would often be detained, then funneled from protective custody into a concentration camp. Homosexuals were not the only people that could be detained indefinitely through *Vorbeugehaft*; unemployed people, Romani, homeless people, and sex workers could also be picked up, detained, then sent to concentration camps without any formal charges being brought against them in court.

In July of 1937, the Gestapo arrested Heckmann in Passau under Paragraph 175. He'd had one prior arrest for homosexuality, so they took him into *Vorbeugehaft*, then quickly shuffled him to the Dachau concentration camp ten miles west of Munich. When WWII started in September of 1939, Willi had already spent over two years in the Dachau concentration camp because he was a homosexual.

When WWII started in 1939, the Gestapo transferred him to the Mauthausen concentration camp in Austria. Mauthausen consisted of a main camp, along with subcamp, and was a *Stufe III* (Grade III) concentration camp, the most brutal camp for the incorrigible political enemies of the Reich. The prisoners worked long hours in quarries, munitions factories, fighter aircraft factories, and mines. Willi was assigned to mining rocks in the quarries for his first year. After a year of hard labor in the quarry, Willi was pulled out to become a camp musician and part of a camp trio that performed for high ranking Gestapo members as they gambled in the local casino, while the kapos (prisoners given roles of leadership and special duties to enforce rules within the camp) were celebrating their birthday, or the SS were carousing in the brothel. By the summer of 1942, Willi was playing an accordion in the "Gypsy Orchestra," and in the fall of 1942, *Reichsführer-SS* Heinrich Himmler ordered Willi to form a Mauthausen camp orchestra. Willi sang and played accordion, while the orchestra played military marches, popular, and classical music. Making music kept Willi spiritually alive.

Although Will got special privileges as a musician, such as better food and less heavy physical labor, he was reviled by the other prisoners and the guards because he was a Paragraph 175, a homosexual. He was brutalized by guards and suffered because of his homosexuality. While Willi was spending his 30s and 40s in the Mauthausen concentration camp, his family in Altena knew he was there, but they were loyal Nazi followers. At least one brother was a member of the *Nationalsozialistische Deutsche Arbeiterpartei* (National Socialist German Workers' Party, a.k.a. Nazi party or NSDAP),[6] and Willi's mother worked with the *Hitlerjugend* (Hitler Youth or HP), all the while aware that their beloved, jovial Willi had been imprisoned in Mauthausen.[7] Altena was a major stronghold of the early Nazi party and his family was conservative, so perhaps this was not a surprise.

By the time the Mauthausen concentration camp complex was liberated by American soldiers on May 5 and 6, 1945, between 122,766 and 320,000 people had been killed there. On May 5th, Willi was released by the 11th U.S. Armored Division of the 3rd U.S. Army. Willi attempted to regain his career as a musician, but suffered rheumatism and nerve damage to his arms and shoulders from his eight years in Dachau and Mauthausen. The pain and inflammation made playing a heavy accordion difficult. In 1954, Willi applied for *Wiedergutmachungspolitik* (German reparation); however, since he was imprisoned under Paragraph 175 for homosexuality, he was denied. The German government would not rule to make reparations to men imprisoned under Paragraph 175 until 2016, over 70 years after WWII ended. In 1995, Willi died at the age of 97.

Resources

Cathcart, Adam "Music and Politics in Hitler's Germany." *Madison Historical Review:* Vol. 3 , Article 1.

Available at: http://commons.lib.jmu.edu/mhr/vol3/iss1/1

Connell, Heather, dir. *Forget Us Not.* Los Angeles: Displaced Yankee Productions. 2016. DVD

Stanjek, Klaus, dir. *Sounds From the Fog: Odyssey of a Gay Musician in Nazi Germany.* Germany: CINETARIUM Babelsberg. 2013.

Stanjek, Klaus. "Musik Und Mord - Ein Berufsmusiker in Mauthausen." Lecture, KünstlerInnen Und WissenschaftlerInnen Im KZ Mauthausen, Linz. Accessed October 4, 2018. http://www.cinetarium.de/downloads/mauthausen-vortrag_musik-und-mord_zusammenfassung.pdf.

Wilhelm Heckmann, drawn by M Rocket

43

This page is intentionally blank to facilitate coloring the reverse side.

Vera Lachmann
1904–1985, Germany/United States
drawn by Avery Cassell

Vera Lachmann was a poet, classicist, scholar, and an educator. She was born in Berlin, Germany into an upper class, well-to-do Jewish family. Her father, Louis Lachmann, was a prominent local architect, designing one of Berlin's opera houses, department stores, and other buildings. In 1910, when Vera was only five years old, her father committed suicide when his firm fell into bankruptcy.[1] There were several suicides in Vera's extended family, and suicide was common amount bourgeois Jewish-German families in that era.[2] Louis' death left Vera, her mother, and her two siblings, Nina and Erick, alone. Vera was studious, attended a private girls' school, then went on to Humboldt University of Berlin and the University of Basel to study philology, language, and literature. In 1931, Vera earned her PhD from the University of Berlin, with an interest in Icelandic saga. Her goal was to teach at the university but, due to the sexist hiring practices of the era, she was denied that opportunity and earned a secondary school teacher's certificate instead. In 1933, Vera founded Jagowstrasse School, a small progressive private school for Jewish and non-Aryan children.[3]

By 1932, the progressive Weimar Republic was slowing down, and Hitler was well on his way toward leading Germans into a conservative, anti-Semitic, fascist regime. Fascism had held sway in neighboring Italy since Benito Mussolini was appointed Prime Minister in 1922 and declared himself the Italian dictator in 1925. Known as *Il Duce* (The Leader), he believed that people were divided into a hierarchy of races and established a police state. In 1933, two countries over in Spain, fascism was also rising, leading to the Spanish Civil War between 1936 and 1939. A violent, conservative movement was sweeping across the continent of Europe. In 1933 in Berlin, Hitler had been appointed Chancellor and quickly begin implementing restrictive laws. The *Gesetz zur Behebung der Not von Volk und Reich* (Law to Remedy the Distress of People and Reich, or Enabling Act of 1933) was the death knell for progressivism.

The years prior to the start of WWII saw the implementation of many laws and repercussions for educators and students, affecting Vera, her colleagues, and their students; in 1933, *Das Reichsgesetz zur Wiederherstellung des Berufsbeamtentum* (The Reich Law for the Restoration of the Civil Service) made it legal to fire Jewish and undesirable teachers and civil servants, massive book burnings took place in Berlin, and a 1.5% cap was put on the admittance of Jewish students into secondary schools and colleges. In 1934, the parents' advisory council was abolished. In 1935, the Boy Scouts and other youth organizations were banned, the Nazi-approved *Hitlerjugend* (Hitler Youth) was the only permitted youth organization, and by 1936, membership in the *Hitlerjugend* was mandatory for children.[4] In 1936, Jewish teachers were banned from teaching in public schools, and in 1937, Jewish students were banned from attending public schools. In 1937, Nazi teachings were fully implemented in schools. Anti-Semitic literature such as *Die Judenfrage im Unterricht* (*The Jewish Question in Education*), which contained guidelines for the identification of Jews, were instituted in the classrooms.[5] 1938 was a turning point leading up to WWII and in Germany's persecution of Jews and undesirables. In November 1938 the bloody, far-right, Nazi uprising *Kristallnacht* (Night of Broken Glass) took place: two days of rioting and violence against Jewish citizens and their businesses, homes, schools, and cemeteries. That year, Vera's school was permanently shut down by the Nazi government, Jewish children were rejected from schools, and Jews were advised to start their own segregated schools.

In the summer of 1939, Vera's sister and parents emigrated from Germany to safety, her sister taking the last flight out of Berlin to London.[6] Even though her family had escaped, Vera was adamant about staying in Berlin to assist folks. Between the summer and winter of 1939, Vera volunteered with *Reichsvertretung der deutschen Juden* (The Representative Body of German Jews), assisting orphaned Jewish children with fleeing to safer countries. Efficient and tender-hearted, Vera gathered the necessary paperwork and booked ship transportation for the children. Despondent at the political climate and the violent Nazi regime in Germany, Vera attempted suicide. Finally, her ex-girlfriend Erika Weigand and colleague Renata von Schelih, a.k.a. "Miss Socrates," intervened and convinced Vera to leave Germany and join them in the United States. Renata pulled strings with her brother Rudolf to get Vera's exit paperwork. Rudolf was a Nazi diplomat, German Resistance fighter, and whistle-blower who arranged for paperwork for hundreds of escapees and leaked documentation of the early Holocaust atrocities to Great Britain. In 1942, the Nazis hung him in Plötzensee Prison for his actions.

Vera arrived in New York in the winter of 1939. Vera's friend Erika and her family were respected academics in the United States and begged the President's wife, Eleanor Roosevelt, to assist in obtaining an extended work visa for Vera and, in the end, Eleanor's intervention paid off.[7] Vera said about the process of emigrating at age 35: "Luckily I had a friend, who managed to get a visa for me, when the quota had long been exhausted, and so I came to the USA via Sweden in 1939 with the 'Gripsholm' from Göteborg. Suddenly there I was on my own, and that even had its good sides. For me exile was a reincarnation. There was nothing of my former life which burdened me. The only thing which counted was what one knew....So I went through this until I finally ended up in my own subject again."[8] Upon landing on foreign soil, Vera also became a poet with her first poem, "Terra Renata" ("Land Reborn").

Before she left Germany, Vera had a dream that affected her deeply. She called it a "prophetic dream," and in this dream, she had seen her future summer camp for boys.[9] Four years later, Vera's dream came true. In 1943, Vera, a dedicated, lifelong caregiver and protector of children, opened a small summer camp for refugee boys whose families immigrated from Nazi Germany. This camp was called Camp Rena, short for the Latin word "renata" or "rebirth."[10] In 1944, Vera founded Camp Catawba, a progressive camp for 6- to 12-year-old boys in Blowing Rock, North Carolina. Camp Catawba ran for 26 years and changed many boys' lives with its combination of love, comradery, art, and drama. The children read Homer around the campfire in their pajamas and performed theatrics, including works by Shakespeare, *The Persians* by Aeschylus, *Philoctetes* by Sophocles, and *The Birds* and *The Frogs*, both by Aristophanes. In the late 1940s, Vera met her partner, Tui St. George Tucker. Tui was 20 years younger than Vera, an avant garde composer, musical instrument inventor, and colleague of composers John Cage and Grete Sulta. Tui soon joined Vera at Camp Catawba during the summers, rising to become the camp's musical director and guiding the children into performing classical work including Bach and Händel. The campers were enthralled with Tui, "I'd never seen a woman in jeans before. She was so outspoken—I'd never heard a woman curse. We absolutely adored her; she was so liberated."[11]

In 1946, Vera became a naturalized American citizen. During the school year, Vera taught the Classics, classical Greek, Greek mythology, German, and Greek theater at colleges including Vassar College, Salem College, Bryn Mawr, Yale University, and Brooklyn College, and published three books of poetry. In 1985, Vera died in Manhattan at age 80. Irascible to the end, Tui retired to Camp Catawba after Vera's death and died there in 2004.

Resources

Bredow, Moritz Alexander Von. *Rebellische Pianistin: Das Leben Der Grete Sultan Zwischen Berlin Und New York*. Mainz: Schott, 2014.

Kreis, Gabriele. *Frauen Im Exil: Dichtung Und Wirklichkeit*. Darmstadt: Luchterhand Literaturverlag, 1988.

Lachmann, Vera. *Homer's Sun Still Shines: Ancient Greece in Essays, Poems, and Translations*. Translated by Charles A. Miller. New Market, VA: Trackaday, 2004.

Archive

Special Collections at Belk Library: Camp Catawba and Vera Lachmann Papers, 1943–2014, undated, http://www.collections.library.appstate.edu/findingaids/ac214

Vera Lachmann, drawn by Avery Cassell

This page is intentionally blank to facilitate coloring the reverse side.

Erika Mann, a.k.a Eri
1905–1969, Germany/United States/Switzerland
Klaus Mann, a.k.a. Eissi
1906–1949, Germany/United States
drawn by Tyler Cohen

Erika and Klaus Mann were siblings, writers, activists, actors, travelers, and heavily involved with the theater. Erika and Klaus were two of the six children of Katia Mann and Thomas Mann, German writer, 1929 Nobel Prize in Literature laureate, and political conservative. The Mann family was well-to-do and intellectual. Katia came from a family of secular Jewish academics, feminists, writers, and musicians, while Thomas' family consisted of Christian politicians, businessmen, and *Hanseaten* (patricians or nobility). Although Katia was Jewish by birth, her husband Thomas was Lutheran, and Erika and Katia were baptized Protestant.

The Mann siblings grew up in Munich, in an unconventional and miserable, albeit creative, household. Thomas was unhappily cold, distant, and closeted as gay or bisexual. Erika, Klaus, and Elizabeth were favored by their parents while the other three children were cruelly disregarded. Erika described an incident during the food shortages of WWI when there was one solitary fig left over for the six children to share, "What did my father do? He gave this fig just to me alone...the other three children stared in horror, and my father said sententiously with emphasis: 'One should get the children used to injustice early.'"[1] The family was also rife with weak sexual boundaries. There were strong indications that there were several incestuous relationships in the Mann family, possibly between Thomas and Klaus, Klaus and Erika, and Katia and her twin brother.[2] Klaus described his relationship with Erika as "[we] acted twin-like in an almost provocative way."[3] Erika and Klaus "shared an exclusive make-believe world in which they created a secret language and role-played a variety of bizarre characters."[4] Suicide and unhappiness also ran rampant in the Mann family; two of Thomas Mann's sisters committed suicide, as did two of his sons, and his brother's wife. Klaus fanaticized about suicide, "In the mornings, nothing but the wish to die. When I calculate what I have to lose, it seems negligible. No chance of a really happy relationship. Probably no chance of literary fame in the near future....Death can only be regarded as deliverance."[5]

In the early 1920s, Erika founded her theater troupe, the *Laienbund Deutscher Mimiker*, and in 1924 she passed her *Abitur* (pre-university exams.) Klaus had a rough time of it in school and was bullied for his homosexuality which was apparent even at a young age. Klaus and Erika moved to Berlin to discover the freedom of Weimar-era Berlin. In 1924, Klaus started writing short stories and plays, including *Anja und Esther*, a play whose four protagonists have convoluted romantic and sexual relationships with one another. When the play opened in 1925, Erika, Klaus, Gustaf Gründgens, and Pamela Wedekind played the parts both in the play and eerily in real life, "Klaus planned to marry Pamela, with whom Erika fell in love, while Erika arranged to marry Gustaf, with whom Klaus began an affair."[6] To add to the scandal, Klaus appeared in promotional photos wearing dark heavy lipstick, and both Pamela and Erika cross-dressed as men in real life. The Weimar Republic in Germany was in full swing, as Klaus and Erika rode its wave of creativity, sexual expression, and permissiveness.

In 1927, Erika and Klaus decided to get the hell out of Dodge and wend their way around the world. They traveled through the U.S. (including Hawaii), Japan, Korea, and Russia, then they wrote a book about it, *Rundherum–Abenteuer einer Weltreise* (*All Around–Adventure of a World Trip*), an anecdotal, humorous travelogue. In 1930, the journalist, writer, and activist Annemarie Schwarzenbach visited Berlin and met the siblings. Erika and Klaus both became enamored with the brilliant and seductive Annemarie and, after Erika had a brief liaison with Annemarie, the trio became lifelong close friends, often traveling and working together until Annemarie's tragic, early death in 1942.

By 1930, the Weimar Republic was winding down, and in 1933, the conservative, populist Nazi party was the largest elected political party in Germany, Hitler was appointed Chancellor, and had passed the *Gesetz zur Behebung der Not von Volk und Reich* (Law to Remedy the Distress of People and Reich, or the Enabling Act of 1933), an amendment to the Constitution that gave the recently formed Nazi Cabinet the power to enact laws for four years without the involvement of the Weimar Republic *Reichstag* (Lower house of the Legislature), essentially handing power carte blanche to Hitler and his band of Nazis.

The Mann family was highly suspect under the new Nazi regime, and not even Thomas Mann's reputation and 1929 Nobel Prize for his novel *Buddenbrooks* could redeem them. The mother's family was Jewish, the entire family were intellectuals, Erika and

Klaus were free-loving, gender-bending homosexuals, and to cap things off, they persisted in living in bourgeois splendor.

In 1933, Erika and Klaus became actively involved with fighting Nazis and fascism. Klaus, Annemarie, and a couple of other writers started a monthly anti-fascist literary magazine called *Die Sammlung* (*The Collection*), whose first issue was published in Amsterdam. *Die Sammlung* was published in German, featured mostly work from exiled German male writers, but also ran work from a few non-German men such as English novelist Aldous Huxley, American novelist Ernest Hemingway, and French poet Jean Cocteau.

Erika and Klaus also formed a new theater group, a political cabaret called *Die Pfeffermühle* (The Peppermill), which caught the disgruntled attention of the Third Reich within weeks of their first performance in Berlin. The troupe fled from Berlin to Zurich, then to Basel, Switzerland where they caused *Schweizer Nationalsozialisten* (a Swiss fascist organization) to riot against them. *Die Pfeffermühle* was getting banned for their strong, anti-fascist political content, but they continued getting bookings and touring, traveling to Czechoslovakia, Belgium, the Netherlands, and Luxembourg. In early 1937, they attempted to tour in America, but could not find a steady venue in New York. From their first performance on January 1, 1933 until they disbanded on August 14, 1936, *Die Pfeffermühle* gave over 1,000 anti-fascist performances across Europe.

In 1934, Klaus was stripped of his German citizenship for his political activities, and in 1935, Erika suffered the same fate. The Mann family fled Germany. In September of 1933, Thomas, Katia, and the other four siblings emigrated to neighboring Küsnacht, Switzerland. In 1935, Erika entered into a marriage of convenience with the English gay poet W. H. Auden in order to gain British citizenship. The gay novelist, pacifist, and memoirist Christopher Isherwood officiated the ceremony, with the handsome, rough-hewn Erika looking considerably butcher than her dapper, effeminate groom. By 1937, Erika was living in New York City with Klaus, Annemarie, and a tattered, yet energetic and creative collection of exiled artists and writers.

In 1938, the Spanish Civil War was raging, so Erika and Klaus traveled to Spain to report on the uprising. That same year, Erika published *Zehn Millionen Kinder: Die Erziehung der Jugend im Dritten Reich*. Published in English as *School for Barbarians: Education under the Nazis*, this fierce critique of the conditions of Adolf Hitler's Third Reich sold over 40,000 copies within three months. Later that year, Klaus and Erika co-wrote another book, *Deutsche Kultur im Exil* (English title: *Escape to Life*) about German pre-WWII exiles. Erika and Klaus also toured American, lecturing passionately on the evils of Hitler and the Nazis, hoping to awaken American citizens to its threat to democracy, human rights, and freedom. A poster advertising a New York 1937 lecture tour with Klaus lists as topics, "After Hitler—What?, A Family Against Dictatorship, and School of Humanity (Democracy and the Youth),"[7] among other things.

In September of 1939, WWII started. During most of the war, Erika lived in England and worked as a BBC radio journalist. In 1942, Thomas, Katia, and Klaus and Erika's siblings moved to Los Angeles. In 1943, Klaus became a U.S. citizen and served in the U.S. Army in Italy. Once the Allied invasion of Normandy, or D-Day, occurred in 1944, Erika became a war correspondent with the Allied forces. D-Day signaled the liberation of German-occupied France and the eventual end of the war a year later. Erika reported from the war front until the end of the war, writing from battlefields in France, Belgium and the Netherlands. After the war ended, Erika was the only woman to cover the Nuremberg trial, military tribunals set up to prosecute Nazi leaders for their actions during the Holocaust and other war crimes. Erika was highly critical of what she considered leniency by the courts towards prominent German figures. In 1946, she moved to Los Angeles to help her parents. Due to their political outspokenness, suspicions of them being Communists, and their homosexuality, Erika and Klaus were investigated by the FBI.

In 1952, the Mann family fled America, the anti-Communist red scare, and McCarthyism for Switzerland. Klaus, having been a depressive his entire adult life, killed himself in France on May of 1949. Erika was devastated, and dedicated the rest of her life assisting her family, specifically her father. Her sister said, "She returned home, because she had exhausted her career, and so devoted herself to the work of her father."[8] In 1955, Thomas Mann died, and Erika died in Zurich of a brain tumor in 1969.

Resources

Hauck, Gerald Gunter. *Reluctant Immigrants: Klaus and Erika Mann in American Exile, 1936-1945*. S.l.: S.n., 1997.

Mann, Erika. *School for Barbarians*. Dover Publications, 2014.

Speck, Wieland and Andrea Weiss, dir. *Escape to Life: The Erika & Klaus Mann Story*. Germany: Jezebel Productions. 2001. DVD.

Spotts, Frederic. *Cursed Legacy: The Tragic Life of Klaus Mann*. New Haven: Yale University Press, 2016.

Weiss, Andrea. *In the Shadow of the Magic Mountain: The Erika and Klaus Mann Story*. Chicago: University of Chicago Press, 2008.

Erika and Klaus Mann, drawn by Tyler Cohen

This page is intentionally blank to facilitate coloring the reverse side.

Hans and Sophie Scholl
Hans Scholl, 1918–1943, and Sophie Scholl, 1921–1943, Germany
drawn by Jon Macy

Hans and Sophie Scholl were two of six children born into a politically and culturally progressive Christian family. Their father, Robert, was a small-town mayor, and their mother, Magdalena, was a housewife who had been a nurse in a military hospital during WWI. Hans was older than Sophie by three years, but they were very close. After the family moved to a nearby town, Robert became a tax consultant. Hans' and Sophie's father was a strong role model for the Scholl siblings; he was known for being uncontrollably outspoken: "He was a big, rather heavyset man, with strong opinions and an unwillingness, if not an inability, to keep those opinions to himself."[1] Robert was a pacifist who disapproved of Hitler and his populist following; however, four of his children became enamored with the Hitler youth groups.

In 1933, 15-year-old Hans joined the *Hitlerjugend* (Hitler Youth, or HJ) and 12-year-old Sophie joined *Bund Deutscher Mädel* (League of German Girls, or BDM), popular youth social groups whose function was to provide populist indoctrination under the guise of wholesome entertainment. Both Hans and Sophie were enthusiastic about change and became Nazi youth group leaders. One of the siblings explained the populist culture within the youth groups in the early 1930s in Germany: "We heard much oratory about the fatherland, comradeship, unity of the Volk, and love of country… Our fatherland—what was it but the extended home of all those who shared a language and belonged to one people. We loved it, though we couldn't say why. After all, up to now we hadn't talked very much about it. But now these things were being written across the sky in flaming letters. And Hitler—so we heard on all sides—Hitler would help this fatherland to achieve greatness, fortune, and prosperity. He would see to it that everyone had work and bread. He would not rest until every German was independent, free, and happy in his fatherland. We found this good, and we were willing to do all we could to contribute to the common effort. But there was something else that drew us with mysterious power and swept us along: the closed ranks of marching youth with banners waving, eyes fixed straight ahead, keeping time to drumbeat and song….We entered into it with body and soul, and we could not understand why our father did not approve, why he was not happy and proud. On the contrary, he was quite displeased with us."[2]

By 1936, the siblings were starting to become became disillusioned with the Nazi government, objecting to its racial legislation, anti-Semitism, and censorship of books and music. 1936 was also the year that legislation was enacted forbidding Jews from becoming tax consultants and school teachers; in 1937, Jewish children were forbidden from attending public schools.[3] It may be possible that their father had words to say about his Jewish colleagues being disallowed from practicing their profession. By 1934, Hans had left the HJ and formed his own non-government sanctioned *die deutsche Jugendbewegung* (German Youth Movement). In 1937, four of the Scholl siblings were arrested. By then, Hans had fulfilled his mandatory service requirement and was now serving in the German Nazi army. Hans was arrested under three charges: affiliation with a banned youth group, traveling with more money than was permitted by the government during a group trip, and homosexuality as stated in Paragraph 175 of the revised German criminal code. Paragraph 175 was written to punish male homosexuals. In 1935, the Nazi regime revised Paragraph 175, broadening the range of illegal behaviors between men. In most cases, the punishment for male homosexual behavior was between three months and up to ten years in prison.[4] Lesbian activity was also illegal, but not punished under this particular code; however, lesbians were arrested as asocials or prostitutes, and lesbianism was considered by the Nazis as a curable condition.

Between 1934 and 1936, Hans had a passionate one-and-a-half years long relationship with Rolf Futterknech, another boy in his youth group. Their obvious affection and unashamed sexual intimacy were noted by the authorities, resulting in Hans' arrest several years later. Hans took responsibility for the affair and tried to protect Rolf by claiming to have seduced him. The homosexuality charges against Hans were dismissed in 1938, but his arrest for homosexuality affected him profoundly and was one of the reasons he questioned Nazi beliefs. Although Sophie was straight, she was also shocked by homophobia directed at her brother.

In 1942, Hans was a medical student at the University of Munich and became a member of the *die Weiße Rose* (the White Rose) resistance group, which was in its embryonic stages of formation. The German Resistance group, the White Rose, was known for Christian passive resistance. Members included University of Munich students, anti-Nazis, and anti-fascists. In the summer of 1942, the White Rose resistance group started printing and publishing political leaflets. The White Rose pamphlets were erudite—quoting from the Bible, Aristotle, and other classic philosophers and poets—and hoped to appeal to the German intelligentsia, sounding the alarm against the Nazi government and Hitler. Their printing press was located in Josef Söhngen's basement, a gay bookstore owner.[5] In the winter of 1942, Professor Kurt Huber became a member and mentor. In the fall of 1942, Sophie became involved after discovering that her idolized brother Hans was writing the pamphlets. In January 1943, the White Rose changed their name to the German Resistance Movement, printed over 5,000 copies of their fifth pamphlet, *Aufruf an alle Deutsche!* (*Appeal to all Germans!*), and distributed them nationally. The name change to German Resistance Movement coincided with a change in pamphlet writing style in an effort to appeal to a wider population.

On February 18, 1943, Hans and Sophie were distributing pamphlets at the University of Munich when they were caught by Professor Jakob Schmid, who held them until the Gestapo arrived. Jakob received a reward and a promotion. On February 20, 1943, Hans Scholl, aged 24, and Sophia Scholl, aged 21, were beheaded by the Nazi government for treason. Professor Kurt Huber was beheaded on July 13, 1943, after publication of the group's sixth pamphlet which Huber helped to write. Several other White Rose members were executed and imprisoned for treason. The bookseller Josef Söhngen was sentenced to six months in prison and lived until 1970. In 1942, Hans' and Sophie's father, Robert, spent four months in prison for calling Hitler the "scourge of God,"[6] and, less than one week after the Nazis killed Hans and Sophie, he was sentenced to 18 months in prison for listening to enemy radio broadcasts.[7] Robert Scholl lived until 1973. Hans' sister Inge wrote several books about her siblings and the White Rose, but deliberately omitted or downplayed Hans' arrest for homosexuality, as she did not want the public to realize that Hans was gay. Hans and Sophie were posthumously awarded the status of Righteous Among the Nations.

Sophie's last words before she was killed by the Nazi government were, "How can we expect righteousness to prevail when there is hardly anyone willing to give himself up individually to a righteous cause? Such a fine, sunny day, and I have to go, but what does my death matter, if through us, thousands of people are awakened and stirred to action?"[8] Hans succinctly proclaimed, "Long live freedom!"[9]

Resources

Rothemund, Marc, dir. *Sophie Scholl, the Final Days*. Produced by Christoph Müller and Sven Burgemeister. By Fred Breinersdorfer. Performed by Julia Jentsch, Alexander Held, Fabian Hinrichs, and Johanna Gastdorf. Germany: X Verleih, 2005. DVD.

Scholl, Hans, Sophie Scholl, and J. Maxwell Brownjohn. *At the Heart of the White Rose: Letters and Diaries of Hans and Sophie Scholl*. New York: Harper & Row, 1987.

Schulz, Stefan. "Der Prozess Gegen Hans Und Sophie Scholl." Karlrobert Kreiten - Roland Freisler - Hans Sophie Scholl. Accessed September 09, 2018. http://karlrobertkreiten.de/roland-freisler/prozess-gegen-hans-und-sophie-scholl.php.

Zoske, Robert M. *Flamme Sein! Hans Scholl Und Die Weiße Rose: Eine Biografie*. München: C.H. Beck, 2018.

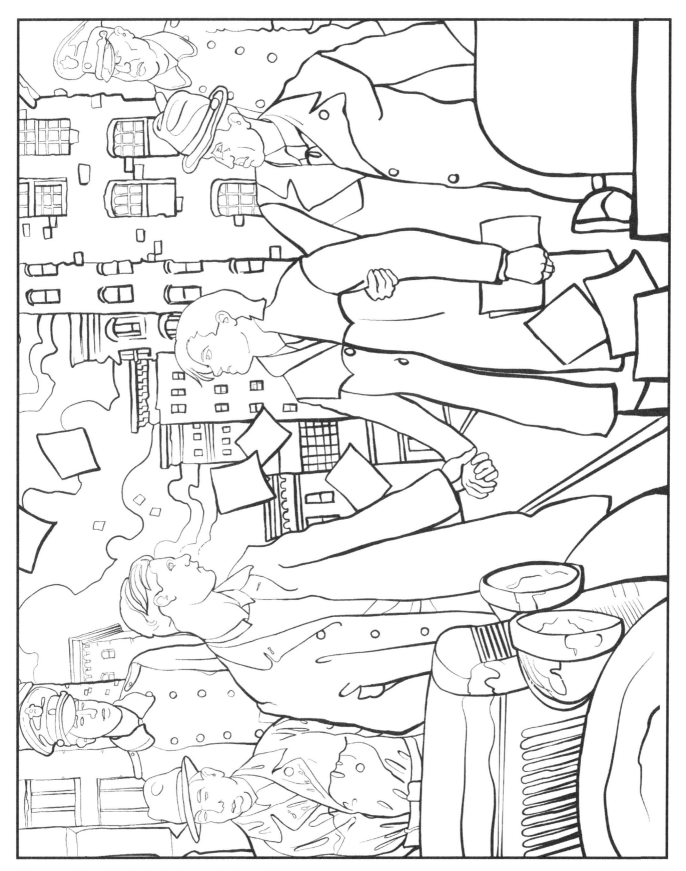

Hans and Sophie Scholl, drawn by Jon Macy

This page is intentionally blank to facilitate coloring the reverse side.

Felice Schragenheim, a.k.a. Lice
1922–1944, Germany
drawn by Soizick Jaffre

Felice Schragenheim was a butch, a poet with a penchant for green ink, and a German Resistance fighter, but she is best known as the dedicated lover to Lilly Wust. Felice was born in Berlin into a liberal, comfortable, loving Jewish family. Her father had served in WWI, both of her parents were dentists, and she had one sibling–an older sister named Irene. In 1930, Felice's mother was killed in an automobile accident. Her father remarried soon after, but Felice and her sister were not fond of their new, younger step-mother. Felice's father was a well-known, popular dentist and held the position of head of the Welfare and Insurance Office of the Reich Association of German Dentists, but this was not going to be enough to save him. Hitler and his populist Nazi government was on the rise. In 1933, the *Gesetz zur Behebung der Not von Volk und Reich* (the Law to Remedy the Distress of People and Reich or Enabling Act of 1933,) was passed, and soon thereafter, the Decree on the Practice of Dentists and Dental Technicians Under the Health Insurance Plan was instituted, which meant that Felice's father could no longer get reimbursement from public health insurance funds for services rendered. In 1933 and 1934, Jewish doctors were forbidden to treat non-Jewish patients, because "…the Jew is the incarnation of lies and deceit."[1]

In 1934, Felice's father bought a home in Palestine with the intention of emigrating. He also made financial arrangements for the teenage girls, Felice and Irene, in case there were any issues. In March 1935, their father died during an air raid and the small family moved into another apartment. Because of her father's service in WWI, Felice remained in school despite the regulations restricting the number of Jews from attending public schools. She had schoolgirl crushes on other girls, but they came to naught. It is believed that in 1936, her older sister left Germany to attend school. The Schragenheim's extended family had several relatives in the U.S. that tried to expedite emigration for Felice, including her Uncle Walter in Chicago.

In October of 1938, Jewish German citizens had their passports revoked by the government, and could only get them back if they agreed to have them stamped with the letter "J" for *Jude* (Jew). In November of 1938, two days of riots and looting against Jews occurred in Germany. During *Kristallnacht* (Crystal Night, or the Night of Broken Glass), Jewish homes, businesses, synagogues, hospitals, cemeteries, and schools were destroyed. The world watched the fiery riots, and although reporters responded with denunciation of the German government-sanctioned riots, assistance for Jewish German citizens was not forthcoming. Newspapers reported extensively on the riots and restrictions against them. *The New York Times* reproduced excerpts of national editorials expressing outrage, including this one from *The Chicago Tribune*, "What is especially significant is that the supposedly all-powerful government has permitted an irresponsible mob to break loose and run riot contrary to law and order. To turn the task over to unrestrained private fury is the negation of civilized political responsibility. It is chaos rather than government. Has the Hitler regime, in fomenting anti-Semitism, bred a beast that it dares not restrain?"[2] Although President Roosevelt said, "I cannot believe that such things can occur in a civilized land in the twentieth century,"[3] it was an empty statement and the President refused to relax U.S. immigration laws to admit fleeing German Jews.

A few days after *Kristallnacht*, Jewish children were completely banned from German public schools. At age 16, Felice's school days were over. Laws and restrictions against German Jews tightened. Jewish citizens continued to flee the budding holocaust in Germany, but most countries were reluctant to take them in or had strict restrictions. WWII started in September of 1939. Felice's step-mother and Felice got approved to emigrate to Palestine in the end of 1940, and her step-mother sailed. Felice chose to stay on in Germany, hoping that Uncle Walter's efforts would soon bear fruit and she could emigrate to the U.S. The U.S. continued to obstruct refugees and immigrants with red tape: "We temporarily can slow the number of immigrants to the United States, and as good as bring that number to a standstill. This will be possible if we instruct our consulates to place all possible obstacles in the applicants' paths, to require additional information and establish various administrative measures, which will serve to delay and delay and delay the approval of visas."[4] In the summer of 1941, Felice was finally approved for emigration to the U.S. She had the money left to her by her father and booked her ship passage over four times, but each time the trip fell through due to cancellations and closed borders. Felice's visa expired before she could successfully book a passage out of Germany.

In October of 1941, Jewish citizens started being assembled into makeshift collection camps in the city, and then transported out of Berlin to destinations unknown. Felice had gotten a factory job, so was exempt from deportation. In August of 1942, Felice's elderly grandmother and her great-uncle were deported to Theresienstadt concentration camp, and in October of 1942, Felice received her notice of deportation. Felice took her possessions, left a tear-stained faux suicide note, and went underground for safety. From 1942 until she was arrested in 1944, Felice lived in Berlin as a one of the *Untergetaucht* (submerged), also called U-Boats or submarines; they lived underground and evaded arrest and deportation, often being helped by sympathetic non-Jewish Germans.

Felice started living with her one of her girlfriends, Inge, at Inge's parent's home. In order to not place herself, Inge, or Inge's family in danger, Felice needed to say indoors away from the eyes of the Gestapo, but she did not always follow these recommendations. The same month that Felice moved in, Inge started a job as a housekeeper for a German family, Lilly Wust, her four children, and her Nazi husband, Günther. Inge soon discovered that Lilly was a hedonistic, bored housewife with a string of male lovers. Günther was a soldier who was away most of the time and also had lovers on the side. Felice, shut up in Inga's parent's home was enchanted with the gossip that Inga brought home about Lilly, and asked to be introduced. In November, Inge introduced Lilly to some of her friends, a lesbian couple, and another woman, Felice. Felice and Lilly took to one another immediately. Soon, Felice was visiting Lilly at her apartment while Inga was working there. In January of 1943, Felice bought a false identification card that identified her as "Barbara Schrader," a "chaperone for children on domestic outings." During this period, Felice worked with a German Resistance group, acting as a courier for false documentation papers.[5]

Between November and March, Felice developed a crush on Lilly; although Lilly considered herself straight and rejected Felice's advances, they remained close friends. In March of 1943 Lilly was hospitalized with an infection and Felice courted her with red roses and hugs. After a few days of illness, Lilly gave Felice a note with her sickbed requests, "skin cream, your handkerchief, correspondence cards, your love for me alone, and needle and thread."[6] Lilly had finally realized that she was in love with Felice and started writing the first of many mash notes to her beloved: "Felice, I love you too much, Felice, my beautiful dark girl…. And when you look at me, Felice, I feel like I'm on fire."[7] On April 2, 1943, Lilly was released from the hospital and they started sleeping together. It was the first time that Lilly had been with a woman, and she was enchanted, they fell into a butch-femme dynamic, with Felice the protective butch and Lilly the glamorous femme. They started going out together as a couple. Felice was closeted about one thing with Lilly; she had not told Lilly that she was Jewish. In May of 1943, Felice moved in with Lilly, occasionally disappearing to do resistance work, until one night Lilly confronted her about her absences and Felice broke down in tears, and confessed that she was Jewish.

Lilly and Felice fell more deeply in love with one another. Felice gave herself the nickname "Jaguar," and Lilly was her "Aimée." Lilly wrote to her lover after she'd discovered that she was Jewish, "When I think of all the years I have wasted! Felice, please don't leave me alone, please take me with you! I know that it would mean that I would leave everything and everyone behind but what does that matter if you love me!"[8] Lilly decided to ask her husband for a divorce, and even came out about Felice to her parents. Her parents were supportive; although they were fine with Lilly and Felice being lovers, they fretted about the dangers of Felice being Jewish. In June 26, 1943, Felice and Lilly made up a marriage contract, vowing their love. Lilly pledged to "be frugal when it is called for"[9] and Felice pledged to "no longer look at pretty girls, at least only to ascertain that you are prettier."[10] In September, they exchanged rings, and in October of 1943, Lilly was granted her divorce from Günther. Felice and Lilly started their life together as spouses.

In early 1944, Felice got a job in the editorial offices at *National-Zeitung*, a newspaper that was affiliated with the Nazi government, and she continued to work with the German Resistance. On August 21, 1944, Felice and Lilly bicycled to a picnic spot near Havel Lake where they spent the day. The Gestapo was waiting for them when they arrived home that night. They arrested Felice and took her to Schulstrasse transit camp in Berlin. In September 4, 1944, Felice was deported to Theresienstadt concentration camp in Czechoslovakia, where Lilly visited her and pleaded unsuccessfully for her release. Felice was sent to Auschwitz concentration camp and, on December 31, 1944, Felice died during a death march. WWII ended less than a year later, on September 2, 1945.

Lilly was heartbroken after Felice's arrest and imprisonment. In 1945, Lilly began her *Book of Tears*, a compilation of all the poems that Aimee and Jaguar had written to each other. In 1995, Lilly was declared Righteous Among the Nations for her efforts to rescue Jewish women and shield them from Nazi persecution during World War II. Lilly died in 2006. Felice is commemorated on Lilly's headstone.

Resources

Clay, Catrine dir. *Love Story : Berlin 1942*. Performed by Gerd Ehrlich, Sara Kestelman, Elenai Predski-Kramer. United Kingdom: BBC: Timewatch, 2000. VHS.

Färberböck, Max dir. *Aimée & Jaguar*. Performed by Juliane Köhler and Maria Schrader. Germany: Antiprod, 1998. DVD.

Fischer, Erica. *Aimée & Jaguar: A Love Story, Berlin 1943*. New York: HarperCollins. 1994.

Felice Schragenheim, drawn by Soizick Jaffre

This page is intentionally blank to facilitate coloring the reverse side.

Charlotte Wolff
1897–1986, Germany/England
drawn by Pat Tong

Charlotte Wolff was a Jewish psychotherapist, sexologist, and chirologist (palm reader) whose work and writing on lesbianism and bisexuality was groundbreaking. She was raised in a liberal, middle-class German-Jewish family in Riesenburg, West Prussia. She knew that she was a lesbian from a young age. She was boyish and had her first romantic and sexual relationship at age 13: "Neither Ida nor I had ever heard of the term homosexuality, nor did we know anything about love between people of the same sex. We experienced our attraction without fear or label, and had no model for love-making. We just loved. Kissing produced the greatest excitement, and we kissed at any hour. When we slept together our legs entwined, while our two mouths molded into one. These were the happiest nights of all my days."[1]

Through Ida, Charlotte later met and fell deeply and obsessively in love with an artist named Lisa. In 1917, in the thick of WWI, 19-year-old Charlotte ran away from her parent's home to join Lisa in Berlin. Lisa was a sculptress and, through her, Charlotte was exposed to the sophisticated art scene in Berlin. Charlotte's life was changed. Lisa moved to Russia and got married, while Charlotte remained in Berlin to study medicine, periodically traveling to Russia to visit Lisa in a frenzy of romantic and sexual passion. In 1924, Lisa forbade Charlotte from further visits and they broke up for good.

In 1926, Charlotte graduated as a physician and went on to work in several practices including the city's first birth control clinic, clinics for working-class people, and clinics for sex workers. She excelled at her work and was appointed deputy director for prenatal services. She volunteered in a marriage counseling center, distributing family planning information and providing low-income women with birth control devices. In 1932, she'd risen to the position of the director of the Institute for Electro-physical Therapy. Charlotte became intrigued by sexology and chirology or hand reading. The modern study of sexology's locus was in Berlin; Magnus Hirschfeld founded the *Institut für Sexualwissenschaft* (Institute for Sexual Science) in 1919, giving scientific clarity to a growing sexual revolution. Charlotte thrived in Weimar Republic Berlin, exclaiming, "At no other time had there been such creative daring among German artists and thinkers alike. Culture flourished while the country seemed at death's door. It was the heyday of erotic pleasures, sophistication and wit, which gave spice to plays, chansons and the cabaret. The 'intimate' theater with its musicals and revues reached a quality never achieved again….Heaven was not somewhere above us, but on earth, in the German metropolis."[2]

By 1931, the Weimar Republic, with its progressiveness and creativity, was almost over with. Hitler and the Nazis were gaining power, and Hitler was appointed as Chancellor of Germany in 1933. Although women were emancipated under the liberal rule of Weimar Republic, their freedoms were curtailed under Nazi Germany. Women's roles were strictly defined; motherhood and procreation were revered, while careers and higher education were discouraged, and in some cases made illegal. Although Charlotte was not politically active, she was a member of the *Verein Sozialistischer Ärzten* (Association of Socialist Physicians) and sympathized with the *Unabhängige Sozialdemokratische Partei* (Independent Social Democratic Party). In 1931, her work with women's reproductive health services was frowned upon by the conservative Nazi government; she was warned and requested to stop.[3] In the fall of 1932, her long-term Aryan lover of the past nine years left her because Charlotte was Jewish and it had become a dangerous liability to be closely associated with Jews. In March of 1933, the *Gesetz zur Behebung der Not von Volk und Reich* (The Enabling Act of 1933, or the Law to Remedy the Distress of People and Reich) was passed, and the decree of the Berlin city commissioner for health suspended Jewish doctors from the city's charity services.[4] Charlotte was effectively banned from working. That same year, the Gestapo arrested Charlotte for cross-dressing as a man and being a spy. By a fluke, she was recognized by the police guard as the doctor who'd treated his wife, and he surreptitiously released Charlotte. Later, when the Gestapo searched her apartment for bombs, she decided it was time to leave Germany.[5]

Many Berliner Jews fled between 1933 and 1939; Berlin originally had a large Jewish community. Approximately a third of the Jews in Germany lived in the capital city of Berlin. By 1939, the metropolis' Jewish population had decreased from 160,000 to 80,000; in 1933 alone, approximately 37,000 Jews emigrated from Germany. Within a month of the passage of the Enabling Act, of 1933, Jewish businesses were boycotted, and people refused to buy Jewish goods and services; Jewish civil servants were fired or made to retire; Jewish doctors were no longer permitted to practice their profession; cultural organizations were purged of Jews and other artists who created art which Nazis labeled "degenerate." Within two months of its passage, all gay bars and clubs were closed, and all LGBT publications ceased to exist.[6]

On May 10, 1933, there was a massive public book burning of "un-German" books in the Opernplatz; specifically, books written by Jews, liberals, and political dissidents.[7] The book burning protest was led by torch-bearing Nazi university students. Over 20,000 books were burned that May in Berlin, including irreplaceable books from the massive sexology library of Charlotte's colleague, Magnus Hirschfeld. Reich Minister Dr. Goebbels spoke to the rabble, "My fellow students, German men and women, the era of exaggerated Jewish intellectualism is now at an end. The triumph of the German revolution has cleared a path for the German way; and the future German man will not just be a man of books, but also a man of character and it is to this end we want to educate you[8]....No to decadence and moral corruption! Yes to decency and morality in family and state! I consign to the flames the writings of Heinrich Mann, Ernst Gläser, Erich Kästner."[9] So-called Jewish and liberal intellectualism was to be replaced by Nazi ignorance. Once her decision to leave was made, Charlotte left quickly and in 1933 she emigrated to Paris.

As an exile from Germany, Charlotte faced many losses. Charlotte found that she was not permitted to practice medicine in Paris, so she turned to chirology as a career. She found her way into Parisian artist circles. Encouraged by the writer Aldous Huxley, and his wife Maria, Charlotte moved to London in 1936, where she expanded her sexuality studies. In the early 1970s, she published *Love Between Woman* and the groundbreaking book on bisexuality, *Bisexuality: A Study*. Her last major publication was the definitive biography of her old colleague, Magnus Hirschfeld, *Magnus Hirschfeld: A Portrait of a Pioneer in Sexology*. In 1986, Charlotte died in London at age 88.

Resources

Wolff, Charlotte. Bisexuality: A Study. London: Quartet Books, 1979.

Wolff, Charlotte. Hindsight: An Autobiography. London: Quartet Books, 1980.

Wolff, Charlotte. Love Between Women. London: Duckworth, 1973.

Wolff, Charlotte. Magnus Hirschfeld: A Portrait of a Pioneer in Sexology. London: Quartet, 1986.

Charlotte Wolff, *drawn by Pat Tong*

This page is intentionally blank to facilitate coloring the reverse side.

Tatamkhulu Afrika
a.k.a. Ismail Joubert, Mogamed Fu'ad Nasif, John Charlton, Jozua Joubert
1920–2002, Egypt/South Africa
drawn by Justin Hall

Tatamkhulu Afrika (Grandfather Afrika or old man of Afrika) was a novelist, a poet, and a chameleon. He was born in Egypt and named Mogamed Fu'ad Nasif by his parents. His mother was Turkish and his father was an Egyptian-Arab. Soon after his birth, the family moved to South Africa, where his parents died of the flu when he was only two years old. He was adopted by a white Christian family in Limpopo, who renamed him John Charlton, raised him as white, and home-schooled him.[1] In 1938, when he turned 18, his parents revealed to him that he wasn't white and that he was adopted. By the time he died at age 82, he'd cycled through a multitude of names, South African racial classifications, and adventures. His names included Mogamed Fu'ad Nasif, John Charlton, Jozua Joubert, Ismail Joubert, and finally, Tatamkhulu Afrika.

In 1940 and at age 17, Tatamkhulu ran away from home, and wrote and published his first novel, *Broken Earth*. Nearly all the copies went up in flames when his publishing house was destroyed during the WWII London Blitz.[2] *Broken Earth* is currently out of print with two known copies in existence, one in the British Library and the other in the Johannesburg Public Library.[3] Tatamkhulu did not publish again until 1991, but once he started, he was prolific. He wrote poetry, novels, plays, and memoirs, and his work was highly acclaimed.

When Tatamkhulu was in his late teens or early twenties, he volunteered with the South African Union Defense Force to fight in WWII.[4] In addition to the fighting in Europe, WWII included a North African Campaign across the Mediterranean Sea, which started in 1940. Nazi Germany and Fascist Italy's goals were to control access to oil. Between 1940 and 1943, there were 2,104 deaths in battle, 3,928 wounded, and 14,247 prisoner of war members in the North African Campaign.[5] In 1940, the British Army's 11th Hussars captured the Italian Fort Capuzzo in Libya. In 1941, the Nazi German Afrika Korps arrived to assist Fascist Italy in North Africa. In 1942 the Americans got involved with the North African Campaign.

Tatamkhulu served in the North African Western Desert Campaign and was captured by German and Italian forces in the second fall of Tobruk in June of 1942. Tobruk is located along Libya's eastern Mediterranean coast near the border of Egypt. After Tatamkhulu was captured in Tobruk, he was interned as an allied prisoner of war (POW) for three years in prisoner of war camps, first in Fascist Italy and then in Nazi Germany. While he was in the POW camps, he was lovers with other male prisoners and wrote about these relationships in his second novel. He wrote his book in secret while huddled on his cot and using a purloined Red Cross pencil, but the Nazi guards discovered the hidden manuscript and ripped it up in front of him.[6] This lost novel was the predecessor to *Bitter Eden*, written 50 years later.

After he got out of the POW camps, Tatamkhulu worked in the Namibia diamond and copper mines in southwest Africa. In the 1960s, he moved to Cape Town and became politically involved with the anti-apartheid movement. In 1964, he converted to Shi'ite Muslim[7] and changed his name to Ismail Joubert. Although he was classified as white under the South African racial classification system, Tatamkhulu refused that classification, rejected the apartheid category of whiteness, and claimed an African and malay (brown) identity.[8] During this time period, Tatamkhulu formed several intense relationships with other men, but was not part of any gay community. He also became more political, joining the banned, anti-apartheid African National Congress (ANC) and founding the anti-apartheid, charitable organization Al-Jihaad in 1967. In 1987, he was imprisoned and banned by the government from writing for four years. Tatamkhulu was a member of *uMkhonto we Sizwe* (MK, or Spear of the Nation), the armed wing of the ANC that was co-founded by Nelson Mandela. His new name, Tatamkhulu Afrika, was gifted to him by the *uMkhonto we Sizwe*.

In 1991, Tatamkhulu published his first volume of poetry, *Nine Lives*. Tatamkhulu also experienced his first exposure to gay and lesbian culture, but continued to maintain a sort of fluid queerness, refusing to be classified as heterosexual, bisexual, or homosexual. He said, "Don't fence me in, you goddam buffoon! I'm a shiftless drifter that needs room—lots of room—to do my hyenaing in!"[9] In 2002, Tatamkhulu wrote *Bitter Eden*, a rewrite of the novel that he'd written when he was a WWII POW more than 50 years before. *Bitter Eden* was a semi-autobiographical novel set in two World War II POW camps in Italy and Germany, detailing a love triangle between three prisoners. Tatamkhulu could not get *Bitter Eden* published in his native country because of the shocking homoerotic content, but got it published in England. Tatamkhulu said that *Bitter Eden* was "*te goed en nie Suid-Afrikaans genoeg nie*" (too good and not South African enough).[10] The trio of men in *Bitter Eden* are not homosexual or bisexual as defined by Western sexual orientation classifications, but they draw upon a rich South African history of men having sexual and romantic relations with men both during World War II and in non-wartime culture.[11]

In 2005, he published a memoir, *Mr. Chameleon*; however, sadly, it is out of print. We learn that *Mr. Chameleon* was "typed by Robin Malan from the original version, consisting of a nearly blind man's handwriting on a range of surfaces: partly-printed newsprint, used envelopes, and the backs of old manuscripts. An examination of the autobiography, which Afrika beguilingly promises to write truthfully, enables one to settle the issue of some of the contradictions, myths and queries surrounding the man, but the old shape-shifter is wily, and gaps, inconsistencies and ambiguities still remain."[12]

In 2002 Tatamkhulu said of his sexual orientation, "Now there are people who ask me if I am homosexual. And I answer that I have known love for women, I have known love for men. I have lived my life long moving through a human landscape without boundaries. This is also why I think these coming-out-of-the-closet-stories are a load of rubbish. Can any person want to categorize himself so restrictively?"[13]

Tatamkhulu published ten volumes of poetry between 1991 and 2002, winning nearly every South African award for poetry, including the CNA Debut Prize, Pringle Awards, the Olive Schreiner, and Sanlam Poetry Prizes. In 2002, Tatamkhulu died at age 82 following a car accident. *Bitter Eden* was a Lambda Literary Award finalist in 2015, posthumously.

Resources

Afrika, Tatamkhulu. *Bitter Eden*. London: Blue Mark Books, 2016.

Afrika, Tatamkhulu. *Mr. Chameleon: An Autobiography*. Johannesburg: Jacana, 2005.

Afrika, Tatamkhulu. *Nine Lives*. Cape Town: Carrefour, 1991.

Horn, Karen. *In Enemy Hands: South Africa's POWs in World War II*. Johannesburg: Jonathan Ball Publishers, 2015.

Archive

The National English Literary Museum, 87 Beaufort Street, Grahamstown, South Africa, A.Torlesse@ru.ac.za

Tatamkhulu Afrika, drawn by Justin Hall

This page is intentionally blank to facilitate coloring the reverse side.

Cecil Williams
1906(?)–1979, South Africa
drawn by Jessica Bogac-Moore

Cecil Williams was an erudite, urbane, gay, anti-fascist, anti-racist, Communist freedom fighter. Although Cecil is best known for his anti-racism activism in South Africa and his friendship and support of Nelson Mandela, the anti-apartheid revolutionary and political leader, the groundwork for his life as a freedom fighter started in 1939 with WWII. The close relationship that Cecil had with Mandela almost certainly led to South Africa becoming the first country in the world to embody LGBT rights in their post-apartheid Constitution.

Born in Cornwall, England to a working-class family, Cecil's father was a blacksmith. In 1928, Cecil left England for Johannesburg, South Africa. Culturally engaged, elegant, handsome, and well-read, he became involved in theater and the arts. He described Johannesburg as a "gangsters marvel of a mining town."[1] He supported himself as an English teacher at King Edward VII Preparatory School. He was popular with his students but decided to leave teaching and become involved with his true love, the theater. The outbreak of WWII in 1939 changed the direction of Cecil's life.

South Africa became fully sovereign from the United Kingdom in 1931. When WWII broke out in 1939, South Africa uneasily declared its alliance with Great Britain against Nazi Germany, instead of declaring themselves neutral. Participation in WWII was contentious, with a large segment of South Africa's population in favor of remaining neutral or being actively pro-Nazi; the Ossewabrandwag was a South African pro-Nazi organization whose members refused to enlist in the military, demonstrated against participation in WWII, harassed soldiers, and formed a paramilitary wing called the Stormjaers (Assault Troops) to vandalize utilities such as electrical power lines, telegraph, and telephone lines. By the time WWII was over with in 1945, approximately 334,000 men volunteered for full-time service in the South African Army, including 211,000 white, 77,000 black, and 46,000 colored (mixed or Asian) and Indian servicemen.

Cecil became a journalist for the South Africa Broadcasting Corporation,[2] a committed anti-fascist, and a South African Navy soldier serving on the front in Italy. As a soldier, Cecil became friends with a close-knit group of men from wildly diverse backgrounds, the comradery between them sealing his commitment to fighting for freedom and equality. Cecil said, "The black soldiers weren't given guns, and they were in the same danger area that we were. They were given spears to carry around, it's unbelievable, but it's true. They were getting half the pay the whites were getting."[3] Cecil was one of the founders of the Springbok Legion, an anti-fascist, integrated soldiers' rights organization that was started in 1941, four years before WWII ended.[4]

After the war, Cecil returned to South Africa and became more heavily involved with activism. He continued his work with veterans and, by 1952, he'd become the chairman of the Springbok Legion. He remained involved with the theater, producing classic plays, including the scandalous *The Kimberley Train*, whose theme was an interracial couple and apartheid. In 1948, the National Party gained control of South Africa and introduced apartheid as the law; apartheid was a legal system of political, economic, and social separation of the races intended to maintain and extend political and economic control of South Africa by the white minority.

In 1953, Cecil was kicked out of the Springbok Legion, the Congress of Democrats, and the Peace Council by the National Party government. Cecil was inflamed, and he wrote them a letter: "I acknowledge the receipt of your two notices prohibiting me from attending gatherings and calling upon me to resign as Chairman from the Springbok Legion, the Congress of Democrats. It gives me great pleasure to inform you that these prescriptions to be of a temporary nature only, since history abundantly shows that purblind reactionary attempts to stop the growth and spread of ideals have failed without exception. I repeat my belief, that my banning will not be for long. I'm surprised that you and your party hasn't learned from your experience. You gave moral support to the Nazi tyrants, who defied the principles of democracy and destroyed civil liberties. I am proud that I play a small part, along with hundreds of millions of democrats to prove the Nazis and your party wrong. I know that your gags and bans will not silence the voices of democracy, nor halt the march forward to liberty, racial harmony, and world peace."[5]

Under the National Party's regime, civil liberties disappeared, and dissent was considered treasonous. Some of the repercussions of the conservative government were that dissidents were banned from organizations, disallowed meeting with other banned people, not allowed to meet in gatherings of more than two people, and were disallowed to leave the Magisterial District of

Johannesburg. Cecil continued his activism, and in 1956 he was arrested for treason. Cecil had always kept his political life and his gay life separate, but in 1959 he met the man who became his life partner, a Johannesburg resident and Scottish man named John Calderwood. John was more than 25 years younger than Cecil, apolitical, smart, and handsome. When the two men fell in love, Cecil begin to integrate his gay life with his political life, introducing John to his political friends, including his close friend and compatriot, Nelson Mandela.[6]

In the early 1960s, Cecil volunteered to be Nelson Mandela's disguise for traveling. Mandela was the commander-in-chief of the South African guerrilla movement. Nicknamed the "Black Pimpernel" by the press, he was the most wanted man in South Africa. Mandela was traveling across the country and into other countries, organizing anti-apartheid activists into armed rebellion. To fool the authorities and make it possible for Nelson to travel safely, Cecil disguised himself as Mandela's "employer," while Mandela disguised himself as Cecil's "chauffeur." In 1962, the CIA tipped off the South African police as to their whereabouts, believing that Mandela was controlled by the Soviet Union. CIA operative Donald Rickard said, "He could have incited a war in South Africa, the United States would have to get involved, grudgingly, and things could have gone to hell."[7] Cecil and Mandela were stopped and arrested near Howick, South Africa. While Cecil spent one night in jail, Mandela spent 27 years in prison.

After Cecil was released from jail, his movements became more restricted by the government, and he was placed under house arrest for five years for being a Communist. He finally decided to become a fugitive from South Africa along with John and was smuggled out with help from his gay networks, leaving with a few meager belongings and an envelope of diamonds stuffed into his underwear.[8] In 1979, Cecil died in exile in England. He wrote to his brother, just days prior to his death, "I've had a wonderful life. I'm glad that I had the good sense to join the Communist Party of South Africa."[9]

Resources

Redgrave, Greta, dir. *The Man Who Drove With Mandela*. Performed by Corin Redgrave. United Kingdom: Jane Balfour Films Ltd., 1998.

Robert Aldrich, Garry Wotherspoon. *Who's Who in Contemporary Gay and Lesbian History: From World War II to the Present Day*. Routledge, London 2001, p. 446.

Roos, Neil. *Ordinary Springboks: White Servicemen and Social Justice in South Africa, 1939-1961*. Milton: Taylor and Francis, 2018.

" your gags
and bans
will not silence
the voices of
democracy,
nor halt the march
forward to liberty,
racial harmony,
and world peace. "
~ Cecil Williams

Cecil Williams, drawn by Jessica Bogac-Moore

This page is intentionally blank to facilitate coloring the reverse side.

Elisabeth Eidenbenz
1913–2011, Switzerland
drawn by Diego Gomez

Elisabeth Eidenbenz was born into a Swiss pastor's family, and grew up to become a teacher. In the early 1930s, Elisabeth was teaching in Switzerland and Denmark. When the Spanish Civil War started on July 17, 1936, like so many other people in Europe, Elisabeth was affected by the horror of the bloodshed between the liberal Republicans and the conservative populist Nationalists. Innocent Spanish civilians were caught up in the crossfire of war, and Elisabeth was eager to assist them. In 1936, she joined the *Asociación de Ayuda a los Niños en Guerra* (Association to Aid Children in War), organized a collection of food, clothing, shoes and money to buy everyday sundries, filled four trucks with the donations, and drove to Spain with a passel of other volunteers to help out.[1]

By 1936, Europe was roiling. In 1933 Germany, the *Gesetz zur Behebung der Not von Volk und Reich* (the Law to Remedy the Distress of People and Reich, or Enabling Act of 1933) was passed, along with the start of a string of legislation to drive out and remove German Jewish citizens. Germany withdrew from the League of Nations. Italy had invaded Ethiopia, Africa in October of 1935, and persisted in massacring Ethiopians until 1939, when the Second Italo-Ethiopian War ended with Italy's victory.

The Spanish Civil War was concurrent with Hitler's rise to power in Germany in the 1930s and Mussolini's dictatorship in Italy in the 1920s and 1930s, and a precursor to WWII. The Spanish Civil War occurred between 1936 and 1939, with WWII following on its heels from 1939 to 1945. The Spanish Civil War was a battle between the democratic, left-leaning Republicans, and the aristocratic, Catholic, Fascist Nationalists. Nazi Germany and Fascist Italy aided the Nationalists and they won, with their leader General Francisco Franco maintaining a military dictatorship until his death in 1975. Germany, Italy, and Spain were geographically close, and together they formed a powerful Fascist entity.

On April 24, 1937, Elisabeth and her fellow volunteers arrived in Madrid in a convoy of trucks, including one named Ulrich Zwingli after the fifteenth century Swiss Reformist pastor, and adorned with the Swiss flag's white cross.[2] She ended up spending two years in Spain. With the Spanish Civil War's end came more violence. Franco was the victor and he unleashed a massive round of executions and imprisonments, killing over 30,000 political foes.

A flood of war-worn Spanish Republicans left the country seeking refuge. Around 500,000 Spaniards fled persecution and death, crossing the border into France; however, France was hostile and disinterested in helping the refugees. France set up fifteen refugee camps. The heavily guarded camps were squalid, sometimes just dirt enclosures surrounded by barbed wire fencing. After crossing the Pyrenees mountains and reaching coastal France, up to 100,000 tattered refugees were forced onto the beach at Argeles-sur-Mer where, cold and starving, people died. Infant mortality in the rough camps was close to 95%.[3] A Spanish refugee survivor related how they were treated like animals: "On one side there was the freezing sea, on the other barbed wire six feet high. For days we weren't given any food or any kind of shelter. I had to dig a hole with my hands in the sand and drink sea water to survive."[4]

The Hungarian journalist Arthur Koestler wrote about the social and political climate in 1939 France against refugees, there was a "tide of xenophobia that swept over France with morbid rabidity…A few years ago we had been called the martyrs of Fascist barbarians, pioneers in the fight for civilization, defenders of liberty…Now we had become scum of the earth."[5]

In 1939, Elizabeth followed the Spanish refugees to France. She traveled to Elne, in the Pyrénées-Orientales region of southern France, two and a half miles inland from the Mediterranean Sea and approximately twenty four miles from the Spain-France border. She wanted to provide children, pregnant women, and young mothers a place to deliver their babies and rest in safety. Although she was inexperienced in newborn care and midwifery,[6] she had vast amounts of determination and chutzpah. Elisabeth looked for a place to squat, settling on a historic abandoned château, the *Château d'En Bardou*.[7] After requisitioning the three-story mansion, she strong-armed 30,000 francs from the *Aide Suisse aux enfants* (Swiss Red Cross) and renovated the building. Elisabeth named the rooms after Spanish cities to help comfort the homesick refugees. Originally built in 1901, the *Château d'En Bardou* made a stunning maternity home, with delivery rooms, an octagonal nursery and octagonal sitting room, a cupola and glass roof, gardens, and more. Elisabeth opened up the doors of the *Maternitat d'Elna* (Mothers of Elne) in September of 1939, and the first baby, José Molina,[8] was born cradled within its confines that December.

When *Maternitat d'Elna* first opened, it took in only Spanish Civil War refugees, but by the time it was shuttered by the Nazis in 1944, it was also sheltering WWII Jewish and Romani refugees. On June 1940, France signed an armistice with Nazi Germany, thus beginning the Nazi occupation of France. In October of 1940, the citizenship of all French Jews was revoked, their property was taken from them, all civil employees were fired, and Jewish businesses were ordered to shut down. In March of 1942, all French Jewish children were required to register with the police, and in June of 1942, all French Jews were ordered to wear yellow stars sewn on their clothing indicating that they were Jewish. In July of 1942, the police begin rounding up crowds of Parisian Jews in order to send them to extermination camps.[9]

As the Nazi Occupation in France grew more restrictive and as WWII started affecting more countries, *Maternitat d'Elna's* private donations dried up and they were forced to collaborate with the Red Cross in order to get material and financial assistance for wartime services. The Red Cross had taken an official policy of neutrality; under their policy, *Maternitat d'Elna* would be disallowed from sheltering fleeing Jewish women and children if they accepted the Red Cross' assistance. In 1941, Elisabeth received notice from the executive committee of the Red Cross ordering her "to give up Jews, Tziganes (Romani) and Spanish refugees if you are requested and do nothing to shield them from the roundups."[10] Elisabeth devised a way around this unjust policy by disguising the identities of the women and children in order to protect them. French historian Grégory Tuban notes that "She hid mothers and gave false Spanish names to Jewish children. She knew the dangers, and she did her best to save and help as many women and babies as she could."[11] Between 1939 and 1944, nearly 600 children were born in *Maternitat d'Elna*. In 1944, the Nazis shut it down.

WWII ended in 1945 and, in 1946, Elisabeth met her life partner and fellow activist and social worker, Henriette "Jetty" Hierhammer. "We met in Vienna in the post-war period, therefore, we have been together for more than fifty years, and since then we have done the same thing…If you had to define Jetty, you would say it was the best gift that my life has made."[12] Elisabeth and Jetty worked together with children for decades, eventually building a home together in Rekawinkel, Austria. Jetty spoke about their life together during an interview on her 103rd birthday, "We took care of about 3,000 children in the course of our lives and we loved helping."[13]

In 2011 and at the age of 97, Elisabeth died of old age, but her partner lived on past 100. Elisabeth received many awards and honors for her humanitarian resistance work; In 2002, she was awarded the status of Righteous Among the Nations by the Government of Israel, in 2006 the *Orden Civil de la Solidaridad Social* by the Spanish Government, in 2006 the *Creu de Sant Jordi* by the Generalitat of Catalonia, and in 2007 star of the *Légion d'honneur* by the French Government.

Resources

Carlos, Assumpta Montellà I. *Elisabeth Eidenbenz: Més Enllà De La Maternitat D'Elna*. Badalona: Ara Llibres, 2011.

Espinosa, Toni and Assumpta Montellà, dir. *El Llegat De La Maternitat D'Elna*. Spain: Enunai Produccions: Televisio De Catalunya. Accessed September 16, 2018. https://www.youtube.com/watch?v=LEX8mIJ1hu0.

Archive

United States Holocaust Memorial Museum, Accession Number: 2017.91.1 | RG Number: RG-58.045 https://collections.ushmm.org/search/catalog/irn558455

Elizabeth Eidenbenz, drawn by Diego Gomez

This page is intentionally blank to facilitate coloring the reverse side.

Annemarie Schwarzenbach
1908–1942, Switzerland
drawn by Soizick Jaffre

Annemarie was an adventurer, dedicated anti-fascist, travel and photographic journalist, writer, and out butch lesbian. Annemarie was raised in a well-to-do conservative Swiss household. Her mother was domineering, and her father was a wealthy businessman in the textile industry. Although her father encouraged his daughter's penchant for dressing like a boy and her mother was a bisexual who had affairs outside of her marriage, her parents did not approve of her adult lesbianism. She was a sickly child, suffering through scarlet fever, whooping cough, and a heart ailment.[1] Annemarie started dressing in boy's clothing as a child and grew up to become a handsome, intellectual, talented, hedonistic, and passionate woman.

Dramatically charismatic, Annemarie led a short life filled with affairs, writing and photography, depression, morphine and alcohol addiction, suicide attempts and hospitalizations, cross-continental travel, and anti-fascist activism. She published her first book, *Freunde um Bernhard* (*Bernhard's Circle*), in 1931 at the young age of 23. *Freunde um Bernhard's* protagonist was a gay man and the novella was well-received.[2] Around the time of the publication of her novella, she met Erika Mann, the daughter of the German writer and Nobel Prize in Literature laureate, Thomas Mann. Annemarie and Erika had a brief but fiery affair, with Erika breaking it off to court actress and anti-fascist activist, Therese Giehse. Annemarie stayed in Berlin during the Weimar Republic, a period from 1931 to 1933. In time-honored lesbian tradition, after her initial heartbreak had worn off, Annemarie remained close friends with her ex-lover, Erika, and eventually became fast friends with Erika's brother, Klaus Mann, who was also gay. Annmarie, Erika, and Klaus soon became traveling companions and, later, anti-fascist co-conspirators. Like so many others, Klaus was enchanted with Annmarie; he said of her, "our 'Swiss child,' Annemarie, the eccentric scion of a patrician house. She is delicate and ambitious and looks like a pensive page."[3]

With the rise of Hitler and the creation of the Nazi government in Germany in 1933, the sexually permissive, bohemian, and creative Weimar Republic gave way to the repressive and fascist Third Reich. Annmarie watched the dramatic changes in Germany with horror. She wrote to Klaus from Germany in 1933, "The statements of the Third Reich are repugnant and [...] inhumane and deeply antipathetic to all concepts of culture. A more or less spiritually oriented person, and a European, belongs, of course, to the opposition [because] we are all involved. Turning away is the same as giving up and suicide."[4] Annemarie and Klaus begin their political collaboration with the formation of the anti-fascist literary review for exiled writers, *Die Sammlun*, which Klaus published while he was exiled in Amsterdam and which Annemarie helped finance. Annemarie's political convictions were at odds with her parents' conservative beliefs; her family sympathized with the far-right Swiss Fronts and were pro-Nazi.[5] When they pressured her to stop her activism and change her beliefs, she fell into a deep depression and attempted suicide.

In 1933, Annemarie traveled from Germany through France to Spain with the Jewish German photographer, Marianne Breslauer, to report on the embryonic start of what would become the Spanish Civil War, a nearly three-year-war that lasted from 1936 to 1939. This bloody internal civil war between leftists and fascists resulted in at least 200,000 deaths and proved to be a violent precursor to WWII.[6] That same year, Annemarie took several road trips with Klaus and sometimes Erika. Seductive, depressed, astonishingly handsome, and broken, Annemarie's love life flourished during her travels, with a trail of women's hearts littered behind her like breadcrumbs, including the daughter of the Turkish Ambassador in Tehran, an archaeologist in Turkmenistan and, later on, Baroness Margot von Opel. Her nephew, Alex Schwarzenbach, said of Annemarie's love life, "The difference with Annemarie is probably that her mother was able to have stable long-term relationships whereas Annemarie never achieved that. Partners were usually exhausted by the end of the year because Annemarie was very demanding and of course the drugs put a lot of strain on the relationships as well."[7] She visited Persia for the first time in 1933, fell in love with the land and the people, then subsequently visited several times while writing the slender travel memoir *Death in Persia* between 1935 and 1936, starting the manuscript when visiting Lar Valley in the craggy but beautiful Persian Central Alborz mountains and finishing it in Switzerland.[8]

Annemarie had flirted with morphine since her time in the Weimar Republic, but she became seriously addicted in 1935, just seven years before her death. She started documenting the rise of Hitler and fascism in 1937, two years before WWII started. By September 1935, the German tricolored flag had been replaced by the swastika-emblazoned Nazi flag and soldiers were goose-stepping through the city streets, and Annemarie was passionately documenting the disturbing changes. WWII started in 1939 and Annemarie traveled to the USA, documenting the American Deep South, along with Southern coal mining regions. She was horrified by the social conditions and the racial conflicts that she saw and documented in America.[9] It was here that she met the iconic Southern American writer Carson McCullers, who formed an immediate crush on Annemarie, so intensely smitten that Carson's husband left her over her pining. Ultimately, the feelings were not reciprocated, although they ended up become close friends and wrote many letters to one another. Carson dedicated *Reflections in a Golden Eye* to Annemarie, saying, "She had a face that I knew would haunt me for the rest of my life."[10]

Annemarie returned to Switzerland, and died from a bicycle-related head injury at the age of 34. Her family, ashamed of Annemarie's political beliefs and lesbianism, burnt her diaries and letters after her death. The German film *Journey to Kafiristan* is based upon Annemarie's travels to the Middle East. Despite her ongoing depression, drug addiction, and the war, Annemarie produced an extraordinary amount of work before her early death in 1942; besides a multitude of books, she produced 365 articles and 50 documentary photo essays for European and American newspapers and magazines.[11]

Resources

Dubini, Donatello and Fosco Dubini, dir. *Journey to Kafiristan*. Performed by Jeanette Hain. Germany: Picture This, 2003. DVD.

McCullers, Carson, and Annemarie Schwarzenbach. *The Correspondence Book: The Letters Of Annemarie Schwarzenbach And Carson McCullers*. Amsterdam: Kunstverein Amsterdam, 2014.

Schwarzenbach, Annemarie. *Death in Persia*. Translated by Lucy Renner. Jones. London: Seagull Books, 2013.

Archive

Archive of Annemarie's photos: "Category:CH-NB-Annemarie Schwarzenbach." Wikimedia Commons. https://commons.wikimedia.org/wiki/Category:CH-NB-Annemarie_Schwarzenbach.

Annemarie Schwarzenback, drawn by Soizick Jaffre

This page is intentionally blank to facilitate coloring the reverse side.

Willem Arondeus
1894–1943, The Netherlands
drawn by Tara Madison Avery

Willem Arondeus was an illustrator, biographer, and Dutch Resistance fighter. He was born in Naarden, a city approximately 28 miles south of Amsterdam, the Netherlands. Willem was one of seven children born into a blue collar family. He knew that he was gay when he was a teen and came out to his family, but his family was unsupportive, homophobic, and judgmental. His parents disowned him when he was 18, threw him out of the home, and he never reconciled with them.[1] Rudi van Dantzig wrote in Willem's biography, "Arondeus was a special and obstinate man from Noord-Holland who, already in 1914 at the age of twenty, contrary to spirit of the age, openly talked about his homosexuality. In those days, even in the circles he frequented, for many this was a bit too much."[2]

After being disowned, Willem traveled around the Netherlands. Inspired by the painters and artists that he met in Laren and Blaricum, Willem moved north to the big city of Amsterdam and took drawing and painting classes at the *Quellinusschool*, a local art school.[3] In his mid-20s, he moved to Paris to be a painter. He did not succeed in Paris and returned to Amsterdam in 1920, disillusioned and downhearted, saying that his "flight from the city of light was one of the wisest deeds in my intelligent life, unfortunately very, very poor life."[4] Between 1920 and 1923, Willem eked out a meager living as an artist, illustrating poems, designing posters and calendars, and designing Christmas stamps for the Dutch postal service. His illustrative style was a blend of the sensuous lines found in the Art Nouveau movement (1890–1910) and the geometric forms of the more recent Art Deco (1910–1939) movement.[5] It's easy to see the influence of fellow gay illustrator Aubrey Beardsley (1872–1898) in Willem's work. In 1923, Willem got his first major art gig and created a large mural in Rotterdam City Hall. He continued to get art jobs; between 1930 and 1932 he designed nine tapestries for the County Seat, and painted a set of murals depicting scenes representing hunting, fishing, shipping, and farming industries for Amsterdam's Bureau of the City Health Department.

In 1928, Willem started writing poetry and short stories, and publishing his work a few years later. In 1932, Willem met his partner Jan Tijssen, and they lived together in rural Apeldoorn for the next seven years. Jan worked as a delivery boy for a grocery store, while Willem wrote and made art. Although Willem was prolific and Jan was hard-working, the couple remained impoverished.

In 1938, he wrote and illustrated two novels, *Het Uilenhuis* (*The Owl House*) and *In de bloeiende Ramenas* (*In the Blooming Wild Radish*), and in 1939 published a biography of Dutch artist Matthijs Maris titled *Matthijs Maris: de tragiek van den droom* (*Matthijs Maris: The Tragedy of the Dream*), followed by *Figuren en problemen der monumentale schilderkunst in Nederland* (*Figures and Problems of Monumental Painting in the Netherlands*) in 1941. Willem identified with and was deeply affected by the story of Matthijs' life: he was rejected by the arts community in Paris and suffered as an impoverished artist. Willem was also inspired by the bravery shown by Matthijs in 1871 when he fought for the revolutionary Paris Communards along the barricades set up by the Army in Parisian working-class neighborhoods.

When Willem published the biography of Matthijs Maris in 1939, his financial situation improved, the couple started living comfortably and moved to Amsterdam. But by then, the social climate in Europe had taken a drastic nose-dive. The Spanish Civil War (1936-1939) ushered in a conservative, fascist, Nationalist regime headed by General Francisco Franco which lasted until his death in 1975. Next door in Germany, Hitler had been appointed Chancellor in 1933. He quickly begin implementing laws; The *Gesetz zur Behebung der Not von Volk und Reich* (Law to Remedy the Distress of People and Reich, or Enabling Act of 1933) was the death knell for progressivism. The *Reichskulturkammer* (Reich Chamber of Culture), was instituted in 1933 in order to control and censor German artists' work, and make sure that it was congruent with Nazi ideals. Artists who did not join *Reichskulturkammer* were banned from making and selling work. On September 1, 1939, the Nazis invaded Poland, with the United Kingdom and France declaring war on Nazi Germany two days later. It was only a matter of time before Germany invaded the Netherlands. Germany fought their way into the Netherlands in May of 1940 with the Rotterdam Blitz, in which over 800 city residents were killed and 80,000 people were made homeless. Over 1,300 bombs were dropped on the thriving Dutch metropolis, resulting in massive fires throughout the city and leveling over one square mile. In the end, more than 20 churches, 2,000+ stores, over 700 warehouses, four hospitals and more than 60 schools were destroyed in the surprise attack.[6] The Nazi occupation of the Netherlands lasted until May 5, 1945. In February of 1941, the first group of Jewish Dutch citizens were arrested and sent to the Mauthausen-Gusen concentration camp.

The Nazis instituted a Dutch sister organization to the German *Reichskulturkammer* called *Nederlandsche Kultuurkamer* (Netherlands Chamber of Culture); as with *Reichskulturkammer*, membership was mandatory for all Dutch artists, and its goal was to control and censor the members' work. Like Dutch composer and musician Frieda Belinfante, Willem was incensed and refused to join the organization. In 1941, worried about Jan's safety, Willem sent Jan back to Apeldoorn for his protection, then joined the Dutch Resistance in Amsterdam. In early 1942, Willem founded *Brandarisbrief*, an underground, illegal newsletter opposing the Nazi occupation and the *Nederlandsche Kultuurkamer*. In 1943, *Brandarisbrief* merged with *De Vrije Kunstenaar* (*The Free Artist*), and continued to be published twice a month until the end of the war in 1945. Willem joined Frieda in the Dutch Resistance group *Groep 2000* (Group 2000). He worked in *De Persoonsbewijzencentrale* (Personal Identity Center, or PBC) branch, whose focus was on forging thousands of non-Jewish identity cards for Jews so that they could avoid deportation, concentration camps, and death.

In March of 1943, Willem, along with other members of the group, including gay fashion designer Sjoerd Bakker and lesbian musician Frieda Belinfante, decided to bomb the Amsterdam municipal registry, destroying all population registry records. The weapons used in the attack were stored in the basement of lesbian bar owner Bet Van Beeren's establishment, *Café 't Mandje*. This was a brave act of resistance and rebellion. They did this because they feared the authorities would realize that thousands of false identity cards were circulating among the Jewish population; in theory, each card was required by law to be registered at the municipal register, but since these were false cards the numbers were not in the municipal register records. All it would take was for one persnickety records clerk to spot the ruse, the jig would be up, and the Nazis would know that false identity cards were being produced.

Several sympathetic firefighters assisted during the attack on the registry, drenching identification records with water and making them illegible. Unfortunately, the Resistance members were betrayed and reported to the Gestapo, who rounded most of them up and arrested them. Twelve men were sentenced to death for the bombing.

Willem attempted to take full responsibility for the bombing. He was executed by the Nazis in the dunes of Overveen in July of 1943, at age 48. His final words were "Let it be known that homosexuals are not cowards".[7] Willem is buried with honors in the *Eeregegraafplaats Bloemendaal* (Honorary Cemetery Bloemendaal) in the dunes of Overveen. In 1984, Willem was awarded the *Verzetsherdenkingskruis* (Resistance Commemorative Cross), and in 1986 he was named as Righteous Among the Nations by Yad Vashem, an organization dedicated to preserving the memory of the Holocaust, its victims, and its heroes.

Resources

Boumans, Toni, dir. *Na het feest, zonder afscheid verdwenen*. VARA/Stimuleringsfonds/Provincie Noord Holland. 1990.

Dantzig, Rudi Van. *Het Leven Van Willem Arondéus 1894-1943: Een Documentaire*. Amsterdam: De Arbeiderspers, 2003.

Entrop, Marco. *Onbekwaam in Het Compromis: Willem Arondéus, Kunstenaar En Verzetsstrijder*. Amsterdam: B. Lubberhuizen, 1993.

Wotherspoon, Garry, and Robert Aldrich. *Who's Who in Gay and Lesbian History: From Antiquity to World War II*. London: Routledge. 2000.

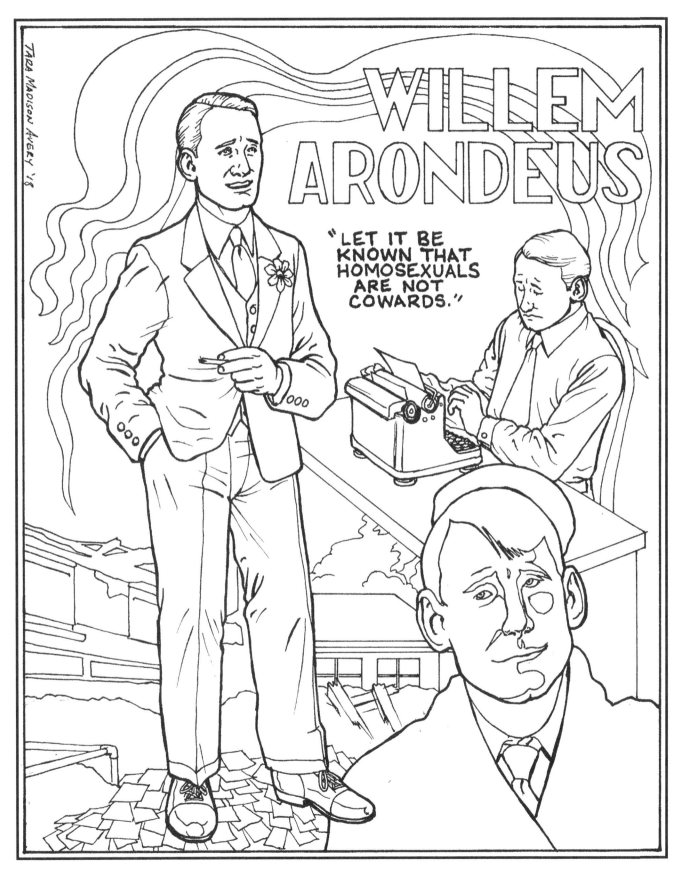

Willem Arondeus, drawn by Tara Madison Avery

This page is intentionally blank to facilitate coloring the reverse side.

Sjoerd Bakker
1915–1943, The Netherlands
drawn by Avery Cassell

Sjoerd Bakker was Jewish, a couture fashion designer, and a member of the Dutch Resistance. Sjoerd came from a prosperous Jewish family of fashion and textile shop owners who owned P.S. Bakker, a chain of stores in Leeuwarden and Groningen, the Netherlands. He was interested in fashion and studied design at Hirsch & Cie, a luxury Belgian fashion house with shops in Brussels, Amsterdam, Cologne, Dresden, and Hamburg. After school, he settled in Amsterdam and lived and worked out of his couture tailoring studio at Vondelstraat 24.[1] Sjoerd was a rising star in the world of Dutch high fashion, and provided work for the Jewish Dutch designer Max Heymans when he was in hiding during the war. Peaceful times did not last for Sjoerd. WWII was about to impact the Netherlands.

Although the Netherlands was initially neutral and had already negotiated a ceasefire, Nazi Germany invaded the country by air in May of 1940, brutally demolishing the city of Rotterdam, 54 miles south of Amsterdam. By the time the Rotterdam Blitz was over with, more than 800 city residents were dead and 80,000 people were homeless. Over 1,300 bombs were dropped on the thriving Dutch metropolis, resulting in massive fires throughout the city and leveling at least one square mile. In the end, more than 20 churches, over 2,000 stores, at least 700 warehouses, four hospitals and more than 60 schools were destroyed in the surprise attack.[2]

Amsterdam was soon invaded by the Nazis who quickly begin registering, deporting, and killing Jewish citizens. In 1941, Amsterdam had a Jewish population of over 79,000. In February of that year, Nazis started decimating Jews in Amsterdam by deporting them to Buchenwald concentration camp in Poland and Mauthausen concentration camp in Austria, where torture and death awaited them. Initially, Sjoerd became involved with activism independently of any Resistance groups, housing Jews, storing their possessions for them, and supplying them with forged identity papers and forged food ration cards. Other members of his family were involved with the Dutch Resistance, his older brother, Popke Bakker and his father's uncle, Paul. In the end, all three Bakker resistance activists were executed by German Nazi forces. By January of 1942, Sjoerd was 26 years old and was working with the Resistance, joining Willem Arondeus with the Resistance group *De Persoonsbewijzencentrale* (Personal Identity Center, or PBC), forging non-Jewish identity cards for Jews so that they could avoid deportation, concentration camps, and death. A year later, Nazis designated a Jewish quarter in Amsterdam and started relocating rural Jews to Amsterdam to monitor their whereabouts.

By summer of 1942, Jews were being rounded up in Amsterdam and deported to Polish concentration camps and killing centers.[4] It was during this reign of terror that Frieda Belinfante came up with the idea to destroy Jewish identification records at the Amsterdam municipal registry. In March of 1943, Sjoerd, along with his friend the gay artist and writer Willem Arondeus, the lesbian musician Frieda Belinfante, and many others, decided to bomb the Amsterdam municipal registry, destroying all population registry records. The weapons used for this act of defiance were stored in the basement of butch bar owner Bet Van Beeren's establishment, *Café 't Mandje*. Sjoerd used his tailoring talents to sew police uniform jackets for the activists. He made two officer uniform jackets for "captain of the State Police" Willem Arondeus, painter and writer; "lieutenant" Gerrit Van der Veen, sculptor; and four for the "constables": Rudolf Bloemgarten, medical student; Karl Gröger, medical student; Coos Hartogh, medical student and editor; and Sam van Musschenbroek, law student. The fabric for the uniforms was donated by an interior designer, Einar Berkovich, who in turn had gotten it from some of her relatives at the Hollandia-Kattenburg garment factory,[5] a Jewish-owned company and one of the largest and most modern garment factories in Europe.[6] Several sympathetic firefighters assisted during the attack on the registry, drenching identification records with water and making them illegible.

Unfortunately, the Resistance members were betrayed and reported to the Nazi authorities, who rounded most of them up and arrested them. Ultimately, only two activists escaped execution after this brave action: Willem Sandberg, and Frieda Belinfante. Twelve men were sentenced to death for the bombing. Sjoerd had just turned 28 the month before, and was accused of collaboration. Although Willem attempted to take full responsibility for the bombing, Sjoerd refuted this.[7] Sjoerd's last wish to his executors was to be killed in a pink shirt, a symbol of his pride and his gayness. Upon hearing of the court's sentence condemning him to death, Sjoerd quoted the last two lines of the poem "Phoenix" by the Dutch poet Hendrik Marsman; "*en laat den moed en uwe vaart niet zakken | het nest is goed, maar het heelal is ruimer.*" "and do not let the courage and your speed drop / the nest is good, but the universe is wider."

Sjoerd was executed by the Nazis in the dunes of Overveen in July of 1943. By the time WWII ended in 1945, the occupying Nazi forces had hastily buried 422 Dutch resistance fighters in mass burial pits in the Kennemer dunes of Overveen, most of whom were also executed in the dunes, but a few that were transported from out of town execution sites. After the war, the bodies of the murdered resistance fighters were reinterred; some were reburied in family plots and some in honorary plots in what became the *Eeregegraafplaats Bloemendaal* (Honorary Cemetery Bloemendaal, or *Ereveld Bloemendaal*). The *Eeregegraafplaats Bloemendaal* was created to commemorate the dead who were executed by the Nazi occupiers and dumped in the dunes. May 4th is a national day of remembrance in the Netherlands, and includes an honorary silent procession of thousands in memory of the Dutch resistors. Sjoerd Bakker, Gerrit Van der Veen, Willem Arondeus, Rudolf Bloemgarten, Karl Gröger, and Sam van Musschenbroek are all buried in *Eeregegraafplaats Bloemendaal*.[8]

In 1986 Sjoerd was named as Righteous Among the Nations by Yad Vashem, an organization dedicated to preserving the memory of the Holocaust, its victims, and its heroes. His memorial stone is engraved with "*Doch de meeste van deze is de liefde. 1 Cor. 13*" ("But the greatest of these is love. 1 Cor. 13")[9]

Resource

Aldrich, Robert F., and Garry Wotherspoon. *Who's Who in Gay and Lesbian History: From Antiquity to World War II*. London: Routledge, 2002.

Sjoerd Bakker, drawn by Avery Cassell

This page is intentionally blank to facilitate coloring the reverse side.

Frieda Belinfante
1904–1995, The Netherlands
drawn by Phoebe Kobabe and Rachel House

Frieda was born in 1904 into a family of musicians and teachers. She was a native of Amsterdam, an out lesbian, a cellist and conductor, and an active member of the Dutch Resistance movement during WWII. Frieda's father was Jewish but her mother wasn't; because Judaism is matrilineal, she was not considered Jewish. Over 70% of the Dutch Jews were killed during the Holocaust of WWII, including many Belinfante relations.

In 1920, Frieda met the composer Henriëtte Bosmans. and they fell in love. Frieda said Henriëtte was "my best friend, girlfriend….I was a high admirer of this wonderful, beautiful looking girl, composer."[1] Henriëtte wrote music for her new love, and they lived together for seven years.

Frieda joined the Dutch Resistance group *Groep 2000* in 1940.[2] She also was a member of *De Persoonsbewijzencentrale* (Personal Identity Center or PBC.) Her close friend and out gay artist Willem Arondeus, along with other members of the group, forged documents including identity cards and food rationing cards and eventually destroyed files including Jewish identity cards. Frieda started forging identity cards for Jews in the early 1940s, removing the "J" for Jewish, thus providing protection from arrest for Jewish citizens. This required a steady hand and some artistic talent. She said, "I was very good at falsifying things. Steady hand to take the glossy part, because the picture had two layers. It's a thick thing, a picture, a passport picture. And the other side, this is the picture, the other side was a seal under which was the fingerprint, the fingerprint on the seal. So, you had to keep the fingerprint because we didn't have the fingerprint of the one who gave his ID to you, so I had to take the glossy part off without injuring the back part, the seal, which I was good at. And then the picture had no stamps on it, stamps, because there were two ink stamps, one in this corner and one in that corner and I had to falsify that with two different colors of ink sometimes."[3]

In March 27, 1943, the Resistance group started to worry the authorities would realize that thousands of false identity cards were circulating among the Jewish population; in theory, each card was required by law to be registered at the municipal register, but since these were false cards the numbers were not in the municipal register records. All it would take was for one persnickety records clerk to spot the ruse, the jig would be up, and the Nazis would know that false identity cards were being

produced. Frieda, always creative and bold, devised a solution. The group planned to bomb the Amsterdam municipal register and destroy all population registry records rooms in March of 1943. Sjoerd Bakker, another gay member of the group and a couture fashion designer, tailored fake police uniforms so that they could successfully infiltrate the building. Butch bar owner, Bet Van Beeren, stored the weapons used for this act of defiance in the basement of her establishment, *Café 't Mandje*. In addition to the bombing of the municipal register, she and her comrades took numerous measures to prevent the Nazis from access to incriminating paperwork and exposing false documentation, thus saving many lives.

After the successful bombing of the municipal register, Frieda disguised herself as a man named Hans[4] to evade the Nazis, even fooling her own mother while passing one another in the streets of Amsterdam. When Willem, Sjoerd, and ten members of her Resistance unit were caught and executed at the sand dunes near Overveen,[5] Frieda—still disguised as Hans—escaped on foot with a traveling companion named Tony to Switzerland. She walked through the woods in the snow from Amsterdam to Switzerland by crossing the Alps, starting in December 1944 and arriving in Switzerland in February 1945. The hike to safety was perilous; she said, "It was February. We had to walk five miles out of the border. You had to walk five miles and then you had to walk all the way north until you get to the place where the bridge was from Switzerland. And the river, the bridge and then you're in France, well, because the bridge was blown up. So, it was only a blown up bridge, and there was a place, a farmers family lived out in nowhere. So, I went with Tony there and we got off the train and we started to walk and we found the farm. And there was snow this high. And there was nobody out. It was a blizzard. And we had to really walk. All I remember I had with me was my music satchel with one towel because I know I had to wade through the river and so I took a towel with me. That was all, and what we had on….We were actually in Switzerland when we crossed the river, because that was the natural border. But we didn't have much profit from that, because on the Swiss side, there was an absolutely steep mountain, so we couldn't get into Switzerland and hide. The forest was completely filled with snow and trees and no way of climbing. So, we had to walk along the river in full sight of anybody. I mean, if there would have been border guards from the Swiss side looking for us, they would have seen us….It was absolute silence. It was gorgeous. It is a trip I will never forget. It was the most wonderful quiet trip of ten or twelve hours that we walked, because we arrived finally to the bridge around dark, 8:00, 9:00, and then we had to walk up the road. See, the road would go down to the bridge and that would be the river, the border, but the bridge was gone."[6] Frieda was granted refugee status in Switzerland and emigrated to the United States two years after the war ended, eventually settling in California.

In 1954, Frieda became the founder, artistic director, and conductor of the inaugural Orange County Philharmonic Society, but was fired from her organization in 1962 due to homophobia and sexism. Interviewed by folks at the United States Holocaust Memorial Museum at the age of 90, Frieda said, "I feel very lonesome if there's nobody I can like and help, and love and protect. I don't understand people that can only live for themselves. How do you get your happiness? What do you do with your life?"[7] In 1995 and at age 90, Frieda died of cancer in New Mexico.

Resources

Boumans, Tony, dir. *But I Was A Girl, The Story of Frieda Belinfante*. Performed by Frieda Belinfante. Vimeo. May 08, 2018. Accessed July 29, 2018. https://vimeo.com/ondemand/friedabelinfante.

Boumans, Toni. *Een Schitterend Vergeten Leven: De Eeuw Van Frieda Belinfante*. Amsterdam: Uitgeverij Balans, 2015.

Archive

United States Holocaust Memorial Museum, The Frieda Belinfante Collection, https://www.ushmm.org/collections/the-museums-collections/curators-corner/the-frieda-belinfante-collection

Frieda Belinfante, drawn by Phoebe Kobabe

91

This page is intentionally blank to facilitate coloring the reverse side.

Frieda Belinfante, drawn by Rachael House

This page is intentionally blank to facilitate coloring the reverse side.

Bet van Beeren, a.k.a Elisabeth Maria van Beeren
1902–1967, The Netherlands
drawn by Maia Kobabe

Bet Van Beeren was the owner of a legendary gay-friendly bar in Amsterdam, a butch, and a flamboyant blue-collar philanthropist. Bet was raised, along with her twelve siblings, in a close-knit blue-collar family in Amsterdam. Her father was a construction worker, while her mother ran a boarding house and sold fish and vegetables door-to-door on the side. Bet quit school during middle school to work and help support her large family. After working as a fishmonger and in a canning factory, during which time she lost two fingertips to factory accidents, Bet started working in her Uncle Toon's bar. By then, the gregarious Caballero-smoking Bet was already out as a butch lesbian, all leathered up in a snappy bespoke double-breasted leather motorcycle jacket and tooling about Amsterdam on her Zündapp motorcycle, her femme du jour riding in back, snugly pressed up against her.[1]

When Bet turned 25, she borrowed some cash, bought out her uncle's business, and renamed the bar *Café 't Mandje* (The Basket Café) after her beloved mother's habit of bringing Bet lunch each day in a covered basket. Bet ran *Café 't Mandje* with a loving hand until her death at age 67, when her sister Greet took over. Bet lived in a cozy apartment over the notorious bar. *Café 't Mandje* was unique within Amsterdam and was the first gay-friendly bar in the city. Located in an older neighborhood called Zeedijk, immediately outside of the *Jodenhoek* (Jewish Quarter) and the Red Light District, it was a mixed bar where lesbians, straight sailors, sex workers, gay men, bisexuals, and artists intermingled. Bet was a prankster with a bawdy sense of humor, and the bar was filled with souvenirs that she beguiled customers into parting with, from mundane business cards to naughtier bras and panties. She had a habit of cutting off male customers' neckties with a butcher knife and hanging them from the ceiling like phallic trophies.[2] Bet had a penchant for straight women, and never had a long-lasting romantic relationship. Bet was known in her neighborhood of social outcasts as a big-hearted caregiver and contributed to many charities, earning the nickname "Queen of the Zeedijk." She took care of the neighborhood children and the elderly, providing them with recreational excursions and necessities, paying for it out of her earnings, or shaking down local pimps and neighborhood businesses for donations. Bet was in her late 30s when the Nazis started their bloody occupation of Amsterdam in 1940.

During the period after WWI and prior to WWII, the Netherlands was ruled by a Christian, right-wing government. With high unemployment and an economic depression between 1929 and 1933, along with the general culture of fascism that was spreading across the continent of Europe, the Netherlands was ripe for a strict fascist movement. Although the Dutch fascist movement was never as strong as the Italian or the Spanish, nevertheless, it was notable. In the early 1930s, the Dutch cabinet instituted an austerity program, reduced unemployment benefits, and instituted laws such as limiting families to one job per household, thus causing married women to lose their jobs and forego employment. Some citizens who were receiving unemployment were required to move to neighboring Nazi Germany for low paying jobs and, if they balked, the government would deny them unemployment benefits. These policies caused mass rioting and dissatisfaction among blue collar workers and the disenfranchised.

When WWII started in September of 1939, the Netherlands proclaimed neutrality; however, the Nazis invaded the Netherlands seven months later and, despite the city having already surrendered, the German Nazi army bombed Rotterdam, killing 900 residents and destroying over 40% of the thriving metropolis. It must have been a horrific shock for the Dutch to have their negotiated surrender disregarded, and their beautiful seaside city bombed. Hitler looked fondly upon the Dutch, considering them to be similar to Germans and racially pure Aryans, and hoped to incorporate them in his vision of the Greater Germanic Reich, a large mass of countries that included Germany, Austria, Bohemia, German-occupied Poland, the Netherlands, the Flemish part of Belgium, Luxembourg, Denmark, Norway, Sweden, Iceland, the German-speaking parts of Switzerland, and Liechtenstein. Ultimately, more than 70% of Jews in the Netherlands were killed during the occupation of that country during WWII.[3] By the time the war ended in 1945, there were 102,000 known Dutch victims of the persecution of Jewish, Sinti, homosexual, and Roma people.

After the Nazis took over the Netherlands, the esteemed Queen Wilhelmina and the royal family fled to London for safety. There, she upheld the spirit of Dutch citizens, became a symbol of the Dutch Resistance, boosting morale and assisted in forming Dutch Resistance groups, and infamously called out Hitler as "the arch-enemy of mankind." Queen Wilhelmina continued to lead the Netherlands and be wildly revered among her citizens, despite being in exile due to the Nazi occupation of her country and her unpopularity with the Dutch government in the Nazi-occupied Netherlands. She traveled to the U.S. and Canada, speaking out against Nazi Germany. According to a historian, Queen Wilhelmina "bolstered morale in her occupied homeland; with her famous emblem of the marguerite flower, she became the focus of national unity for hundreds of other Dutch exiles."[4]

Never one to back down and always one to help, Bet assisted the Dutch Resistance in fighting the Nazi occupation. We know that at least one of Bet's brothers, Co Van Beeren, was a member of the artist Gerrit van der Veen's Dutch Resistance group, *De Vrije Kunstenaar* (*The Free Artist*), which published an underground newspaper and made false identity cards for persecuted Jews. Bet assisted the Resistance by allowing her attic to be used as an arms depot, providing storage for the weapons used in the bombing of the Amsterdam municipal register records office by Frieda Belinfante, Willem Arondeus, Sjoerd Bakker, and several other members of the Dutch Resistance group in 1943.[5] The storage basement of *Café 't Mandje* was also used as a refuge to hide Jews from the occupying Nazi forces where, if they were caught, they would face certain imprisonment in concentration camps and probable death. *Café 't Mandje* became a distribution point for black market items and stolen and forged food ration cards. Helpfully, *Café 't Mandje* was considered off limits to Nazi troops due to its proximity to the Jewish quarter and its reputation as catering to sex workers, thus also offering some degree of protection to its gay patrons.

In 1940, food rationing became law in occupied Amsterdam. Citizens were issued books of coupons that they could exchange for food, with pregnant women and mothers of young children being issued extra rations of coupons. When the Nazis stopped food and fuel supplies from being imported into the country in the winter of 1944, the result was the *Hongerwinter* (Hunger Winter) of 1944-1945, a period of great starvation and suffering in the Dutch cities. It is estimated that at least 22,000 Dutch people starved or froze to death during that long, bitter winter, many of them weakened elderly men. Desperate for food, people ate tulip bulbs and burnt their furniture and housing to keep warm. Many citizens made their way through the winter with the aid of charity soup kitchens and the assistance of women like Bet.

Bet continued to run *Café 't Mandje* after the war, with assistance from her sister Greet as she grew older. Bet died in 1967 from complications of a lifetime of heavy drinking, and her body was laid out for public viewing upon the bar's billiard table for three days for the loving crowds to pay their respects. Bet continues to be a much loved icon of gay culture in Amsterdam. There is a bridge in Amsterdam named for her, Bet Beer Bridge, and a plaque on the site of *Café 't Mandje* in commemoration of her progressiveness and her charity. In 1998, the Amsterdam Museum created a tribute to Bet and the *Café 't Mandje* with a display containing some original mementoes from the bar, including a selection of the infamous purloined neckties.[6]

Resource

Bosch, Tibbe. *Bet Van Beeren, Koningin Van De Zeedijk*. Amsterdam: PMP, 2007.

Bet Van Beeren, drawn by Maia Kobabe

This page is intentionally blank to facilitate coloring the reverse side.

Valentine Auckland, a.k.a. Molly Ackland
1906–1969, United Kingdom
drawn by Pat Tong

Valentine Ackland was born Mary Kathleen Ackland to an upper class English family. She was a feminist, Marxist, historical novelist, journalist, polyamorous, alcoholic poet. Her father's favorite child, she was nicknamed Molly; the androgynous name "Valentine" came later. Her father treated her as a boy; she was taught to shoot, box, and drive. She was a shy tomboy who had her first crush on a girl at 13, when she met an older girl while on vacation in Italy. Valentine daydreamed that she would return to England and, when she was older, would dress as a man, travel to Italy, and reclaim the girl. Other crushes followed, driving a wedge between Valentine and her father. He was angry and felt that her lesbianism was "filthy" and "unnatural."[1] In 1922 and at age 16, Valentine kissed a girl for the first time. She was enthralled, "…my blood burned me, my heart-beat stifled me; I felt as though something exploded beside me and I had been blown to atoms."[2]

In 1924, Valentine started her first serious lesbian relationship with Bo Foster, a well-to-do speaker of the Conservative Party.[3] This affair continued for six years, and only ended when Valentine met Sylvia Townsend Warner. Pressured to marry and conform to heteronormative standards, Valentine married Richard Turpin in 1925, but continued her relationship with Bo. The day of her wedding, she scandalously got her hair cut into a boyish bob. Richard was a closeted gay or bisexual man, and sex between the two became problematic; they never consummated their marriage. Valentine was not sexually attracted to Richard and acted out by not eating, by smoking, and by drinking heavily.[4] Unable to bear penetrative sex with Richard and still seeing Bo, Valentine was persuaded to get her hymen removed surgically. The day she left the hospital, Valentine bought her first pair of men's flannel trousers at an Army and Navy Store and drove to the freedom of the countryside village of Chaldon in Dorset County with a friend, two suitcases packed full of books, records, and a gramophone. From then on, Valentine dressed mannishly. Although Valentine was interested in literature, she had not yet become a writer. She continued to be a heavy drinker for another 19 years, marking her drinking habits in her diaries with "DD" (Devoid of Drink) and "TMD" (Too Much Drink). TMD always outnumbered DD.[5]

She said, "The extraordinary pleasure of sleeping alone: I have never been happier, never known a greater rapture in my life than when I shut the door of my bedroom that night! I lay in bed and by the light of the candle looked around the tiny room: sloping ceiling, the overhanging eyebrow of a thatch above it; a text on the wall above my washstand that said 'GOD IS LOVE'. I blew out the candle and lay on my back, listening to the owls until I fell asleep."[6]

Valentine convalesced in Chaldon from the surgical loss of her virginity, playing dance tunes on the gramophone, smoking a pipe, drinking tea, reading poetry, and taking walks. She realized that she could not return to Richard, and on the fourth day wrote him a letter telling him so. Richard arrived the following day to fetch Valentine, but she stood fast and he returned alone on the train to London. Her parents gave her a small allowance and she remained in Chaldon, discovering herself and finally meeting other artists and writers. Valentine started writing and publishing poetry to some acclaim and was awarded a divorce decree from Richard in 1926.

In 1930 she met her lifelong partner, Sylvia Townsend Warner, and gave up Bo. Valentine and Sylvia settled in Chaldon, got a cat, and wrote erotic love poetry together. In January of 1931, they married. In 1933, Valentine and Sylvia's collaboratively written collection *Whether a Dove or a Seagull: Poems* was published. None of the poems were signed, leaving the reader to guess who wrote which one. In the mid-1930s to the mid-1940s, Valentine had her poetry published in the popular magazines *The New Republic*, *The New Masses*, and *The New Yorker*.

In 1933 Hitler was appointed Chancellor of Germany, and the *Gesetz zur Behebung der Not von Volk und Reich* (Enabling Act of 1933, or the Law to Remedy the Distress of People and Reich) was passed, fascism was rising in Europe, Spain was on the verge of a civil war, and Valentine was becoming politically aware. After reading *The Brown Book of the Reichstag Fire and Hitler* (Otto Katz, 1933), Valentine wrote to an artist friend in 1933, "Have you read the Brown Book of Nazi terror? If not, you should read it, and I will lend it to you. Apart from the consideration of my own fate, and others like me, if the Fascist State came to rule us in England, it is a Party I abhor so roundly that I can hardly contain myself when there is any discussion of it….I think perhaps there is a true danger of the madness spreading to England…"[7]

In 1935, Valentine and Sylvia joined the Communist Party to help fight the spreading fascism. Valentine started writing political poetry, including "Communist Poem, 1935" and "Instructions from England," which addressed England's nonchalance towards the uprising in Spain, "Teaching to Shoot," and started writing political editorials for leftist news journals including *The Daily Chronicle*, *The New Statesman*, *Time and Tide*, *The Daily Worker*, and *Left Review*.[8] In 1935, her first political editorial was published. It was titled "Country Dealings," appeared in *Left Review*, and advocated for high quality state-run hospitals and the benefits of Communism. Valentine started a local political book lending club to educate people about Socialism[9] and, in 1936, she and Sylvia traveled to Spain to assist in the Spanish Civil War efforts. Together, they volunteered with the British Medical Aid Committee supporting the Spanish Republican Army.

Concurrent with Hitler's rise to power in Germany and Mussolini's dictatorship in Italy, the Spanish Civil War was a precursor to WWII. The Spanish Civil War occurred between 1936 and 1939, with WWII following on its heels between 1939 to 1945. The Spanish Civil War was a battle between the democratic, left-leaning Republicans, and the aristocratic, Catholic, Fascist Nationalists. Nazi Germany and Fascist Italy aided the Nationalists and they won, with their leader, Francisco Franco, maintaining a military dictatorship until his death in 1975. The three countries were geographically close, and together they formed a powerful fascist entity. Valentine's premonitions about the spread of fascism throughout the continent of Europe were spot on.

In 1937, Valentine and Sylvia attended, as delegates, the anti-fascist Second Congress of the International Association of Writers for the Defense of Culture in Madrid and Valencia, and both of them continued to write politically aware fiction. That year the couple moved 140 miles away to the microscopic village of Lower Frome Vauchurch. In 1939 they traveled to the United States for the Third Congress of American Writers and, later that year, WWII started. During WWII, Valentine worked as a civil defense clerk and continued to write political poetry. One potent poem is "Teaching to Shoot." Published in *The New Yorker* in 1942, "Teaching to Shoot" talks about teaching Sylvia to shoot at possibly invading Nazis:

> This thing you hold as you once held my hand if ready to kill.
> We intend to finish those who would finish us—we who are not ill,
> Are not old, are not mad; we who have been young and who still
> Have reason to live, knowing that all is not told.

In 1938, Valentine met the other love of her life, an American named Elizabeth Wade White. They had a volatile relationship, often causing Sylvia considerable pain. In 1947, Valentine heroically stopped drinking alcohol after attempting sobriety for years. In 1949, Valentine, Sylvia, and Elizabeth tried living together for one month, then when that didn't work, Sylvia moved out to give Valentine some space. When Valentine realized that she could not have both women, she chose Sylvia, and Elizabeth moved back to the United States. Although Valentine wrote poetry that was a witness to political injustice, including work that protested war, work that addressed Soviet dissidents, the Vietnam War, the bombing of Hiroshima, and other human rights issues, she became conservative as she got older, causing dissent between her and Sylvia, but they found ways to compromise. From 1952 to 1966, Valentine and Sylvia operated an antique shop together selling mostly overseas to the United States, all still in the tiny hamlet of Lower Frome Vauchurch. They were known as the two strange elderly ladies of Lower Frome Vauchurch. In 1968, Valentine died at home of metastasized breast cancer, and Sylvia died in 1978. They are buried together in St. Nicholas Churchyard in Chaldon under a plain headstone that reads, *Non omnis moriar* (I shall not wholly die).

Resources

Ackland, Valentine. *For Sylvia: An Honest Account*. London: Methuen, 1989.

Jackson, Angela. *British Women and the Spanish Civil War*. London: Routledge, 2014.

Judd, Peter Haring. *The Akeing Heart: Passionate Attachments and Their Aftermath: Sylvia Townsend Warner, Valentine Ackland, and Elizabeth Wade White*. New York: P. Haring Judd, 2013.

Mulford, Wendy. *This Narrow Place: Sylvia Townsend Warner and Valentine Ackland: Life, Letters and Politics 1930-1951*. London: Pandora, 1988.

Warner, Sylvia Townsend, and Valentine Ackland. *Whether a Dove or a Seagull: Poems*. London: Chatto and Windus, 1934.

Valentine Auckland, drawn by Pat Tong

This page is intentionally blank to facilitate coloring the reverse side.

Joe Carstairs, a.k.a Marion Barbara Carstairs, a.k.a. Tuffy
1900–1993, United Kingdom
drawn by Rachael House

Joe was born into a wealthy family in turn-of-the-century London. Given the name Marion, her mother was Fannie Bostwick, a prominent New York heiress, and her father was Captain Albert Carstairs, an officer in the Scottish army. Joe's parents divorced soon after her birth, and there is some doubt that Caption Carstairs was indeed Joe's father. Joe's mother came from a family of strong, stubborn women; Joe said about her beloved Grandmother Nellie, "She was a wicked old lady, rough, tough, she wanted her own way. She was a wonderful person. She had great power."[1] Eccentric Grandmother Nellie would grandly descend the staircase in the family mansion singing operatic arias at the top of her lungs. Joe's mother Fannie was romantically adventurous and jaded, marrying a total of four times. Unfortunately, Fannie was also an alcoholic and a heroin addict, prone to mood swings and rages. Intelligent, creative, and raised in a dysfunctional home by a string of nannies, a drug-muddled mother, and a series of step-fathers, Joe was a wild child. Joe was always aware of her difference, stating, "I was never a little girl. I came out of the womb queer."[2]

Because Joe's family was rife with alcoholism and drug abuse, and her divorced mother was unable or unwilling to parent Joe, Joe was shunted off on a transatlantic ocean liner to a girls' boarding school in Connecticut when she was 11. Joe thrived in boarding school, relieved to be away from her mother; during school holidays she would often stay with her much loved Grandmother Nellie in New York.

WWI broke out in 1914 when Joe was 14. When Joe turned 16, she pleaded with her grandmother to let her join the war efforts on the front until her grandmother relented, pulled some strings, and enlisted Joe in the American Red Cross ambulance unit in France.[3] Upon arriving in Paris, Joe moved into a glass-roofed artist's loft in Maupassant with four other female ambulance drivers, and was promptly seduced by one of her roommates, Dolly Wilde. Dolly was the niece of gay writer and dissolute, Oscar Wilde, and was a wit in her own right. Joe was a devilishly handsome teenage butch ambulance driver, five years younger and infinitely less experienced than the hedonistic and brilliant Dolly. Modernist writer Gertrude Stein's lover, Alice B. Toklas, described Dolly as having a "pristine freshness,"[4] and Dolly's life-long lover, writer, and salon hostess, Natalie Barney, said that Dolly was "half-androgyne and half-goddess."[5] Joe was a virgin, and came reeling from Dolly's bed exclaiming, "My God, what a marvelous thing. I found it a great pity I'd waited so long."[6]

Joe served for four years in the ambulance corps. She described the heavy bombing of Paris, with destroyed homes, Parisians dying in the streets, and aircraft being shot out of the sky and falling onto the Paris cobblestones. Early on during her service, Joe described rescuing a French pilot from his plane wreckage, only to discover that he was already dead. In January of 1918, Germans dropped two hundred bombs on Paris and its suburbs, not realizing that in 11 months the war would be over. Many records were destroyed, so we'll never know whether Joe drove with Toupie Lowther's infamous Hackett-Loather all-women ambulance unit. Toupie, when interviewed, said, "…We were often 350 yards from the German lines awaiting the wounded, under camouflage."[7] Like the Women's Army Corps (WACS), the all-women units were populated by a high proportion of lesbians, including butch movie director Dorothy Arzner.[8] In addition to being speedy and safe drivers during dangerous wartime conditions, the women were required to be mechanics for their trucks, and tend to elderly and sick civilians as they were forced from their homes by German Nazi soldiers.

When the war ended in 1918, Joe moved to Ireland and worked with Edith Vane-Tempest-Stewart's Women's Legion.[9] In 1919, she and several fellow legionnaires traveled back to France to assist with clearing battlefields, burying the dead, transferring prisoners of war, reburying the dead, and other post-war necessities. In 1921, Joe returned to England and started a business with her friends and flatmates, the X Garage, an all-woman rental and chauffeur service.

In 1939, Joe became long-time lovers with the German-turned-American actress Marlene Dietrich. Marlene described the first time she saw Joe as they were sailing in the South of France: "At the helm, a beautiful boy, bronzed and sleek—even from a distance, one sensed the power of his rippling muscles of his tight chest and haunches…The first thought on seeing him had been 'pirate'—followed by 'pillage' and 'plunder'." As Carstairs came closer, though, "…he turned from a sexy boy into a sexy, flat-chested woman."[10] No wonder Joe caught Marlene's eye. Marlene and Joe ended up having a passionate affair for several years, with Joe offering to buy an island for Marlene and Marlene purchasing a sailboat for Joe.

By 1925 Joe had inherited an immense amount of money from her mother and grandmother, freeing Joe to reinvent herself once again, this time as a tattooed, out, butch dyke speedboat racer, with a string of glamorous and powerful femme admirers and lovers, including Greta Garbo, Gwen Farrar, Tallulah Bankhead, and Marlene Dietrich. Joe was racing speed boats and sometimes winning competitions; her boat, the Estelle II, crashed during a race for the Harmsworth Trophy. She was pulled from the churning waters still chewing gum and with three cracked ribs, but spiritedly went out dancing that night. The newspapers reported, "While her misfortune was disastrous and came with amazing suddenness, Miss Carstairs gave a demonstration of piloting ability never before equaled by a woman."[11]

In that same year, Joe was also given a Steiff doll by her first serious girlfriend, wild woman, heroin addict, and socialite Ruth Baldwin. Joe named the doll Lord Tod Wadley, and the toy became her beloved, pampered constant companion, whom she outfitted in tiny bespoke suits and wee Italian leather slippers. Joe traveled between London and New York, living with Ruth in London, and living with Isabel Pell, another glamorous socialite and girlfriend, in New York.

In the early 1930s between WWI and WWII, there was a rash of conservatism in England. Joe's masculine behavior became noted disparagingly in the press. Whereas before, the public was either bemused or admiring of Joe's cigar smoking, gum chewing, tattoos, masculine attire, and athleticism, now they were rude and biting. One article said, "She smokes incessantly, not with languid feminine grace, but with the sharp decisive gestures a man uses."[12] Additionally, a fortune teller had foretold disaster in her career, her home, and in her car in Joe's future; when the predictions came true, Joe superstitiously decided to leave England. The unflattering, homophobic press, the fortune teller's prediction and the proceeding disaster, and the uneasy political fascist climate that was spreading across Europe were strong impetus to find a new home.

She looked 4,500 miles away from London for her new home, to an island in the Bahamas. In the early 1930s, Joe fell in love with and purchased an island named Whale Cay and moved there in 1934. It was near the start of WWII and fascism was spreading across Europe. Hitler was Germany's Nazi Chancellor, Benito Mussolini was Italy's fascist dictator; and the Spanish Civil War would start in two years. Joe had served for four years during the first World War, and may have wanted to put some distance between herself and the rise of Nazism and fascism. Many soldiers returned from WWI with the newly named "shell shock," defined as a physical or psychological injury, and with four years in service in occupied France, it's possible that Joe suffered from shell shock.

She lived on Whale Cay until close to the end of her life. In 1975, she sold Whale Cay and moved to Miami, bringing with her a Victorian hodge-podge of mementos of a life well lived, including 120 photographs of ex-girlfriends that she displayed in a glass-topped table.[13] Joe was adventurous, generous to her pals, and eccentric to a fault. In 1993, Joe died. Joe and her beloved Lord Tod Wadley were cremated together.

Resource

Summerscale, Kate. *The Queen of Whale Cay*. London: Bloomsbury, 2012.

Joe Carstairs, drawn by Rachael House

This page is intentionally blank to facilitate coloring the reverse side.

Ian Gleed, a.k.a. Widge
1916–1943, United Kingdom
drawn by Jon Macy

Ian Gleed was born in rural England, and his father was a doctor who had served in WWI. Ian loved sailing boats and writing but was determined to become a pilot. When Ian was still a teen, he flew for the first time as a daredevil joyrider at the London Aeroplane Club.[1] In 1935, Ian completed his flying lessons and got his pilot's license, and in spring of 1936 he enlisted in the British Royal Air Force (RAF). Ian quickly became a proficient, confident pilot. He earned the nickname "Widge" or "Wizard Midget" because of his diminutive height and his habit of using the slang term "wizard" when expressing enthusiasm.[2]

In 1938, Ian's love for sailing took him to France, where he met the gay English novelist Somerset Maugham. Somerset had served in WWI in an ambulance unit, then in 1916 and 1917 worked undercover with the British Secret Intelligence Service. By the time Ian and Somerset met, Somerset was a highly successful writer and living with his lifelong partner, Gerald Haxton at the Villa La Mauresque on the French Riviera. Somerset was suave and more than 40 years older than the young, self-assured pilot. Somerset described Ian in his memoir, "I knew one somewhat more intimately; he was a little older than the others, twenty-four, and quite a little chap, not more than five foot four, I should guess (just the right height for a pilot, he said), jaunty, with a care-free look in his impudent blue eyes….I asked him if he wasn't scared. 'Not then,' he said. 'I've never been scared in a scrap—it's too damned exciting.' He thought for a moment. 'But I'll tell you when I have been scared. When I was on a reconnaissance by myself. When you're up there all alone, hour after hour. Gosh, my knees shook. You feel there's no one in the world but you, and the sky looks so damned big. There's nothing to be afraid of really, I don't know why it should make you feel funny.' 'Infinity,' I suggested. He was a jovial, cheery soul. He was in tearing spirits because he had two days' leave and was determined to have the time of his life. He was full of plans for the future. After the war was won, he was going to buy a sailing-boat, forty foot long, and sail with a friend to the South Seas."[3]

Although Ian joined the RAF during peacetime, that did not last long, and WWII arrived far too quickly. On September 1, 1939, Germany invaded Poland. On September 3, 1939, England, France, New Zealand, and Australia declared war on Germany. On September 4th, Nepal declared war on Germany. On September 6th, South Africa declared war on Germany. On September 10th, Canada, Bahrain, and Oman declared war on Germany. It wasn't until two years later, on December 12, 1941, that the United States joined the fray and declared war on Nazi Germany. Between 1939 and the war's end in 1945, every continent in the world except for Antarctica was fighting in WWII.

Ian was a remarkable and dedicated pilot; he was promoted to Flying Officer in the fall of 1938, Flight Lieutenant in fall of 1940, and Squadron Leader in fall of 1941. Ian suffered an airplane accident in May of 1939; then, on his first day back as a solo pilot in May of 1940, he fought successfully in the Battle of France, and went on to fight in the Battle of Britain just a few months later in early July 1940. He was awarded the Distinguished Flying Cross medal in September 1940 for his part in the Battle of Britain, and was promoted to commander of No. 87 Squadron RAF in December of 1940. In May of 1942, Ian was awarded the Distinguished Service Order medal.[4]

Many fighter pilots decorated their planes with art. Ian had enjoyed Disney's 1940 animated film Pinocchio and adopted the black and white cartoon cat, Figaro, as his unofficial coat of arms which he had painted on his fighter plane's cockpit door. Ian's mascot Figaro made his thoughts on Nazis known, and was depicted deservedly smashing a swastika with his paw.

Because of the anti-gay laws of the day, Ian was not out about being gay and took pains to disguise his homosexuality. In the 1930s and 1940s, homosexual sexual activity was illegal in England and was not decriminalized until 1967, when the Sexual Offences Bill 1967 was passed. The Sexual Offences Bill 1967 decriminalized private homosexual acts between two men who were both over 21 years of age. In 2000, it became legal for LGBT people to serve in the military, including the RAF, but in Ian's time, homosexual acts were illegal; Ian would have been punished by court martial law, imprisoned, and discharged if it was discovered that he was a gay RAF member. A fellow pilot commented during an interview in 2015 about gay military personal in the 1940s said that "…homosexuality was a 'dirty word' and discussed in 'hushed tones and absolute horror'."[5]

In May of 1942, Ian's semi-autobiographical novel *Arise to Conquer* was published. Ian decided to add a girlfriend to his book because his publisher was worried that his "confirmed bachelor" status might make him appear gay. When his relatives and friends asked who the mysterious girlfriend was, Ian explained glibly that he made her up because "readers like a touch of romance."[6]

In 2015, Ian was outed as gay, posthumously and publicly, by one of his fellow pilots and an ex-lover, Christopher "Chris" Gotch, in a BBC interview. Chris spoke fondly of Ian. It was 1942 when Chris caught Ian's eye in the mess hall. When Chris returned to his room, there was the flirtatious and forward Ian waiting for him, "…and who should be sitting there on my windowsill, looking at my photograph album, but Commander Ian Gleed. He just leaned over and gave me a kiss, which took me by surprise, but being the product of a public school, it wasn't exactly strange. So we started having sex together. He was a great character, an incredible character. He was the first bloke who ever buggered me, and it went extremely well. He had charm, he had personality, and he had a car and used to take me up to London and introduce me to people."[7] Chris and Ian hit it off and remained lovers for some time.

In April of 1943, Ian was injured in an aerial fight, headed towards Tunisia, but crashed on the sand dunes of Cap Bon, a peninsula in the far northeastern region of the country. His body was not found in the sand, only the debris from his Spitfire. Ian was awarded the Distinguished Service Order (DSO), Distinguished Flying Cross (DFC), *Croix de Guerre* (Belgian), and *Croix de Guerre* (French, posthumously) for his heroic service in the war. As Ian said when receiving his DSO from King George VI, "Nazis, you may blow London and every town in our country to smithereens—if you can. You shall never rule the British Isles."[8]

Resources

Bourne, Stephen. *Fighting Proud: The Untold Story of the Gay Men Who Served in Two World Wars*. S.l.: I B TAURIS, 2018.

It's Not Unusual: Age of Innocence. YouTube. March 5, 2015. Accessed September 10, 2018. https://www.youtube.com/watch?time_continue=1929&v=Z9NQbZlKfY4.

Franks, Norman L. R. *Fighter Leader: The Story of Wing Commander Ian Gleed, DSO, DFC, Croix De Guerre*. London: Kimber, 1978.

Gleed, Ian. *Arise to Conquer*. London: Grub Street, 2010.

Reeve, Jonathan. *Battle of Britain Voices: 37 Fighter Pilots Tell Their Extraordinary Stories*. Stroud, Gloucestershire: Amberley, 2015.

Ian Gleed, drawn by Jon Macy

This page is intentionally blank to facilitate coloring the reverse side.

Evelyn Irons
1900–2000, United Kingdom
drawn by Rachael House

Evelyn Irons was a butch, cat loving, Scottish journalist, known for her heroic wartime reporting, dramatic story scoops, and for breaking Vita Sackville-West's heart. Evelyn was born in Glasgow to a stockbroker and a housewife. Her father drowned at sea when she was only nine, possibly by suicide, and she was not close to her mother.[1] She graduated from high school, winning an award for best scholar, and went on to study at Somerville College, one of the one of the constituent colleges of the renowned and highly respected University of Oxford. In 1921, she graduated with a degree in English, a love of canoeing, and the intentions of becoming a great writer.

Fortunately, fate had something different in mind for Evelyn; instead of becoming a novelist, she became a wartime correspondent. Needing to earn a living and pay the rent, Evelyn started taking small writing assignments for a couple of local newspapers, then worked as a public relations officer, as a sales clerk in a bookstore, and writing short stories for magazines. Finally, in 1927, she got a full-time gig at the *Daily Mail* as the women's page editor, a job that she was dubiously suited for, having no interest in frippery, fashion, or cosmetics. Although she was a sharp writer, Evelyn's hair was cut mannishly short and she never wore makeup.

By the early 1930s, Evelyn was accumulating lovers as rapidly as bylines. She was securely entrenched in the English lesbian community and rubbing more than just elbows with the women in the artistic Bloomsbury group. Evelyn met the author of the 1928 banned lesbian novel *The Well of Loneliness*, Radclyffe "John" Hall after interviewing her for a 1927 article that was intended to soften her image, entitled "How other women run their homes" in which John confessed that she's a "super" homemaker, who enjoys dusting and polishing her furniture—while her partner Una was the family cook.[2] Evelyn was also friends with Virginia Woolf, the bisexual author of the magnificent time-traveling and gender-bending *Orlando*, and had just met the novelist and poet, Vita Sackville-West. Vita's grand affair with depressive writer Virginia Woolf was finally over with, although they remained friends until Virginia's death in 1941.

Evelyn was living with her lover, the consumptive painter Olive Rinder in Chelsea, but she was obsessed with Vita, so she invited the poet over. As Evelyn served cocktails to Olive and Vita, she murmured to Vita, "I suppose you know that I'm desperately in love with you."[3] This became the start of a brief *ménage à trois* between Evelyn, Vita, and Olive, awash with extravagant gifts from Vita to Evelyn of men's silk pajamas and love poems. It was not an easy triad, but fraught with jealousy and drama. Vita complained to Virginia, "Life is too complicated,—Sometimes I feel that I can't manage it all."[4] That summer, the three of them took a Cornish vacation together, rife with quarrels and hurt feelings.

In July 1932, Evelyn met her life partner, fellow journalist Joy MacSweeney, at a cocktail party, fell deeply in love at first sight, and broke up with Vita and Olive in August. This left Vita desolate; she wrote in a poem that was published the following year, "Do not forget, my dear, that once we loved, / Remember only, free of stain or smutch, / That passion once went naked and ungloved, / And that your skin was startled by my touch."[5] Vita had instigated the inclusion of Olive into the threesome, resulting in some resentment. As Olive noted to Vita once the dust settled, "You do like to have your cake and eat it,—and so many cakes, so many, a surfeit of sweet things."[6] By that fall, Evelyn had moved on, leaving Vita to support the homeless and tubercular Olive in a rural bungalow for the rest of her life.

Despite the messy breakup, Evelyn remained friends with Olive, Vita, Virginia, and the rest of the close-knit English lesbian community. In 1932, Evelyn showed Virginia Woolf around the offices of the then au courant, intellectual magazine *The New Yorker*, "There seemed to be little that was wan or mothlike, delicate or remote, about her now. Her long, slender fingers were smudged with black ink, and her behavior was that of a mechanically minded man."[7]

In 1935, Evelyn left the *Daily Mail* for the *London Evening Standard*, a rival newspaper, although she continued with the position of women's editor. By then she was blissfully living with Joy. In 1936, the couple bought a historic 16th-century rural home together, Lodge Hill Cottage. Years later, after moving to New York in 1952, Evelyn reminisced, "How many times have I closed my eyes and felt—I can almost touch it—that I am once again in the timbered drawing-room of Lodge Hill Cottage? In my mind's eye, I always seem to be draped languorously across the overstuffed sofa before the fire, my fingers smoothing the rust velvet cushions or straightening the rust silk shade of the lamp above my head. I am curiously always alone in that magnificent room, the same room that had been the kitchen of the cottage when it was built some 400 years before."[8]

The spread of fascism and WWII was about to interrupt their cozy, domestic life. In September of 1939, the United Kingdom declared war on Nazi Germany. Evelyn decided that she was tired of covering women's issues and, inspired by a recent trip and interview with First Lady Eleanor Roosevelt, she announced to the *Standard* news editor that from now on she was a war correspondent (warco), and then acted accordingly. She covered the war from the front lines and was one of the first journalists to enter liberated Paris after the occupation was toppled in 1944. When Field Marshal Montgomery refused to be allow her to travel with the British Army, she accompanied the First French Army as their only regular British warco,[9] traveling with General de Gaulle and General de Lattre de Tassigny through France, Belgium, Austria, and Germany. She was known for her sense of humor, ability to deflect sometimes misogynist officers, and her level-headedness.[10] When she was awarded the French *Croix de Guerre* it read, "War correspondent of great professional valor and coolness, not hesitating to go into the thick of the fighting to get the best description of the First French Army in action. At the taking of Pforzheim on 13 April, 1945, under violent enemy fire, went into the town with advance troops, volunteering to serve as liaison officer and taking part in the transport of the wounded. Example of calm and modest courage."[11] Evelyn described an incident to Australian historian and warco Phillip Knightley where she helped the First French Army capture a village from the German Nazis: "We somehow had got ahead of the advance, and four of us in a jeep came to this village and found no Allied troops had arrived. So we took it ourselves. We were armed—the French would have none of this nonsense about war correspondents not carrying weapons—so we held up everyone at gunpoint and accepted their surrender. Then we helped ourselves to all the radios, cameras and binoculars we could find and drove off."[12] As the war ended in 1945, she was the first female warco to arrive at Hitler's mountain retreat at Berchtesgaden, where she celebrated the capture of the base by tippling a glass of the Fuhrer's "excellent Rhine wine."[13]

Evelyn did not slow down after WWII. She continued her work as a warco and an exemplary journalist, and spent time at her beloved Lodge Hill Cottage with Joy. She played as hard as she worked. Critic, biographer, and novelist Victoria Glendinning said of Evelyn, "I always thought she was like a little bulldog—and a terrific enjoyer."[14] During an interview, Evelyn said, "My idea of heaven is a Sunday on the Thames in a canoe, without Sunday papers. My idea of hell? Investigative assignment!"[15] In 1952, Evelyn and Joy moved to Brewster, New York where they settled down. In 1954, Evelyn was the first journalist to cover the revolution and overthrow of Guatemalan President Jacobo Arbenz Guzmán, illegally crossing the border through rebel territory on a mule for over twelve hours, while the other journalists waited meekly in a bar for the go ahead.[16] Dean Rusk, the Head of State Department, noted her derring-do in a telegram: "Miss Irons not lady in restricted sense, but seasoned War Correspondent who valiantly covered Guatemalan Liberation in 1954….Department requests transport Miss Irons lest she arrives San Domingo by breaststroke or canoe."[17]

Evelyn was the first woman journalist to be awarded the French *Croix de Guerre* for her reporting during WWII. Joy, nearly ten years younger, died first. In 2000 and at age 99, Evelyn died. Her ashes were scattered in her beloved rose garden in Brewster.

Resources

Dennison, Matthew. *Behind the Mask: The Life of Vita Sackville-West*. New York: Griffin, 2016.

Glendinning, Victoria. *The Life of V. Sackville-West*. London: Phoenix, 2005.

Sebba, Anne. *Battling for News: The Rise of the Woman Reporter*. London: Sceptre, 1995.

Archive

The Dobkin Family Collection of Feminism, Dobkin Collection Item 7035 http://www.glennhorowitz.com/dobkin/archive_
     evelyn_irons_archive._5_large_slipcases

Evelyn Irons, drawn by Rachael House

This page is intentionally blank to facilitate coloring the reverse side.

Alan Turing
1912–1954, United Kingdom
drawn by Ashley Guillory and Burton Clarke

Alan was born in 1912 into an upper-middle-class English family in London, England. Alan was a child genius whose brilliance continued through adulthood, leading him to become the father of artificial intelligence (otherwise known as AI or machine intelligence) and theoretical computer science. He had an uneventful childhood and, although he was clearly exceedingly bright, his grades were often mediocre.[1] As a child, Alan was fascinated with repetition and patterns in nature, specifically the petals of the common daisy, which led to an adult interest in morphogenesis, the biological process by which organisms take their shape.[2] He excelled in science and frequently neglected his other studies, leading the headmaster to say, "If he is to be solely a Scientific Specialist, he is wasting his time at a Public School."[3]

Alan realized that he was gay in his mid-teens, forming his first crush on fellow boarding school student Christopher Morcom. Although their friendship remained platonic, the two boys shared important intellectual and deep emotional bonds. They were fellow science students: "During the term, Chris and I begin setting one another our pet problems and discussing our pet methods." Alan fell deeply in love with Chris; he "worshipped the ground he trod on."[4] Alan was an unusually smart-alecky teen with a quirky sense of humor, traits that he carried into adulthood. He was much loved by his classmates; at a house supper that December they dedicated a song to 17-year-old Alan, "The maths brain lies often awake in his bed / Doing logs to ten places and trig in his head."[5] Just two months after that December dinner, Chris suddenly died of bovine tuberculosis from tainted milk. Alan grieved, losing himself in science and relying on support from Christopher's mother.

Alan entered Kings College, Cambridge in 1931 where he immersed himself in his studies of science and mathematics, long distance running, and had his first sexual experiences with men. Homosexuality was illegal; Alan lived in varying degrees of being out during his adult life and was unashamed of his homosexuality. Hitler was rising to power in Germany, though, and by 1933, although he was not a pacifist, Alan was participating in anti-war demonstrations.[6] Alan visited Nazi Germany in 1935, the year

after he graduated and a few years before the start of WWII in 1939. By the time of his visit, Hitler had been the Chancellor of Germany for two years, swastika flags had just been declared the official German national flag rather than merely the Nazi party flag, and citizens were greeting one another with exclamations of "Heil, Hitler."

It was while he was at Cambridge that Alan started the mathematical work that eventually became known as the Turing machine, and which helped defeat Hitler and his bloody reign. After earning his Ph.D. from Princeton in 1938, Alan returned to England. WWII started September 1, 1939 and Alan begin working in Bletchley Park, a heavily turreted Victorian Buckinghamshire mansion and Britain's codebreaking center for the Government Code and Cypher School (GC&CS). The Germans had the uncrackable Enigma machine, which Alan managed to crack in 1939. The methods that he used to crack the code were finally utilized in 1941, after additional data and statistical processes made regular decryption possible. Alan also sponsored a young Jewish boy and aspiring chemist from a refugee camp at Harwich, Robert "Bob" Augenfeld. Alan arranged for a family to take the child in and provided both English lessons and Bob's secondary education.[7]

Alan's mathematical work at Bletchley was covert; as Geoffrey O'Hanlon wrote in Alan's obituary in *The Shirburnian*, "During the war he was engaged in breaking down enemy codes, and had under him a regiment of girls, supervised to his amusement by a dragon of a female. His work was hush-hush, not to be divulged even to his mother."[8] WWII was the deadliest war in history, lasting for six years from 1939 to 1945 and with over 60 million people killed, which was approximately 3% of the world population in 1940.[9] Alan's work with breaking the code at Bletchley Park was of vast importance, shortening WWII by over two years and saving over fourteen to twenty-one million lives.[10] By the invasion of Normandy on June 6, 1944 at the end of WWII, Alan had developed three ideas that were the basis for the modern computer or, as Alan called it, the "brain"; the concept of a universal machine which was the principle for the computer, reliable electronic technology which was the practical means for the computer, and the inefficiency in designing different machines for different logical processes which was the motivation for the computer. Alan continued his work in mathematics and computing after the war ended; however, he quickly lost his security clearance due to changing security guidelines. In 1950, Alan developed the Turing Test, a component of the philosophy of artificial intelligence which looked at a machine's ability to exhibit intelligent behavior similar to that of a human.

When the Cold War started post-WWII, political tension between powers in the Soviet Union (now known as Russia and its satellite states) and powers in the Western Bloc (the United States and its NATO allies) created an alliance between Great Britain. Unfortunately, this alliance occurred during the repressive 1940s and 1950s McCarthy era in the United States. Once this alliance was formed, the influence of McCarthyism caused known homosexuals/sexual perverts to be explicitly banned from receiving security clearance.[11] After his powerful covert work with Bletchley Park, Alan had been thoughtlessly discarded by his country.

In December of 1951 and a couple of years after Alan was abandoned by his country's secret service, he picked up a nineteen-year-old man in front of a cinema while cruising on Oxford Street. Arnold was uneducated but bright, lower class, and unemployed. After hooking up a few times and a failed attempt at dating, the affair fizzled, but not before Arnold broke into Alan's home and stole some household goods and clothing. Alan reported the theft to the police, told them that he suspected Arnold, and that he'd had sexual relations with him.[12] Alan's crime was that not only was he a homosexual, but also that he was out as gay, and totally unrepentant about his sexual perversions and his apparent penchant for friendly, casual sexual pleasure. Alan and Arnold were charged with and found guilty of several counts of gross indecency on March 31, 1952. Arnold was sentenced to twelve months' probation and submitted to treatment by a 'duly qualified medical practitioner,' while Alan was sentenced to a year of estrogen injections that were intended to suppress and control his sexual urges, as an alternative to a prison sentence. The hormone injections made him impotent although he continued to carry on flirtations with other men.[13]

Alan's probation and hormone treatment ended April 1953, and he committed suicide by eating a cyanide-coated apple on June 7, 1954 at the youthful age of 41. There have been those that dispute whether it was indeed suicide; there was a perfunctory inquest, no suicide note, and the half-eaten apple was never analyzed for cyanide, but he was deeply depressed, seeing a therapist, had organized his correspondence, and had rewritten his will recently.[14] Queen Elizabeth pardoned Alan in 2014. The "Alan Turing Law,"[15] an amnesty law that retroactively pardons men who were cautioned or convicted under historical legislation that outlawed homosexual acts, received royal assent in January 2017. Alan received many awards and honors, some during his life, but the majority were granted posthumously.

Resources

Hodges, Andrew. *Alan Turing, the Enigma*. London: Burnett Books, 1983.

Hodges, Andrew. "Alan Turing: The Enigma." Alan Turing Internet Scrapbook. http://www.turing.org.uk/index.html.

Tyldum, Morton, dir. *The Imitation Game*. Performed by Benedict Cumberbatch and Keira Knightley. Roma: VIDEA-CDE, 2015.

Archive

"The Turing Digital Archive." The Turing Digital Archive. http://www.turingarchive.org/.

Alan Turing, drawn by Ashley Guillory

This page is intentionally blank to facilitate coloring the reverse side.

Alan Turing, drawn by Burton Clarke

This page is intentionally blank to facilitate coloring the reverse side.

Dolly Wilde, a.k.a. Dorothy Ierne Wilde
1895–1941, United Kingdom
drawn by Diane Kanzler

Dolly Wilde was born in London, England into the Wilde family. Her mother, Lily, was beautiful yet indigent and indolent, and her unhappy marriage to Willie Wilde was the result of an unwanted pregnancy. Dolly's parents were impoverished and neglectful. Her father, Willie, was Oscar Wilde's brother. Willie shared a clever wit with his brother, but little else. Unlike Oscar, Willie was not a kind and generous man. Willie was a ne'er-do-well, alcoholic slacker; he relied upon his mother for financial sustenance and broke into children's piggy banks to steal money so that he could party. He was prone to anger with the women in his life, and often abusive. Willie was married once prior to marrying Dolly's mother, Lily, but the marriage only lasted six months before his first wife, a well-to-do American publisher, divorced him. Willie's brother Oscar was a hard-working, successful novelist and playwright best known for his novel *The Picture of Dorian Grey* and his legal troubles as the result of being homosexual during an intolerant era. Willie is quoted as arrogantly boasting, "What America needs is a leisure class and I am determined to introduce one."[1]

In April 1895, Oscar Wilde was arrested for "gross indecency" under Section 11 of the Criminal Law Amendment Act of 1885, and in May he was imprisoned for two long years for homosexual behavior. This tragedy occurred just months after Dolly's birth, indelibly marking the Wilde family. From an early age, Dolly took after her Uncle Oscar in temperament, intellect, and looks. When Willie died, four-year-old Dolly was sent away by her mother to be reared in a "country convent" or foster home. Reticent about her family and her youth, only one anecdote from Dolly's childhood lives on: As a young child, Dolly doused lumps of sugar with her mother's perfume and ate them.[2] In 1930, journalist Janet Flanner, upon meeting Dolly dressed as her uncle Oscar at a Paris bal masqué, wrote in her *The New Yorker* "Letter from Paris" column that Dolly was "looking both important and earnest".[3] Sardonic and hedonistic, Dolly wrote and was a gifted raconteur, but she never published. A depressive, she attempted suicide four times and there are those who say that she succeeded with her eventual death at age 45.

When WWI started in 1914, teenage Dolly immediately joined the war efforts by sending her mother a succinct and excited telegram that read "SAILING!", crossing the English Channel to France to volunteer as an ambulance driver, and eventually ending up driving with an all-women ambulance driving unit.[4] Dolly traveled to Paris and moved into a glass-roofed artist's loft in Maupassant with four other female ambulance drivers. Dolly immediately seduced one of her roommates, and how could she resist? Young Joe Carstairs was a devilishly handsome teenage butch ambulance driver, five years younger, charmingly oblivious to his considerable sexual charisma, and ignorant of the power of sexuality. Joe was a virgin and came reeling from Dolly's bed exclaiming, "My God, what a marvelous thing. I found it a great pity I'd waited so long."[5] After Dolly's seduction, Joe discovered the power of sexuality and became a rake, with over 120 lovers. Later, Joe reminisced fondly about Dolly, saying that she was one of the four women who changed her life, and considering that the compelling singer and actress Marlene Dietrich was undisputedly one of the remaining four women, this was no small claim to Dolly's abilities.

Many records are destroyed, so we'll never know whether Dolly and Joe drove with Toupie Lowther's infamous Hackett-Loather all-women ambulance unit or another all-woman unit. Toupie when interviewed said, "…We were often 350 yards from the German lines awaiting the wounded, under camouflage."[6] Like the WACS, the all-women units were populated by a high proportion of lesbians, including butch movie director Dorothy Arzner.[7] The Hackett-Loather unit with its rash of lesbian drivers was said to have inspired Radclyffe Hall's lesbian novel *The Well of Loneliness*.[8] Women were not allowed to fight in combat; for the adventurous and passionate Dolly this was the closest she could get to battle. Dolly had never driven anything before she started driving an ambulance, so she learned to drive while on the Front while being shot at and bombed as she drove wounded and dying soldiers and civilians to treatment.[9] In addition to being speedy and safe drivers during dangerous wartime conditions, the women were required to often drive 24 to 36 hour shifts, be mechanics for their trucks and tend to elderly and sick civilians as they were forced from their homes by German Nazi soldiers.[10] Dolly served in WWI for four years until the war ended in 1918, and was discharged with honors.

It was not unheard of for wartime service personal to turn to opioid use to assuage the horrors experienced while working on the front. Dolly started using drugs either during the war or immediately afterward. In a mirror of her refusal to discuss her dysfunctional childhood, she also refused to discuss her wartime experiences. It is highly likely that the sensitive Dolly suffered from war-induced post-traumatic stress disorder (PTSD), or shell shock as it was called back then. It seems that each war had a name for the psychological afflictions of soldiers and service personal. The American Civil War had the army disease which referred to opioid addiction, WWI had shell shock, WWII had combat fatigue or battle exhaustion, and the Vietnam War had PTSD. The psychological and physical manifestations of shell shock came about as the result of the modern warfare of WWI, specifically the soldiers' and service personnels' close proximity to repeated massive explosions and heavy artillery bombardments. It was believed that such exposure caused hidden brain injuries. More recently, a doctor noted, after describing the brain injuries in modern Iraqi war veterans, "Doctors treating IED [improvised explosive device] survivors often see depression, anxiety, post-traumatic stress, and substance abuse or adjustment disorders."[11] If Dolly suffered from shell shock, this could be one of the major factors in her later slide into drug addiction.

In 1927, Dolly started an 18-year affair with the glamorous, seductive, and literary Parisian expatriate from Dayton, Ohio and salonnière, Natalie Barney. Dolly was one of Natalie's several lovers, a situation which riled her and caused furious fighting between the two. The butch lawyer and spy Nadine Hwang caused her spectacular grief and fits of jealousy. Dolly was thinly disguised as "Doll Furious" in Djuna Barnes' *The Ladies Almanack*, a dishy novel documenting the tight-knit and incestuous Paris and London lesbian community,[12] and Natalie called Dolly her "puppy."

In 1939, WWII broke out. During this time Dolly discovered lumps in her breast and was diagnosed with breast cancer, but she doubted the doctors' diagnosis. Broken and ill, she decided to return to England. Back home, she volunteered for the Polish Relief Fund, one of the largest wartime assistance organization. Her guardian, Tancred Borenius, was the Polish Relief Fund's secretary until he took off to do intelligence work on the Front.[13] Dolly relied upon alternative treatments for her cancer rather than the invasive surgery that the doctors recommended. In England, Dolly struggled with drugs and drinking, finally succumbing to a combination of untreated breast cancer, alcoholism, and drug addiction. Dolly died of a drug overdose in 1941, at age 45.

Resources

Barnes, Djuna. *The Ladies Almanack*. New York: Kessinger, 2013.

Rodriguez, Suzanne. *Wild Heart: A Life: Natalie Clifford Barney and the Decadence of Literary Paris*. New York: HarperCollins, 2002.

Schenkar, Joan. *Truly Wilde: The Unsettling Story of Dolly Wilde, Oscar's Unusual Niece*. New York: Basic Books, 2000.

Dolly Wilde (right) and Joe Carstairs, drawn by Diane Kanzler   123

This page is intentionally blank to facilitate coloring the reverse side.

Ernestine Davis, a.k.a. Tiny Davis
1909/1910–1994, United States
drawn by Ajuan Mance

Tiny Davis was a musician and singer from Tennessee, born into a large family with six siblings. In 1923 and age 13, Tiny started playing the trumpet. "I saw the boys in the high school band playing the horn, and I liked the way it looked," she said, "So I asked my mother to buy me one, and she did. People thought I was crazy, practicing up on top of the barn like I did. But I wanted to learn to blow that horn more than anything. More than anything."[1] Tiny never stopped, eventually earning the nickname "the female Louis Armstrong." Tiny played almost exclusively in all-female bands; Louis Armstrong himself even attempted to hire Tiny by offering her ten times her salary, but she turned him down to stay with the girls saying, "I loved them gals too much. Them was some sweet gals - you know."[2]

She married, bore a daughter named Dorothy, and divorced. In the 1930s, she moved to Kansas City and formed a band called the Torrid Eight, and in 1935 joined the Harlem Playgirls, an acclaimed all-black, all-female, jazz music dance band. The band appeared in such venues as the Apollo Theater in New York City and the Savoy ballroom in Chicago. Tiny lasted for one year with the Harlem Playgirls then, in the early 1940s, she joined the highly popular, 16-piece, racially mixed, traveling International Sweethearts of Rhythm, billing themselves as "International Sweethearts of Rhythm. The World's Greatest All-Girl Band – All Nationality Band."[3]

The International Sweethearts of Rhythm's mixed racial line-up was highly controversial and unique, particularly offending and confounding white segregationists. The interracial band included Chinese-American, Mexican, Native American, Jewish, and native Hawaiian musicians, along with black, mixed, and, in 1943, the first white musician. The inclusion of the word 'International' was to tip off the local authorities that there were white-appearing women in the band, so the band would hopefully get harassed less. In the American south, touring was dangerous. Jim Crow laws specifically banned black and white people from traveling or working together, so any white-appearing members would need to take care to appear black with make-up and hair styling. Tiny told a reporter from the *Chicago Times* in an interview in 1988, "Our sound was so tight - nobody could argue with us. We were just like sisters, traveling on a bus, sleeping on it to keep from getting arrested in the South for mixing the races. The white gals had to wear that heavy makeup, trying to pass for black. Most of the time, they just looked orange."[4]

Tiny started getting rave reviews with the International Sweethearts of Rhythm. The *Chicago Defender* wrote this review: "Tiny Davis, the 245 lb. 'girl with a horn' whose trumpet renditions are a sensation. Miss Davis, aside from her horn tooting is a natural born entertainer."[5] Short and round, Tiny thumbed her nose at the expectations that female performers needed to be slender and glamorous, and billed herself as "245 pounds of jive and rhythm,"[6] even singing about her sweetness in her signature song "How 'Bout That Jive": "Mama's round and brown and can roll just like a ball / Yes mama's round and brown and can roll just like a ball / She's got a lot to give and daddy you can have it all / I'm sister five by five and I'm known all over town / I'm sister five by five and I'm known all over town / I ain't much when I stand but oh when I lay it down."[7]

Another song that the International Sweethearts of Rhythm performed was an instrumental called "Diggin' Dykes" written by Maurice King, so I'm guessing there was more than one lady lover in the traveling troupe. Tiny explained that although many of the musicians considered themselves straight, the long days and nights touring led to hook-ups and relationships with one another. Tiny said, "But it was them girls – white, light, bright, brown, tan, and yellow. Yes sir, that's who I grinding my axe for."[8]

The United States entered into WWII in 1941 with the bombing of Pearl Harbor. When the all-male draft was instituted, men went off to war, leaving fewer male musicians to play and tour. Suddenly, all-girl bands became more visible. In 1945, the International Sweethearts of Rhythm started touring with the United Service Organizations (USO), becoming the first black women to travel with the organization. The USO was formed under President Roosevelt to provide respite and entertainment to soldiers who were on the battlefront, with a lengthy roster of American artists donating their time to fight fascism by boosting morale with entertainment (and sometimes even more covert actions). The list of USO performers included hundreds of popular American comedians, singers, actors, and dancers, and such notable POC entertainers as Alberta Hunter, Anna May Wong, Adelaide Hall, Marion Anderson, Lena Horne, Count Basie, Noble Sissle, and Al Jolson. In July of 1945, the International Sweethearts of Rhythm toured Germany and France. Their audience was segregated, white soldiers to one side and black soldiers to the other side.[9] The International Sweethearts of Rhythm also recorded for the Armed Forces Radio broadcasts of *Jubilee*, a radio show geared towards soldiers in the all-black U.S. Army's 92nd Infantry Division.

After WWII ended, the International Sweethearts of Rhythm disbanded and Tiny formed another band, Tiny Davis and the Hell Divers, touring the United States and the Caribbean.

Sometime in the late 1940s, Tiny met her life partner, fellow musician and bassist Ruby Lucas. Tiny explained, "The Sweethearts would come to Kansas City every Easter, and I would sell food and drinks from wherever we were staying. Ruby came over one day and never left. Hell, she stayed for 42 years."[10] In the 1950s, the couple opened a gay bar in Chicago called Tiny and Ruby's Gay Spot. Tiny continued to perform through her 70s, sometimes with her daughter Dorothy Davis on keyboards and bass.

Towards the end of her life, Tiny talked about her career as a musician: "I don't like to hear that 'plays like a girl' or 'plays like a sissy'. I had more chops than most men….So no, we never got the credit we deserved. But women have a hard time in anything. There's nothing you can do. Just keep on keeping on."[11] In 1994, Tiny died in Chicago at the age of 87.

Resources

Davis, Tiny, Julian Dash, Jack Pettis, Ben Bernie, George Gershwin, Fats Waller, and Erskine Hawkins, writers. *Hot Licks: 1944-1946*. International Sweethearts Of Rhythm. 2006, CD.

Handy, D. Antoinette. *The International Sweethearts of Rhythm: The Ladies Jazz Band from Piney Woods Country Life School*. Lanham (Ma.): Scarecrow Press, 1998.

Schiller, Greta and Andrea Weiss, dir. *International Sweethearts of Rhythm*. Jezebel Productions: Channel 4 (UK). 1986. Accessed September 26, 2018. https://www.kanopy.com/product/international-sweethearts-rhythm.

Schiller, Greta and Andrea Weiss, dir. *Tiny and Ruby: Hell Divin' Women*. Jezebel Productions: Channel 4 (UK). 1996. Accessed September 26, 2018. https://www.kanopy.com/product/tiny-and-ruby-hell-divin-women.

Tucker, Sherrie. *Swing Shift: "All-Girl" Bands of the 1940s*. Durham, NC: Duke University Press, 2001.

Ernestine
"Tiny"
Davis
1910-1994

Tiny Davis, drawn by Ajuan Mance

This page is intentionally blank to facilitate coloring the reverse side.

Marlene Dietrich, a.k.a Lili Marlene
1901–1992, United States
drawn by Phoebe Kobabe and Justin Hall

Marlene Dietrich was a bisexual, iconic actress and singer. Although she was born a German citizen, she adamantly opposed Hitler, and took proactive steps to demonstrate her revulsion of Hitler and the German Nazi government and to support the resistance. Marlene was one of two children born in Berlin, Germany to a well-to-do family. Her older sister's name was Elizabeth, nicknamed Liesel. Her mother's family owned a jewelry and clock-making factory, and her father had served in the Franco-Prussian War (1870-1871) and was a police lieutenant; he died in 1907 when Marlene was only six. Her mother remarried, but her new husband died shortly after their marriage of injuries sustained in WWI. Marlene played violin as a teenager, and switched to musical saw when she injured her wrist. She knew that she wanted to go into the entertainment business.

In 1922, Marlene started acting in films, but none were hits. In 1923, she married her assistant director, Rudolf Sieber, and in 1924 they had one child. Marlene and Rudolf did not live together and remained in an open marriage. Marlene performed in cabaret shows and was deeply involved in the blossoming, louche, sexually ambiguous German Weimar Republic era. In 1928, Marlene performed a campy duet "*Wenn Die Beste Freundin*" ("We're the Best of Friends") with her pal Margo Lion for the show, "*Es Liegt in Der Luft*" ("It's In The Air"). The couple both wore violets in the show, a popular indication that one was a lesbian, and the tune became a lesbian anthem in Berlin.[1]

Always androgynous and adventerous, in the late 1920s Marlene joined Turkish fighter Sabri Mahir's *Studio für Boxen und Leibeszucht* (Studio for Boxing and Physical Culture) and learned to box. Fellow pugilist Vicki Baum said, "I don't know how the feminine element sneaked into those masculine realms, but in any case, only three or four of us were tough enough to go through with it (Marlene Dietrich was one)."[2]

This creative and sexually free time period lasted from 1919 until the early 1930s, dwindling to nothingness when Hitler was appointed Chancellor of Germany in 1933. Hitler moved quickly, dismantling every social and cultural advancement of the Weimar Republic. In 1933, the first movie to be premiered in Berlin under the new Nazi regime was *Morgenrot* (English title *Dawn*), with Cabinet Minister and creator of the Gestapo Göring and Minister of Public Enlightenment and Propaganda Goebbels in attendance. Blond-haired, blue-eyed, Jewish actress Camilla Spira was the star and received a wreath with a ribbon reading "The representative of the German woman." Two weeks after the premier of this blockbuster movie, Camilla was shipped off to Westerbork concentration camp for being Jewish.[3] This should have been a strong signal of things to come for German entertainers and artists, but many paid no heed.

Volker Kuehn, a historian specializing in German cabaret, talked about the political climate concerns among entertainers in early 1930s Berlin, "He [Kurt Robicek, head of the *Kaberet Der Komiker* (Comedians' Cabaret,)] had a comedian who was in the play whose name was Kurt Lilien, both of them were Jews. In 1932, Robicek said, 'Hey Kurt, don't you think we ought to look around for a country where we could go if things continue the way they are?' And Lilien said, 'I don't know what you mean. Why?' 'Well, don't you think there could be a situation here in Berlin, in Germany, where we'd have to leave?...Haven't you read *Mein Kampf*, that book by Adolf Hitler?' Kurt Lilien said, 'I don't read bad books.'"[4] Robicek fled Germany for America and lived, but Lilien stayed in Germany and in 1943 was killed at Sobibór extermination camp.

In 1930, Marlene appeared in her first popular film, *Der Blaue Enge* (*The Blue Angel*). Marlene, a regular at Berlin lesbian and gay nightclubs, found out she got the lead role in *Der Blaue Enge* while hanging out at The Silhouette, a mixed gay, lesbian, and drag club. When she got the good news, the orchestra played the tango "*Schöner Gigolo, armer Gigolo*" ("Just a Gigolo") and Marlene "ordered so much champagne that you could bathe in it."[5] Marlene attended the January 30th opening of *Der Blaue Enge* in an elegant white gown and a fur wrap and left Berlin the same night. She collected her thirty-six pieces of luggage that were waiting by the stage door, then boarded a train to sail on the ocean liner *S.S. Bremen* to America.[6]

Marlene had signed up with Paramount Pictures, and started producing hit films. In 1930, she starred in *Morocco*, sizzling as she kissed another woman while dashingly sporting a men's white evening dress suit. When in Hollywood, Marlene joined "the Sewing

Circle," a secret social group of bisexual and lesbian actresses and movie folks, including Dolores del Ráo, Mercedes de Acosta, Katherine Hepburn, Greta Garbo, Barbara Stanwyck, Dorothy Arzner, and Tallulah Bankhead. In 1937, Marlene became an American citizen.

Never one to neglect the ladies, Marlene had a lusty sexual appetite. In 1936, she visited Paris and seduced a handsome, young, Parisian butch named Frede Baulé, then bought Frede *La Silhouette*, a nightclub in Pigalle, as a token of her affection. In 1939, English rake and butch Joe Carstairs sailed by Marlene's cove on her boat. Marlene took one look at Joe in the sunlight, "At the helm, a beautiful boy. Bronzed and sleek – even from a distance, one sensed the power of his rippling muscles of his tight chest and haunches….The first thought on seeing him had been 'pirate' – followed by 'pillage' and 'plunder'." As Joe came closer, though, "he turned from a sexy boy into a sexy, flat-chested woman."[7] Their passionate affair lasted for years, with Joe wistfully offering to buy an island for Marlene and Marlene purchasing a sailboat for Joe.

WWII did not start until Germany invaded Poland in 1939, and the United States did not join the war until 1941. Although Germany pleaded with Marlene to do her patriotic duty and return to her homeland, when she angrily refused Germany banned her movies. Marlene avidly hated Hitler and everything he stood for, but Marlene's sister Liesel in Germany was pro-Nazi and maintained that the Nazis had "moral integrity," and even ran the canteen with her husband Will near Bergen-Belsen concentration camp where German soldiers and SS officers watched films.[8] Their political differences caused an enormous rift between Marlene and Liesel, and they spoke infrequently. Unlike Liesel, Marlene's mother was not pro-Nazi. She stayed in Berlin during the war and sheltered Jews in her apartment.[9]

While Elizabeth was serving the Gestapo soldiers tankards of beer, Marlene was doing everything in her power to thwart Hitler. During WWII, Marlene made over 500 personal appearances before Allied troops between 1943 and 1946 with the United Service Organization (USO) in Europe and North Africa; sold a record number of war bonds, debt securities that helped finance military operations; made anti-Nazi radio broadcasts in German to demoralize the German Nazi troops; joined Billy Wilder, an Austrian-American filmmaker, to set up a fund to assist Jews and dissidents escape from Germany; donated her salary from the film *Knight Without Armor* ($450,000) to help refugees; housed German and French refugees in America; and made several appearances on Armed Forces Radio Services shows like "The Army Hour" and "Command Performance." Marlene earned the U.S. Medal of Freedom and the French *Legion d'Honneur* for her wartime work.

After the war, Marlene continued to record and make movies. She performed mostly live cabaret work during the 1950s, 60s, and 70s. She collaborated with Burt Bacharach as her musical arranger starting in the mid-1950s. In 1965, Marlene was suffering from physical ailments beginning with cervical cancer, then she had a series of debilitating falls along with alcohol and opioids issues. She spent the last 11 years of her life holed up in her apartment in Paris, reclusive, dependent upon alcohol and opioids, and bed-ridden. In 1992 and at age 90, Marlene died. Over 1,500 mourners appeared to pay their respects at *La Madeleine*, a Roman Catholic church in the 8th arrondissement of Paris, and thousands more lined the streets outside.

Resources

Dietrich, Marlene, and Salvator Attanasio. *Marlene*. New York: Avon, 1990.

McLellan, Diana. *The Girls: Sappho Goes to Hollywood*. Seattle: Booktrope Editions, 2013.

Madsen, Axel. *The Sewing Circle: Hollywood's Greatest Secret—Female Stars Who Loved Other Women*. New York, NY: Open Road Media, 2015.

Riva, Maria. *Marlene Dietrich: The Life*. New York: Pegasus Books, 2017.

Riva, J. David, and Guy Stern. *A Woman at War: Marlene Dietrich Remembered*. Detroit, MI: Wayne State University Press, 2006.

Schell, Maximilian, dir. *Marlene*. Produced by Zev Braun and Karei Dirka. Germany: Futura Film, 1984. DVD.

Archive

Deutsche Kinemathe, Marlene Dietrich Collection Berlin, https://www.deutsche-kinemathek.de/en/archives/marlene-dietrich-colecction-berlin/permanent-exhibition

Marlene Dietrich, drawn by Phoebe Kobabe

This page is intentionally blank to facilitate coloring the reverse side.

Marlene Dietrich, drawn by Justin Hall

This page is intentionally blank to facilitate coloring the reverse side.

Janet Flanner, a.k.a. Genêt
1892–1978, United States/France
drawn by Jennifer Camper

Janet Flanner was born in the American Midwest to a mortician and a housewife. Janet was the Paris cultural and political correspondent for *The New Yorker* magazine from 1925 until 1975, writing political and cultural commentary. She wrote "Letter From Paris" under the rather romantic nom de plume Genêt because Harold Ross, the magazine's editor, mistakenly thought that it was the French version of Janet.[1] Janet's writing for *The New Yorker* was erudite and sophisticated, bringing joy to American Francophiles everywhere.

In 1918, Janet lived in bohemian Greenwich Village, New York, trying fruitlessly to sell her writing. She married a man, then almost immediately met the writer and critic, Solita. The marriage dissolved quickly, but her open romantic and sexual relationship with Solita lasted a lifetime. Janet blamed herself for the divorce and considered that she'd acted "criminally."[2] In 1921, Solita and Janet moved to Europe to travel, explore, and escape American conservatism. The couple settled in Paris in autumn of 1921, falling in with the rollicking international lesbian community there and becoming notorious enough to be portrayed as Nip and Tuck in Djuna Barnes' dishy novel, *The Ladies Almanack*.[3] Janet started writing her column for *The New Yorker* in 1925. A lifelong practitioner of polyamory, Janet got around. When in Paris, Janet loved to go out, dance and flirt, picking up women, "her attitude toward casual sex was essentially that of a single young male."[4] Janet became close pals with fellow expatriate Parisians Gertrude Stein and Alice B. Toklas, even caretaking Alice after Gertrude's death. But these carefree and delightful times were coming to an end. Fascism was rising, and Janet noticed. After eight years of charming and lighthearted reporting from Paris, the political climate began to change, and Janet felt compelled to write about the escalation of hatred and political turmoil.

In 1933, Hitler was appointed Chancellor of Germany, and civil liberties gradually eroded. In February, the Reichstag or parliamentary building was burnt, and Hitler blamed the Communists, a political party that held 17% of the house seats. On February 28, 1933, Hitler was awarded emergency powers under the presidential decree, *Reichstagsbrandverordnung* (Decree of the Reich President for the Protection of People and State), effectively removing many of German citizens' civil liberties. Less than one month later, the first concentration camp opened, Dachau concentration camp, which initially accepted political prisoners. In the beginning, efforts were concentrated at separating desirables from undesirables; the government established an office of racial hygiene later that month. Book burnings soon followed. Hitler said of the arsonists, "These sub-humans do not understand how the people stand at our side. In their mouse-holes, out of which they now want to come, of course they hear nothing of the cheering of the masses."[5] In March, the the *Gesetz zur Behebung der Not von Volk und Reich* (the Law to Remedy the Distress of People and Reich, or Enabling Act of 1933) was passed which gave Hitler the power to pass laws without the approval of the Reichstag or German Parliament. In October 1933, Germany left the League of Nations; in October 1934, members of the German military begin swearing a personal oath of loyalty to Hitler instead of to the German constitution; in 1935, the Nuremberg Laws were passed, institutionalizing legal discrimination against Jews in order to identify and prosecute them; and in 1936, the Spanish Civil War started. Democracy in Germany and Spain was smashed, fascism was rising, but no one was stopping the carnage; WWII did not start until 1939.

In 1936 and three years prior to WWII, Janet wrote a series of three columns for *The New Yorker* documenting Hitler's rise to power. This series was titled "Führer," and although she feared retaliation from Hitler, Janet signed all three with the name Janet Flanner rather than Genêt. She was making a political statement about the current danger. Janet was a dedicated antifascist and watched Hitler's rise with horror: "The only job on the magazine that I am really proud of was the fact that I had sufficient apprehension…to propose to write about Hitler as an important man."[6]

In the *New Yorker* article "Führer II," dated March 7, 1936, Janet wrote about Hitler's anti-Semitism as documented in his statement of ideology, "Only those who are of German blood can be considered our countrymen, regardless of creed. Hence no Jew can be regarded as a fellow countryman."[7] Janet then noted some recent repercussions of this hate speech from Nazi Germany's leader; Jewish business owners were demoted, their businesses had been taken away from them, and they had been forced to work as managers because "firing them from their own businesses might result in incompetent management of the business, perhap even bankruptcy and closing, and thus more Christian unemployment."[8] Janet also talked about Nazi Germany no longer renewing Jewish passports, thus leaving them without identity papers, and small towns where businesses were refusing to serve Jews and putting signage in their windows saying *Juden Sind Hier Nicht Erwünscht* (Jews are Not Wanted Here). Hitler wondered at America's animosity towards Nazi Germany and speculated that it was because in America Jews ran all the press, banks, businesses, and entertainment industry. By 1936, several major foreign newspapers had been banned in Germany, including *The New York Times* and *The Guardian*. As Janet noted in her three-part article about Hitler, control of the press, anti-Semitic laws, and government sanctioned hate speech were the norm in 1936 Nazi Germany. In "Führer III," Janet wrote that Hitler "...regards liberalism as a form of tyranny, hatred and attack as part of men's civic virtues, and equality of men as immoral and against nature."[9]

Hitler was not taken seriously by many, but seen as a "blood-and thunder Teutonic political clown."[8] Janet struggled with the series on Hitler, and writing in a letter to her editor Harold Ross said, "Those who hate Fascism better start knowing he is not a mere hysterical heliotrope: he's the fanatic and dangerous exalte he says he is, and his sobbing occasionally doesn't interfere, alas."[10]

After WWII broke out, Janet moved back to the United States. In 1940, Janet met her other lifelong lover, Natalia Danesi Murray, at a cocktail party in Manhattan, where their relationship quickly became serious. Soon, Natalia replaced Solita as Janet's primary partner. Janet co-parented Natalia's teenage son William, forming a family of three. Natalia divided her time between Rome and the U.S. Janet moved back to Paris in 1944, moving in with Solita again, but continuing to see Natalia as romantic lovers. The deep bond and love between Solita, Natalia, and Janet continued until Solita's death in 1975.[11] That year, Janet returned to Natalia in New York and died just three years later. Janet received many honors for her journalism including being made a knight of *Legion d'Honneur* and the U.S. National Book Award.

Resources

Barnes, Djuna. *Ladies Almanack*. New York: Kessinger, 2013.

Flanner, Janet. *Paris Was Yesterday: 1925-1939*. London: Virago, 2003.

Murray, William. *Janet, My Mother, and Me: A Memoir of Growing up with Janet Flanner and Natalia Danesi Murray*. New York: Simon & Schuster, 2000.

Wineapple, Brenda. *Genêt, A Biography of Janet Flanner*. London: Pandora, 1994.

Janet Flanner, drawn by Jennifer Camper

137

This page is intentionally blank to facilitate coloring the reverse side.

Alberta Hunter
1895–1984, United States
drawn by Ajuan Mance

Alberta Hunter was an American jazz singer, actress, journalist, and songwriter. She was raised fatherless and in poverty in Tennessee, left home at age 11 or 12 for a career as a singer in the big city of Chicago, where her beloved mother soon followed and moved in with her. Alberta shunned alcohol, cigarettes, and drugs. By age 15, Alberta was singing the blues publicly and writing songs. An accomplished songwriter, her songs include such classics as "Downhearted Blues." She eventually sang with such greats as Louis Armstrong and Sidney Bechet, and branched off into theater, performing to rave reviews in London. She was driven, adventurous, and talented, moving to New York in 1923 to become part of the Harlem Renaissance arts movement.

Alberta was not closeted as a lesbian; however, she was an extremely private person. Alberta was considered unattractive by the public, most likely because she was on the mannish side of the fence, although she was not a bulldagger like fellow blues singer Gladys Bentley. Her lack of conventional sex appeal caused issues with getting gigs, but her raw talent, stage presence, and ambition worked in her favor. Sometime between 1915 and 1917 and, after a two-month-long failed marriage to a man, Alberta met and fell in deeply love with Lottie Tyler at the Panama Café where Alberta was singing in Chicago. Lottie was the daughter of a well-liked comedian and according to Alberta had, "…the most beautiful legs that were ever on a person."[1] Alberta and Lottie remained lovers and close friends their entire lives, even after their initial flurry of new relationship lust dissipated. After traveling to Europe together, Lottie left Alberta to return to the United States in order to start seeing her lawyer's wife.

Alberta toured Europe as an entertainer for the first time at age 22. Alberta was in good company in Europe, as it was a popular destination for black Americans wanting to escape American racism, and she toured extensively. The exodus of black Americans between the two World Wars and beyond, during the 1920s through the 1950s, led to the formation of "Black American Paris." Many Harlem Renaissance movement artists and writers moved to Paris. Entertainer and resistance fighter Josephine Baker moved to France in 1925, where her ex, the infamous bisexual businesswoman and performer Ida "Bricktop" Smith opened a bar in Paris called Chez Bricktop. The renowned writer James Baldwin moved to France in 1948 in order to write, talking about his escape from America's racism, "It wasn't so much a matter of choosing France—it was a matter of getting out of America."[2] Some black American soldiers even elected to stay in France rather than return to the States after WWI ended.

After moving to Paris, Alberta said, "The Negro artists went to Europe because we were recognized and given a chance. In Europe they had your name up in lights. People in the United States would not give us that chance."[3] and "I don't know when I'll be home. I am mad about the freedom of Paris. Color means nothing over here. If anything they treat the colored people better."[4] Eventually, Alberta grew quite fond of England during her time in Europe, becoming an Anglophile and developing a taste for tweed and tea.

In 1927, Alberta started writing for the *Amsterdam News*; her first article was a Paris travelogue.[5] As Hitler gained power in the early 1930s, racism spread in Germany. Alberta warned fellow black performers to stay away from Germany, citing her experiences in Hamburg of being taunted by children who chased her down the street, while yelling racial slurs.[6] With the rise of Fascism in Italy, racism became legal and by 1937, Mussolini or *Il Duce* in Italy had banned "undesirable" performers, including black folks. Alberta was alarmed, educated, and vocal about the approaching fascism. Starting in the early 1930s, she tracked the rise of antisemitism and racism in Europe by saving newspaper articles,[7] and warned black American newspapers that the American Consulate in Paris was advising "race" performers to refuse contracts to appear in Italy.[8] In the fall of 1938, the American Embassy sent performers telegrams admonishing them to leave, "In view of the complicated situation prevailing in Europe, it is considered advisable to recommend that American citizens who have no compelling reason to continue their sojourn here to arrange to return to the U.S."[9]

Alberta sadly sailed back to the U.S. in 1939. Hitler banned all people of African descent from Paris in the fall of 1940 and even Francophile Josephine Baker fled.[10] Although WWII started in 1939, America did not become involved until 1941. Desperate to assist during the war, Alberta joined the newly minted United Service Organizations Inc. (USO), which was formed under President Roosevelt to provide respite and entertainment to soldiers who were on the battlefront. Alberta enjoyed her time in the USO saying, "I'm going to be with Uncle Sam till he takes this uniform off me. I've never been so satisfied and had so much protection in my life. If you're with the USA, everything jumps."[11] Alberta performed for the troops nearly 300,000 times in the four years between 1941 and 1945, when the war ended. The roster of American artists donating their time to fighting fascism by boosting morale with entertainment (and sometimes even more covert actions) was lengthy, and included hundreds of popular American comedians, singers, actors, and dancers. Alberta toured Europe, the Middle East, and Asia. Alberta was put in charge of Unit 342 because she was a leader, and a stickler for regulations and order.[12] She performed with the USO relentlessly, becoming one of 40 recipients of the Asiatic Pacific Campaign Ribbon for "Outstanding Service" for her extensive resistance work with the USO.

When her beloved mother died in 1954, Alberta declared that she was done with show business and trained to become a nurse. She worked as a nurse until she was in her 80s, while remaining in the closet about her previous career as a singer. She was an excellent nurse; a nursing colleague exclaimed "She was as good a nurse as she was an entertainer. Maybe there's some parallel there, in that to do both well, you have to make people feel good."[13] Alberta returned to singing accidentally. She went to a party for fellow cabaret singer and one of Joe Carstair's exes, Mabel Mercer, and casually broke into "Down Hearted Blues." Alberta's voice and phrasing in her 80s were as brilliant as when she was young, and the party-goers were stunned with her talent and the unexpected serenade. She immediately was offered a gig at a Greenwich Village club named the Cookery, and based on her success in the club, returned to entertaining for nine spectacular, award-winning years. Alberta signed up with Columbia Records, cut three albums, and toured Europe and South America. She was inducted into both the Blues Hall of Fame and the Memphis Music Hall of Fame. Alberta died in 1986 at age 89.

Resources

Goldman, Stuart A. dir. 1988. *Alberta Hunter: My Castle's Rockin.* DVD.

Keaton, Trica Danielle, et al. *Black Europe and the African Diaspora.* University of Illinois Press, 2009.

Monahan, Patrick. "Alberta Sings the Blues." *The Paris Review.* March 01, 2012. https://www.theparisreview.org/blog/2012/03/01/alberta-sings-the-blues/.

Moore, Lisa C. "Whither Lottie Tyler?" The Untitled Black Lesbian Elder Project. September 13, 2012. http://ubleproject.tumblr.com/post/31419751452/whither-lottie-tyler.

Taylor, Frank C. *Alberta Hunter: a Celebration in Blues.* McGraw-Hill Book Company, 1988.

Archive

"Alberta Hunter Papers." New York Public Library Archives and Manuscripts. Accessed July 15, 2018. http://archives.nypl.org/scm/20645.

ALBERTA HUNTER 1895-1984

Alberta Hunter, drawn by Ajuan Mance

141

This page is intentionally blank to facilitate coloring the reverse side.

Vincent Miles
b. 1924 (?), United States
drawn by Ajuan Mance

We know very little about Vincent Miles except that he was from Davenport, Iowa, joined the United States Army in 1943 against his parents' wishes, dropped out of college to enlist, was wounded in the side by shrapnel, and fought in the all-black 92nd Infantry Division in Italy and in North Africa while serving as an Army medical clerk. Vincent had a religious upbringing and had faith in god; he said, "The whole time the fight was going on, it didn't seem to really get me panicky….it's all in god's hands. What's going to happen is going to happen."[1] He was interviewed for the book *Coming Out Under Fire: The History of Gay Men and Women in World War II*; it was published in 1990, so he was alive in the decade preceding publication. Vincent appears to be the only representative from the 92nd Infantry Division in that book, perhaps a sign of the depth of the closet for black servicemen of that era.

The 92nd Infantry Division was first activated in WWI in October, 1917 as the 92nd Division, then changed its name to the 92nd Infantry Division during WWII. A segregated unit, they were active in WWI between 1917–1919, and for WWII between 1942–1945. Although the soldiers and junior officers were black, most of the higher officers were white. Approximately 909,000 black Americans served in the U.S. Army during WWII, but the U.S. Army 92nd Infantry Division became the only Army military unit which allowed black Americans to serve in combat. Previous to being activated for battle in October of 1942, it was felt that black soldiers did not have the aggressiveness, courage, discipline, and intelligence that was necessary to fight effectively, so they were instead given menial service jobs such as burying the dead, cooks, stewards, and laborers. Vincent enrolled in 1943, after the 92nd Infantry Division had been activated as an infantry division. We do not know with certainty which regiment Vincent belonged to, but since we know that he was a medical clerk, we can safely speculate that it was the 317th Medical Battalion, the 92nd Infantry Division's only medical battalion. Medical clerks, nurses, and hospital corpsmen worked under direct fire, but were unarmed. This meant that they had a higher likelihood of dying during battle. A war journalist noted, "A special fortitude is needed by the man who goes into battle as a noncombatant….These unarmed forces—trained to defend themselves with their bare hands in emergency—form a vital part of Uncle Sam's mighty fighting machine."[2]

The soldiers in the U.S. Army 92nd Infantry Division were nicknamed Buffalo Soldiers, a nickname that was created in the late 1860s, when the all-black 10th Cavalry Regiment of the United States Army were nicknamed "Buffalo Soldiers" by the Comanche.[3] They saw them as "black white men" and compared their appearance to buffalos, with their darker skin and curly hair. Buffalos were associated with strength, endurance, and protection by most Native American tribes, so this nickname for the soldiers was given with great respect for the black soldiers that the Native Americans were battling.[4] A black buffalo silhouette on an army drab background was the shoulder sleeve emblem for the 92nd Division, and the division magazine was *The Buffalo*, edited by Ted Shearer, an artist and a sergeant in the 92nd Infantry Division. After the war, Ted went on to create *Quincy*, one of the earliest mainstream comic strips with a black protagonist.

Although WWII started in 1939, U.S. Army military soldiers did not officially start fighting in Europe or North Africa until the North African Campaign in 1942, and then after that they fought under the U.S. Fifth Army in the Italian Campaign between 1943 and 1945. The North African Campaign, across the Mediterranean Sea, was concurrent with the fighting in Europe and started in 1940. Nazi Germany's and Fascist Italy's goals were to control access to oil. In 1940, the British Army's 11th Hussars captured the Italian Fort Capuzzo in Libya. In 1941, the Nazi German Afrika Korps arrived to assist Fascist Italy in North Africa, and in 1942 the Americans got involved with the North African Campaign.

Vincent served overseas from the start of his enlistment. As a medical clerk in the division, Vincent and his fellow Buffalo Soldiers rubbed shoulders with segregated military personal from many other countries including segregated troops of the both the British and the French colonial empires (Black Africans, Moroccans, Algerians, Indians, Gurkhas, Arab, and Jewish Palestinians) and Italian anti-fascists. I like to imagine Vincent happily drinking coffee with Tatamkhulu Afrika, who served with the South African Union Defense Force, but sadly this never happened as Tatamkhulu was captured in 1942 during the North African Campaign.

All-American racism followed the 92nd Division to Italy. In *The Buffalo Saga*, a memoir written by another black 92nd Infantry Division soldier named Pat Daugherty, a white officer was asked why they couldn't call up white replacements after heavy black losses in battle. The officer's reply was, "Look, bud, they don't train colored soldiers to fight. They train them to load ships, and you don't expect them to put white boys in a Negro outfit, do you? What do you think this is, a democracy or something?"[5] Racism followed the soldiers as the war ended; historian Daniel Gibran said, "It was an experience that a lot of white officers didn't really want, and they might as well soon forget that kind of experience."[6]

In August of 1944, the 92nd Infantry Division's 370th Infantry Regiment arrived in Italy to fight. When Buffalo Soldier Harold Montgomery arrived in Italy in 1944, he said that he "began to make out a new sound 'like the roar of a crowd in a ballpark.' Hundreds of black service troops—cooks, stewards and laborers—had gathered to cheer the arrival of the first black combat soldiers in Italy."[7] If the white military was not welcoming, the black service troops were overjoyed to see the 92nd Infantry Division's arrival.

By late September of 1944, the division was stationed in Po Valley in Northern Italy, an agricultural region that extended from the Western Alps to the Adriatic Sea. The Normandy Landing, or D-Day, occurred on June 6, 1944, starting the liberation of France from Nazi forces and signaling the end of WWII a year later. While neighboring France was being liberated, things were rough in Italy; Italy was in a state of civil war and there was strong resistance from multiple groups of Nazis and Fascists, including the German Fourteenth Army and its Italian Fascist soldiers, the 90th Panzergrenadier Division and the 16th SS Panzergrenadier Division. Soldiers from the 370th Infantry Regiment cleared minefields, worked on fords, and constructed a floating bridge across the Arno River in Tuscany so that infantry could cross the river to do battle against the Nazis and the Italian Fascist soldiers. After the Italian Campaign ended, of the 12,846 Buffalo Soldiers who saw action during the campaign, 2,848 were killed, captured or wounded, nearly 24,000 prisoners were captured, and the soldiers in the division received more than 12,000 decorations and citations for bravery in combat.[8]

One solder said of the racism he experienced in the Army during and post-WWII, "I was really disgusted with this country. I was angry, and I stayed angry for years."[9] Although American troops were desegregated in July of 1948, three years after the end of WWII, this was not the end of racism in the American military.

Resources

Barnes, Charline J., and Floyd Bumpers. *Iowa's Black Legacy*. Charleston, SC, 2000.

Bérubé, Allan, John DEmilio, and Estelle B. Freedman. *Coming Out Under Fire: The History of Gay Men and Women in World War II*. Chapel Hill: University of North Carolina Press, 2010.

Daugherty, James Harden. *The Buffalo Saga: A Story from World War II U.S. Army 92nd Infantry Division Known as the Buffalo Soldiers*. Place of Publication Not Identified: Xlibris, 2009.

Deeds Not Words: The Buffalo Soldiers in World War II. 2011. Accessed October 13, 2018. https://www.youtube.com/watch?v=ZildUeisGqQ&feature=youtu.be.

Gibran, Daniel K. *The 92nd Infantry Division and the Italian Campaign in World War II*. Jefferson, NC: McFarland, 2001.

The dog tag reads:
Vincent Miles
92nd Infantry
Enlisted:1943

Vincent Miles, drawn by Ajuan Mance

145

This page is intentionally blank to facilitate coloring the reverse side.

Reed Peggram
1914–1982, United States
drawn by Burton Clarke

Reed Peggram was born in Dorchester, Massachusetts to parents originally from Virginia. His father was an artist and a WWI veteran; he suffered long-lasting effects from wartime gas poisoning which required hospitalization at Central State Hospital in Petersburg, Virginia[1] when Reed was a child. Reed's parents divorced, and Reed and his three brothers were taken in by his maternal grandmother.

Reed was an intellectually brilliant and curious boy. His interest in the classics was cultivated while attending middle and high school at the elite, predominantly white, Public Latin School in Boston. He was a dedicated student, earning honors in many courses, including Elementary Latin, French, German, and Advanced Latin. He was the only black student in the schools literary and drama clubs. Fortunately, Reed's grandmother saw his intellectual potential and had the foresight to save the Veterans Aid program benefits that he received for his father's service in WWI; this money helped pay for Reeds attendance at the prestigious Harvard University.

In 1931, Reed was admitted to Harvard University. Reed was one of just a few black students to be admitted to Harvard that year. Harvard University was founded in 1636, but it wasn't until 1870 that it had its first black student. It was known for being a university catering nearly exclusively to white Anglo-Saxon Protestants (WASPs), and although all freshmen were mandated to live in the freshman Harvard dormitory, black students were forbidden from the dorms and told to find a room elsewhere. Two black students were accidentally admitted to the freshman dormitories during WWI, but after the war ended, the black student dorm ban was strictly reenacted. In 1921, Harvard's administration and President Lowell started getting pressured to exclude black men from the university completely, but this suggestion was shot down after much protest. The dorm ban remained, with President Lowell justifying it by distinguishing between social and educational integration, "…it seems to me that for the colored man to claim that he is entitled to have the white man compelled to live with him is a very unfortunate innovation which, far from doing him good, would increase prejudice."[2] In 1923, the dorm ban policy was officially overturned after a rigorous nationwide protest led by the National Association for the Advancement of Colored People (NAACP), although it wasn't until the mid-1950s that black students routinely lived in the freshman dorms.[3]

In 1933, Reed, a talented scholar, was admitted as a member of the prestigious Phi Beta Kappa Society (motto: Φιλοσοφία Βίου Κυβερνήτης, or "Love of learning is the guide of life"), the oldest academic honor society in the United States. In 1934, Reed applied for a Rhodes Scholarship, the international postgraduate award for students to study at the University of Oxford. His application was interceded by Harvard's Dean Hanford, who supplemented his recommendation of Reed with an addendum noting that, "I wish to supplement my letter of May 29th to you about Mr. Reed Peggram by stating that he is a negro[sic]. It seemed to me that you should know that fact." The folks at Rhodes were unhappily startled to hear that Reed was black and replied, "Thank you for your testimonial and letter about Reed Peggram. I should like to thank you however for telling me that Peggram is a Negro. I should certainly have been somewhat taken aback if I had admitted a man with such a name unwarned."[4] Reed was not awarded the fellowship. Although writer, philosopher, and "Dean" of the Harlem Renaissance Alain Leroy Locke was awarded a Rhodes Scholarship in 1907, it would not be until 1960 until that another black person was awarded the distinguished Rhodes Scholarship.

In 1935, Reed earned his Bachelor of Arts in Romance Languages and Literature, graduating *Magna cum laude*. In 1936, he earned is Masters degree in Comparative Literature from Harvard, and in 1937 and 1938 went on for his PhD in Comparative Literature. Reed's thesis was, "A comparison of the personal element in Madame Bovary and *L'Éducation Sentimentale*," in which Reed compared elements of French writer Gustave Flaubert's novel *L'Éducation Sentimentale* (1869), to his debut novel, Madame Bovary (1856). In 1935, future composer and conductor Leonard Bernstein started studying at Harvard. Leonard had also attended Boston Latin School, but he was four years younger than Reed so it's doubtful that they knew one another then. Although Leonard was gay, at the time he was closeted and he never was completely out. Reed and Leonard became close friends, and Reed developed an unreciprocated crush on him, becoming devastated and ashamed when cruelly rejected. Reed wrote back to Leonard after the rejection, "The revelation of your letter was after all, a great shock to me, and your use of the words 'repulsive' and 'shudder' an insult to the tenets which I hold sacred. May I also request that, as a favour to me, you destroy all my letters and any other material that I have sent or given you during this regrettable incident?"[5]

In 1938, Reed was awarded a scholarship to study at the Sorbonne in Paris, France. The exodus of black Americans to Paris between the two World Wars and beyond, during the 1920s through the 1950s, led to the formation of "Black American Paris."

Many Harlem Renaissance movement artists and writers moved to Paris to escape America's racism. Although WWII would not start for another year, fascism was spreading across Europe like a malevolent fungus, and Paris would be occupied by armed Nazi Gestapo troops by June of 1940. In 1938, the general unrest caused the American Embassy in Paris to admonish Americans to leave France, "In view of the complicated situation prevailing in Europe, it is considered advisable to recommend that American citizens who have no compelling reason to continue their sojourn here to arrange to return to the U.S."[6]

Despite the rise of fascism, anti-Semitism, concentration camps, and Nazi Germany's violent military occupation of several European countries, it wouldn't be until December 7, 1941 that the United States joined WWII. Despite the holocaust in Europe, the U.S. was reluctant to accept refugees from the war. The prevalence of racism and anti-Semitism in America affected policies towards refugees and immigrants, making immigration policies even more restrictive.[7] The connections between racism and Nazism were noted, but that wasn't enough. In July 1943, one month after a major Detroit race riot, United States Vice President Henry Wallace spoke to a crowd of union workers and civic groups, "We cannot fight to crush Nazi brutality abroad and condone race riots at home. Those who fan the fires of racial clashes for the purpose of making political capital here at home are taking the first step toward Nazism."[8]

Despite the impending war and dire warnings from the State Department, Reed flourished intellectually and emotionally in Paris. In 1938, he met Gerdh Hauptmann, a Danish painter, poet, and scholar. They exchanged English and Danish lessons, and within a year, they were lovers and intellectual collaborators. WWII was declared in September of 1939, and France and Great Britain joined the fray immediately. Italy declared war on France in June of 1940. In 1929, Reed and Gerdh took heed and fled to Denmark. His vastly understated letter to a friend read, "Recent European events have caused me to leave France for Copenhagen, Denmark. I hope you will also join your prayers to mine for humanity, civilization, and culture."[9] Reed and Gerdh continued with their collaborative projects, notably a manuscript, "Poems and Sketches," a translation of the work of Danish Modern Breakthrough novelist, poet, and scientist J. P. Jacobsen. Reed's friends and family pleaded for him to return home to safety from the war, but he refused to leave his love. On April 9, 1940, merely hours before the Nazis crossed the Danish border to occupy Denmark, the lovers fled Copenhagen for Florence, Italy. Once in Fascist, war-torn Italy, they tried to find a way to move to America together, but were broke and unsuccessful. In September of 1940, Reed inherited a substantial amount of money, but needed to return to America to claim it, could not get an advance, and was unwilling to leave Gerdh to a wartime fate of possible arrest and death. He tried to find a way to access the funds, but to no avail. Unfortunately, their time was running out; the Germans had chased Reed and Gerdh across Europe like a cat chases a mouse, and soon after, they pounced. Sometime between April of 1941 and 1943, the Nazis arrested them because they felt "a Dane has no right to be a friend of a Negro."[10]

The Nazis offered to set Reed free, but he refused to leave his lover. Reed and Gerdh were imprisoned by the Gestapo in the Bagni Di Lucca concentration camp near Pistoia, Italy until it was closed down in January of 1944. They then spent a year in another camp, possibly near Colle di Compito. At that point, they were put in solitary confinement until the Nazis could decide whether or when to kill them. Reed told reporters after their unexpected release from the concentration camp, "We didn't know how long we stayed there, but it was really hell. Just enough soup to lead a miserable existence. For months we did not see a single human being. In fact, we saw nothing that was living. Not even bugs. There was no light, no action—nothing but a great deal of time to think about what was in store for us."[11] In 1944, the concentration camp that they were imprisoned in was attacked by members of the *la Resistenza* (the Italian Resistance), and Reed and Gerdh were released into the Italian countryside. Without identity papers, passports, or money, they were helpless. They tramped across the countryside, hoping to stumble upon allies, sleeping in barns, being shot at by German Nazi soldiers, and depending upon the kindness of passing Italian Resistance members. In March of 1945, the pair stumbled upon the safety of the U.S. Army, segregated 92nd Infantry Division. Reed told them that all they wanted was to be together to work on their projects, "We are not principally concerned with going to America. We only want to go someplace where we can be assured remaining together to work in peace,"[12] but this never happened.

Reed was sent back to the United States. In August of 1945, he set foot on U.S. soil, but without Gerdh. They never saw one another again. Reed was hospitalized for four years with wartime-induced PTSD, then moved in with his mother and half-brother. He was an introvert, tinkered with languages, worked as a translator, and sang in a church choir. Gerdh lived after the war and, in 1971, published a book of poetry. Reed died in 1982 at age 67.

Resources

Hauptmann, Gerdh. *Declaration*. Strube, 1971.

Peggram , Reed. "The First French and English Translations of Sir Thomas More's 'Utopia.'" *The Modern Language Review*, vol. 100, 2005, pp. 51–61

Sollors, Werner, Caldwell Titcomb, and Thomas A. Underwood. *Blacks at Harvard: A Documentary History of African-American Experience at Harvard and Radcliffe*. New York: New York University Press, 1993.

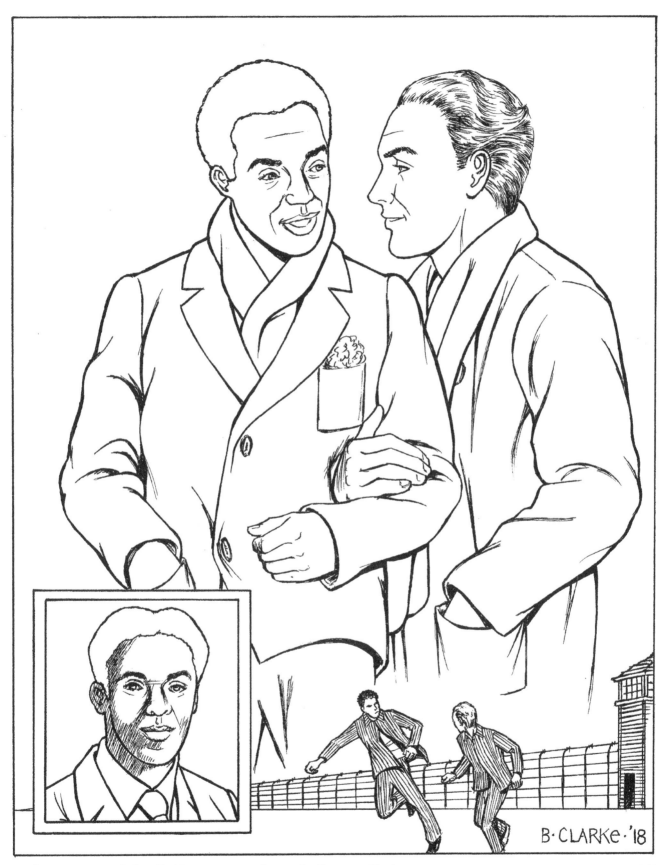

Reed Peggram and Gerdh Hauptmann, drawn by Burton Clarke

149

This page is intentionally blank to facilitate coloring the reverse side.

Isabel Townsend Pell, a.k.a. Fredericka, *la femme à la mèche blonde*
1900–1951, United States/France/United States
Claire Charles-Roux De Forbin, a.k.a. Marquise De Forbin
1908–1992, France
drawn by Jon Macy

Isabel Pell was striking—a tall athletic American adventuress, known in the Resistance as Fredericka or *la femme à la mèche blonde* for her forelock of white hair. Isabel was an East Coast socialite born into wealth, but her parents divorced when she was young due to her father's compulsive philandering, who then died when she was thirteen. After attending a series of prep schools, Isabel moved to Manhattan and went through several jobs. Bored with the frivolity of socialite circles, she said, "Life had grown stupid. I was very bored with it all. I had done all the usual things a girl does after she is 'out,' and I am very tired of it."[1] Glamorous, handsome, and tough, she wore slacks and tailored clothing, kept her blond hair short, and was fond of the sultry perfume, Tabac Blanc, a smoky scent of leather and tobacco. She had a strong-willed and sometimes self-centered personality. She was athletic, charming, and owned over forty pairs of riding boots. In America, Isabel got a reputation for dalliances and misadventures with a multitude of women. Between being rescued at sea from a small plane crash off the coast of Sweden with Dorothy Fleitmann, a married, upper-crust, English woman,[2] and the unexpected scandal of getting outed about an affair with a NY Metropolitan Opera soprano, Isabel decided in the mid-1930s to flee to the more permissive France.

Once in France, Isabel joined the large community of lesbian expatriates led by Gertrude Stein, Radcliffe Hall, Natalie Barney, and others. There, she met Claire De Forbin. Claire De Forbin was born in Avignon, France to an upper-class family of bankers and businessmen, but Claire was raised in Morocco. Her father, Charles Wulfran Marie Louis Roux was a Lieutenant Colonel of Cavalry in WWI who died of wounds suffered during the liberation of La Fere, and Claire had three siblings. In 1932, under the pressure of her parents, she married Antoine de Forbin des Issarts La Barben, the last marquess of Forbin-la Barben and a member of French Provencal nobility, granting her the title of Marquise. Theirs was a *mariage blanc*, that is an unconsummated marriage, as both Antoine and Claire preferred their own sex.[3]

Soon, Isabel moved to be near her new lover. When WWII started in 1939 and the Nazis occupied France in 1940, Isabel and Claire immediately became activists, joined by their friend Dickie Fellowes-Gordon, a Scottish socialite, opera singer, talented home cook, and bisexual.[4] In Auribeau, the couple lived in Dickie's home, a hilltop mill house called *La Domaine du Sault*. Dickie left France in 1940, leaving Isabel and Claire to watch over *La Domaine du Sault*. Before the occupation of France in 1940, their activities were limited to raising funds to aid the dashing *chasseurs alpins*, the mountain infantry of the French Army, but they quickly deviated to other, more dangerous activities.

Women were heavily involved with the French resistance and with Allied resistance activities, partially because such a large number of men were fighting in the military. There were three Allied resistance intelligence groups that worked with women in WWII, the British Special Operations Executive (SEO), the American Office of Strategic Service (OSS), and the French *Bureau Central de Resiegnements et d'Action* (BCRA). Women coded and decoded messages, gathered information for Allied armies, edited newspapers for accurate news (rather than propaganda), and assisted over 5,000 downed fighter pilots by housing, feeding, clothing, and providing them with life-saving travel documents. Women managed cryptography sections, infiltrated enemy lines to gain information and tactical intelligence, published underground newspapers, sabotaged enemy bases, served in paramilitary units, acted as couriers, and were often leaders of resistance groups.[5]

By December of 1941, when America declared war on Germany, the couple used *La Domaine du Sault* as a center for distributing anti-Nazi propaganda and as a meeting place for Maquis Resistance groups, while they stored weapons and a communication radio in the basement. One of Claire's brothers was in the French Resistance in London, and Claire joined a local Maquis Resistance group. French Maquis Resistance group members were often Communists and composed of rural French Resistance fighters that were active in the remote or mountainous areas of Brittany and southern France.

Isabel and Claire both started working with the American Office of Strategic Service (OSS.) Isabel was fond of children, and made sure that the village children were protected, had medical treatment, and that their schools had adequate supplies and money.

Claire had the valuable skill of being trilingual, and spoke French, German, and English. She helped establish Allied Resistance headquarters in Grasse, then in Nice, becoming the chief of the intelligence section in charge of processing reports from over one hundred fellow field agents and overseeing five other women translators.[6] Claire had sharpened her English with the American G.I.s, so it tended towards the tough and the colloquial; a refined French noblewoman talking about "guys" and "dolls."

In 1942, Isabel was commanded by the Nazis to remove herself to the French Alpine town of Puget-Théniers. They were aware of some of her illicit activities and wanted her to stop, yet did not take the more aggressive step of sending her to prison or a concentration camp. Although she was a prisoner of the Gestapo, she was allowed to take walks throughout the town. During these walks she continued her Resistance work, smuggling classified information to other Resistance members, organizing local residents that were fleeing being deported under the *Service de Travail Obligatoire* (Compulsory Work Service, or STO), and organizing an underground Resistance cell inside the prison. By 1943, *Service de Travail Obligatoire* was affecting more and more of the local men in the Puget-Théniers area. *Service de Travail Obligatoire* was the compulsory mechanism of enlistment and deportation of French men to Germany for labor in exchange for releasing French prisoners of war. Over 600,000 French laborers ended up being deported to Germany in the two years between 1942 and 1944. Many fled the mandatory deportation, living rough in the surrounding forests and countryside.

In fall of 1943, Isabel was allowed to return to Auribeau, but was placed under house arrest at *La Domaine du Sault*. She continued to relay messages to Maquis Resistance groups and store guns, ammunition, and fugitives in her cellar. In July of 1944, the Gestapo searched the home, but did not find the stash of papers, guns, and ammunition in her cellar. Fortunately, Isabel decided to flee into the mountains to find refuge with the Auribeau Maquis. The Gestapo revisited her home, but this time, her home was vacant. Claire and Isabel relocated twenty five miles away from Auribeau to Nice, where Isabel continued transporting weapons and Claire brazenly snuck into the front lines to rescue American paratroopers and German prisoners. Captain Rupert Graves of Civic Affairs said of Isabel during this period, "…there are some people who seem peculiarly out of step during uneventful times but whose lives achieve sharp meaning during extraordinary periods, Isabel Pell was one of these."

In 1947, the writer Mercedes de Acosta visited Isabel from America. Mercedes said of meeting Claire for the first time, "Once or twice during the war I had seen her name mentioned in the American newspapers as one of the French women doing remarkable work in the Resistance movement….When, however, she came into the house this evening and introduced herself to me. I was at first struck by her extreme fragility. She was so thin and looked so ill that I wondered how it was possible for her to actually be alive under these conditions. I saw at once, however, that she had great nervous vitality—even a kind of nervous strength."[8] Upon meeting Claire, Mercedes became smitten and courted her. Claire was war-worn and exhausted, but Mercedes succeeded in tearing her away from Isabel and bringing her to America. Much later Claire returned to Europe and lived in Switzerland until her death in 1992 at age 84.

Isabel was decorated with *Ordre national de la Légion d'honneur* (French National Order of the Legion of Honor) for her work with the Resistance during the war. The children of Puget-Théniers composed a song in Isabel's honor, "*Miss Pell, vous etes une fée / Et des milles difficulties / Pour nos chers enfants de Puget / Vous avez su triompher.*" ("Miss Pell, you are a fairy and over the thousand problems of our dear children of Puget, you have triumphed").[9] With Claire gone and the war over with, Isabel returned to Manhattan, but 1950s America was puritanical and placid compared to war-time France and she had difficulties. In 1952, Isabel died in Manhattan at age 51, unexpectedly and tragically after falling from her chair while eating dinner.

Resources

Acosta, Mercedes De. *Here Lies the Heart: A Tale of My Life*. Mansfield Centre, CT: Martino Publishing, 2016.

Emerson, Maureen. *Riviera Dreaming: Love and War on the Côte D'Azur*. London: I.B. Tauris &, 2018.

Pell, Eve. *We Used to Own the Bronx: Memoirs of a Former Debutante*. Albany: Excelsior Editions/State University of New York Press, 2009.

Rossiter, Margaret L. *Women in the Resistance*. New York U.a.: Praeger, 1986.

Schanke, Robert A. *"That Furious Lesbian": The Story of Mercedes De Acosta*. Carbondale: Southern Illinois Univ. Press, 2004.

Isabel Townsend Pell and Claire Charles-Roux De Forbin, drawn by Jon Macy

This page is intentionally blank to facilitate coloring the reverse side.

ENDNOTES

Nadine Hwang:

1. Acme. "Diplomat." *Daily News* (New York), April 23, 1933, Main ed. https://www.newspapers.com/image/416066303/?terms=Nadine hwang.

2. "Chinese Girl Is Colonel in Army." *Santa Ana Register*, September 1, 1927. Accessed September 20, 2018. https://www.newspapers.com/image/88059253/?terms=Nadine hwang.

3. "Laínñuencia de Una Madrileña." *ABC en París y Roma*. Ed. de L'a anana. Accessed September 20, 2018. http://hemeroteca.abc.es/nav/Navigate.exe/hemeroteca/madrid/abc/1928/03/03/023.html

4. Acme. "Diplomat." *Daily News* (New York), April 23, 1933, Main ed. Accessed September 20, 2018. https://www.newspapers.com/image/416066303/?terms=Nadine hwang.

5. Schenkar, Joan. *Truly Wilde: The Unsettling Story of Dolly Wilde, Oscar's Unusual Niece* (London: Virago Press, 2000), 301.

6. Brooks, Victoria. *Literary Trips: Following in the Footsteps of Fame* (United Kingdom: GreatEscapes.com, 2001), 330.

7. Harmsen, Peter. "A Chinese Woman in Ravensbrueck Concentration Camp." Shanghai 1937. October 9, 2013. Accessed September 23, 2018. http://www.shanghai1937.com/a-chinese-woman-in-ravensbrueck-concentration-camp/.

8. Schenkar, Joan. *Truly Wilde: The Unsettling Story of Dolly Wilde, Oscar's Unusual Niece* (London: Virago Press, 2000), 302.

9. Ibid., 302-303.

10. "Nadine Hwang – Every Face Has a Name." Every Face Has a Name. Accessed September 24, 2018. http://everyfacehasaname.com/nadine-hwang/.

11. Ibid.

12. "Nadine Huong." Wikipedia. August 12, 2018. Accessed September 24, 2018. https://fr.wikipedia.org/wiki/Nadine_Huong.

13. Helm, Sarah. *Ravensbrück: Life and Death in Hitler's Concentration Camp for Women* (New York: Anchor Books, 2016), LOC 3895.

14. Ibid., LOC 2110-2128.

15. "Nadine Hwang – Every Face Has a Name." Every Face Has a Name. Accessed September 24, 2018. http://everyfacehasaname.com/nadine-hwang/.

16. Ibid.

Josephine Baker:

1. Baker, Jean-Claude, and Chris Chase. *Josephine: The Hungry Heart* (New York: Cooper Square Press, 2001), 46.

2. Nugent, Bruce, and Thomas H. Wirth. *Gay Rebel of the Harlem Renaissance: Selections from the Work of Richard Bruce Nugent*. Durham, NC: Duke Univ. Press, 2002.

3. Baker, Jean-Claude, and Chris Chase. *Josephine: The Hungry Heart* (New York: Cooper Square Press, 2001), 63–64.

4. Ibid., 48.

5. Murari, Tim. "From the Archive, 26 August 1974: An Interview with Josephine Baker." *The Guardian*, August 26, 2015. Accessed September 19, 2018. https://www.theguardian.com/stage/2015/aug/26/josephine-baker-interview-1974.

6. Crosley, Sloane. "Exploring the France That Josephine Baker Loved." *The New York Times*, July 12, 2016. Accessed September 19, 2018. https://www.nytimes.com/2016/07/17/travel/josephine-baker-paris-france.html.

7. "Josephine Baker." Victoria and Albert Museum The World's Leading Museum of Art and Design. May 26, 2015. Accessed September 19, 2018. http://www.vam.ac.uk/content/articles/j/josephine-baker/.

8. Baker, Josephine, Jo Bouillon, and Jacqueline Cartier. *Joséphine* (Paris: Robert Laffont, 1976), 177.

9. Papich, Stephen Papich. *Remembering Josephine* (New York: The Bobbs-Merrill Company, Inc.: 1976), 210–213.

Marcel Moore and Claude Cahun:

1. Downie, Louise. "Sans Nom: Claude Cahun and Marcel Moore." *The Heritage Magazine*, 9-17. Accessed October 14, 2018. https://www.jerseyheritage.org/media/PDF-Heritage-Mag/Sans%20Nom%20Claude%20Cahun%20%20Marcel%20Moore.pdf

2. Downie, Louise. "Marcel Moore, Her Art and Life." The Heritage Magazine, 51-61. Accessed October 14, 2018. https://www.jerseyheritage.org/media/PDF-Heritage-Mag/Marcel Moore.pdf.

3. Gewurtz, Michelle. *Equivocally Jewish: Claude Cahun and the Narratives of Modern Art*. 2012. Accessed October 14, 2018. https://www.brandeis.edu/hbi/publications/workingpapers/docs/gewurtz.pdf.

4. Ibid.

5. Downie, Louise. "Marcel Moore, Her Art and Life." *The Heritage Magazine*, 51-61. Accessed October 14, 2018. https://www.jerseyheritage.org/media/PDF-Heritage-Mag/Marcel Moore.pdf.

6. Asif, Noor A., "Women Surrealists: Muses or Seekers?" (2016). *Scripps Senior Theses*. Paper 826. http://scholarship.claremont.edu/scripps_theses/826

7. Downie, Louise. "Marcel Moore, Her Art and Life." *The Heritage Magazine*, 51-61. Accessed October 14, 2018. https://www.jerseyheritage.org/media/PDF-Heritage-Mag/Marcel Moore.pdf. 59.

8. Ibid.

9. Ibid.

10. Hammer, Barbara, dir. *Lover Other: The Story of Claude Cahun and Marcel Moore*. New York: An Outcast Films, Barbara Hammer Films Production, 2006. DVD.

Thérèse Pierre:

1. Fougères. "Heroines de la Resistance Fougeraise: Odile Gautry, Thérèse Pierre, Mme Bouffort." Société D'Histoire Et D'Archéologie Du Pays De Fougères. September 21, 2012. Accessed September 30, 2018. http://shapfougeres.blogspot.com/2012/09/heroines-de-la-resistance.html.

2. Ibid.

3. Ibid.

4. "V - LA S.P.A.C. (Service De Police Anti-communiste) ET L'ENFER JACQUES-CARTIER." La Resistance En Ille-et-Vilaine: La SPAC. Accessed September 30, 2018. http://memoiredeguerre.free.fr/cvr/ch5.htm#deb.

Pierre Seel:

1. Anarchist Federation. "The Zazous, 1940–1945." Libcom.org. October 1, 2006. Accessed September 03, 2018. http://libcom.org/history/1940-1945-the-zazous.

2. Loiseau, Jean-Claude. *Les Zazous* (Paris: Le Sagittaire, 1977) 155–158.

3. Seel, Pierre. *I, Pierre Seel, Deported Homosexual: A Memoir of Nazi Terror* (Translated by Joachim Neugroschel. Perseus Books Group, 2011), 16–19.

4. Ibid., 30.

5. Ibid., 123.

6. Ibid., 128.

7. Rapp, Linda. "Seel, Pierre (1923–2005)." GLBTQ. 2008. Accessed September 3, 2018. http://www.glbtqarchive.com/ssh/seel_p_S.pdf.

Édith Thomas:

1. Kaufmann, Dorothy. *Édith Thomas: A Passion for Resistance* (Ithaca, NY: Cornell University Press, 2004), 148.

2. Ibid., 47.

3. Ibid., 67.

4. Ibid., 88.

5. Ibid., 122.

6. Ibid., 129.

7. Ibid., 130.

8. Kaufmann, Dorothy. "The Story of Two Women: Dominique Aury and Edith Thomas." Signs 23, no. 4 (1998): 883-905. http://www.jstor.org/stable/3175197.

Rose Valland:

1. Heit, Judi. "Rose Valland (1898-1980)." Heroines of the Resistance. September 03, 2015. Accessed August 26, 2018. http://resistanceheroines.blogspot.com/2015/08/rose-valland-and-monuments-men.html.

2. Bouchoux, Corinne. *Rose Valland: Resistance at the Museum* (Translated by Robert M. Edsel. S.I.: Laurel Publishing, LLC 2013), Loc 300.

3. Ibid., Loc 296-306.

4. Ibid., Loc 327.

5. Evans, Richard J. *The Third Reich in Power* (Penguin, 2006) p168-169.

6. Adam, Peter. *Art of the Third Reich* (New York: Harry N. Abrams, Inc. 1992), 53.

7. Spotts, Frederic. *Hitler and the Power of Aesthetics* (The Overlook Press, 2002), 151.

8. Bouchoux, Corinne. *Rose Valland: Resistance at the Museum* (Translated by Robert M. Edsel. S.I.: Laurel Publishing, LLC 2013), Loc 416.

9. Nicholas, Lynn. *The Rape of Europa: The Fate of Europe's Treasures in the Third Reich and the Second World War* (New York: Vintage Books,1994), 135.

10. Bouchoux, Corinne. *Rose Valland: Resistance at the Museum* (Translated by Robert M. Edsel. S.I.: Laurel Publishing, LLC 2013), Loc 551.

11. Ibid., Loc 599.

12. Ibid., Loc 1017.

13. Yaelle. "14. Rose Valland." Panthéonistas. January 01, 1970. Accessed August 27, 2018. http://pantheonistas.blogspot.com/2015/04/14-rose-valland.html.

14. "Monuments Men: Rose Valland, L'héroïne Lesbienne Oubliée." Yagg. March 17, 2014. Accessed August 26, 2018. http://yagg.com/2014/03/17/monuments-men-rose-valland-lheroine-lesbienne-oubliee/.

Gad Beck:

1. United States Holocaust Memorial Museum. "ID Cards: Gad Beck." United States Holocaust Memorial Museum. Accessed August 27, 2018. https://encyclopedia.ushmm.org/content/en/id-card/gad-beck.

2. Interview. Gad Beck on Coming out to His Family. Accessed August 26, 2018. https://sfi.usc.edu/video/gad-beck-coming-out-his-family.

3. United States Holocaust Memorial Museum. "Nuremberg Race Laws." United States Holocaust Memorial Museum. Accessed August 27, 2018. https://encyclopedia.ushmm.org/content/en/article/nuremberg-laws.

4. United States Holocaust Memorial Museum. "Kristallnacht: A Nationwide Pogrom." Holocaust Encyclopedia. Accessed August 17, 2018. https://encyclopedia.ushmm.org/content/en/article/kristallnacht.

5. United States Holocaust Memorial Museum. "Page 2." United States Holocaust Memorial Museum. Accessed August 27, 2018. https://www.ushmm.org/collections/the-museums-collections/collections-highlights/do-you-remember-when/page-2

6. United States Holocaust Memorial Museum. "Cover." United States Holocaust Memorial Museum. Accessed August 27, 2018. https://www.ushmm.org/collections/the-museums-collections/collections-highlights/do-you-remember-when/cover.

7. United States Holocaust Memorial Museum. "Cover." United States Holocaust Memorial Museum. Accessed August 27, 2018. https://www.ushmm.org/collections/the-museums-collections/collections-highlights/do-you-remember-when/cover.

8. Interview. Gad Beck on Rescuing His Lover Manfred Lewin. Accessed August 26, 2018. https://sfi.usc.edu/video/gad-beck-rescuing-his-lover-manfred-lewin.

9. United States Holocaust Memorial Museum. "Back Cover." United States Holocaust Memorial Museum. Accessed August 27, 2018. https://www.ushmm.org/collections/the-museums-collections/collections-highlights/do-you-remember-when/back-cover

Annette Eick:

1. Safier, Scott. "The History of the Gay Male and Lesbian Experience during World War II: Lesbians." Pink-triangle.org. Accessed August 16, 2018. http://www.pink-triangle.org/.

2. Groden, Suzy Q. "Eleven from Sappho." *Arion: A Journal of Humanities and the Classics 3*, no. 3 (1964): 23-26. http://www.jstor.org/stable/20140423.

3. Schoppmann, Claudia, and Annette Eick. "Annette Eick (1909-2010)." Lesbengeschichte. December 03, 2005. Accessed August 15, 2018. https://www.lesbengeschichte.de/Englisch/bio_eick_e.html.

4. Schoppmann, Claudia. *Days of Masquerade: Life Stories of Lesbians During the Third Reich* (New York: Columbia University Press, 1996), 104.

5. Ibid., 106.

6. Ibid., 106.

7. United States Holocaust Memorial Museum. "Voyage of St. Louis." Holocaust Encyclopedia. Accessed August 18, 2018. https://www.ushmm.org/wlc/en/article.php?ModuleId=10005267.

8. United States Holocaust Memorial Museum. "Kristallnacht: A Nationwide Pogrom." Holocaust Encyclopedia. Accessed August 17, 2018. https://www.ushmm.org/wlc/en/article.php?ModuleId=10005201.

9. Giovanni, Sue, dir. *Immortal Muse*. 2005. Accessed August 17, 2018. http://www.cultureunplugged.com/play/3795/Immortal-Muse.

10. Schoppmann, Claudia. *Days of Masquerade: Life Stories of Lesbians During the Third Reich* (New York: Columbia University Press, 1996), 114.

Lotte Hahm:

1. Lybeck, Marti M. *Desiring Emancipation: New Women and Homosexuality in Germany, 1890–1933* (New York: State University of New York Press, 2015).

2. Magee, Maggie, and Diana C. Miller. *Lesbian Lives: Psychoanalytic Narratives Old and New* (New York, NY: Routledge, 2014), 350.

3. Zagria. "Lotte Hahm (1890 - 1967) Activist, Bar Owner, Ball Organizer." A Gender Variance Who's Who. March 02, 2018. Accessed August 06, 2018. https://zagria.blogspot.com/2018/03/lotte-hahm-1890-1967-activist-bar-owner.html#.W-S_odVKhMA.

4. Brendon. "Berlin's Lesbische Frauen." Cabaret Berlin. January 10, 2012. Accessed August 11, 2018. http://www.cabaret-berlin.com/?p=546.

5. Magee, Maggie, and Diana C. Miller. *Lesbian Lives: Psychoanalytic Narratives Old and New* (New York, NY: Routledge, 2014), 350.

6. Whisnant, Clayton J. *Queer Identities and Politics in Germany: A History, 1880–1945* (Harrington Park Press: New York. 2016), 209.

7. Tamagne, Florence. *A History of Homosexuality in Europe. Berlin, London, Paris 1919–1939* (New York: Algora Pub., 2006), 79.

8. "Lesbengeschichte - Biografische Skizzen - Lotte Hahm." Lesbengeschichte - Biografische Skizzen - Claire Waldoff. January 16, 2009. Accessed August 11, 2018. https://www.lesbengeschichte.de/bio_hahm_d.html.

9. Zagria. "Lotte Hahm (1890 - 1967) Activist, Bar Owner, Ball Organizer." A Gender Variance Who's Who. March 02, 2018. Accessed August 06, 2018. https://zagria.blogspot.com/2018/03/lotte-hahm-1890-1967-activist-bar-owner.html#.W9cUxy-ZN0I.

10. "Persönlichkeiten in Berlin 1825 - 2006." Persönlichkeiten in Berlin 1825 - 2006 - Digitale Landesbibliothek Berlin - Zentral- Und Landesbibliothek Berlin. 2018. Accessed August 11, 2018. https://digital.zlb.de/viewer/metadata/15916855/1/.

Wilhelm Heckmann:

1. Strupp, Christoph. "Hamburg in de Eerste Wereldoorlog". *Cahiers Bruxellois–Brusselse Cahiers*, vol. xlvi, no. 1N, 2014, 198–219.

2. Stanjek, Klaus, dir. *Sounds From the Fog: Odyssey of a Gay Musician in Nazi Germany*. Germany: CINETARIUM Babelsberg. 2013. Accessed October 04, 2018. http://forgetusnotmovie.com/2010/12/31/wilhelm/

3. Walter Abendroth, "Kunstmusik und Volstümlichkeit." *Die Musik*. März 1934, s. 413–414. 359.

4. *Das Deutsche Podium. Fachblatt für Ensemble-Musik und Musik-Gaststätten*, Nr. 31, S.15 + Nr. 36, S. 10. Brückner-Verlag München, 1935.

5. "Repression Gegen Homosexuelle Männer." LSBTTIQ in Baden Und Württemberg. Accessed October 04, 2018. https://www.lsbttiq-bw.de/historischer-kontext/repressionen/repression-gegen-homosexuelle-maenner/.

6. Stanjek, Klaus, dir. *Sounds From the Fog: Odyssey of a Gay Musician in Nazi Germany*. Germany: CINETARIUM Babelsberg. 2013. Accessed October 04, 2018. http://forgetusnotmovie.com/2010/12/31/wilhelm/

7. Stanjek, Klaus. "Musik Und Mord—Ein Berufsmusiker in Mauthausen." Lecture, KünstlerInnen Und WissenschaftlerInnen Im KZ Mauthausen, Linz. Accessed October 4, 2018. http://www.cinetarium.de/downloads/mauthausen-vortrag_musik-und-mord_zusammenfassung.pdf.

Vera Lachmann:

1. Bodenheimer, Rosemarie. *Edgar and Brigitte: A German Jewish Passage to America*. (Tuscaloosa: University of Alabama Press, 2016), 158.

2. Ibid., 159.

3. Thiel, Guenter. "THE CAMP CATAWBA Founded by Vera Lachmann." Wolfguenterthiel. February 20, 2014. Accessed August 29, 2018. http://wolfguenterthiel.blogspot.com/2014/02/the-camp-catawba-founded-by-vera.html.

4. "Auszüge Aus Gesetzen Und Verordnungen, Die Das Schulleben Zur Zeit Des Nationalsozialismus Veränderten." Schule Im Nationalsozialismus. Accessed August 31, 2018. http://www.grunewald-grundschule.de/html/Schule/Schulgeschichte/2Nationa.html.

5. Simkin, John. "Education in Nazi Germany." Spartacus Educational. Accessed August 31, 2018. http://spartacus-educational.com/GEReducation.htm.

6. Cook, Blanche Wiesen. *Eleanor Roosevelt: The War Years and After* (New York: Viking, 2016), 222.

7. Ibid., 223.

8. Schoppmann, Claudia. "Www.lesbengeschichte.de Vera Lachmann (1904-1985)." Lesbengeschichte - Biografische Skizzen - Claire Waldoff. 2005. Accessed September 01, 2018. https://www.lesbengeschichte.de/Englisch/bio_lachmann_e.html.

9. Barnieck, Jens, and Wheeler Sparks. "Between Two Worlds: A Time at Camp Catawba." Editorial. 2008. Accessed August 30, 2018. http://www.periodicals.narr.de/index.php/real/article/viewFile/1591/1570.

10. Thiel, Guenter. "THE CAMP CATAWBA Founded by Vera Lachmann." Wolfguenterthiel. February 20, 2014. Accessed August 29, 2018. http://wolfguenterthiel.blogspot.com/2014/02/the-camp-catawba-founded-by-vera.html.

11. Ibid.

Erika and Klaus Mann:

1. Tóibín, Colm. "I Could Sleep with All of Them." *London Review of Books 30*, no. 21 (November 06, 2006): 3. Accessed October 7, 2018. https://www.lrb.co.uk/v30/n21/colm-toibin-i-could-sleep-with-all-of-them.

2. Ibid.

3. Weiss, Andrea. *In the Shadow of the Magic Mountain: The Erika and Klaus Mann Story*, excerpt (University of Chicago Press, 2008). Accessed October 07, 2018. https://www.press.uchicago.edu/Misc/Chicago/886725.html.

4. Ibid.

5. Tóibín, Colm. "I Could Sleep with All of Them." *London Review of Books 30*, no. 21 (November 06, 2006): 3. Accessed October 7, 2018. https://www.lrb.co.uk/v30/n21/colm-toibin-i-could-sleep-with-all-of-them.

6. Ibid.

7. Spotts, Frederic. *Cursed Legacy: The Tragic Life of Klaus Mann* (New Haven: Yale University Press, 2016), plate 10.

8. Tóibín, Colm. "I Could Sleep with All of Them." *London Review of Books 30*, no. 21 (November 06, 2006): 3. Accessed October 7, 2018. https://www.lrb.co.uk/v30/n21/colm-toibin-i-could-sleep-with-all-of-them.

Hans and Sophie Scholl:

1. Dumbach, Annette, and Jud Newborn. *Sophie Scholl and the White Rose*. Oneworld Publications, 2018.

2. Scholl, Inge, and Dorothee Sölle. *The White Rose: Munich, 1942-1943* (Middletown, CT: Wesleyan University Press, 1985), 7.

3. United States Holocaust Memorial Museum. "ANTISEMITIC LEGISLATION 1933–1939." United States Holocaust Memorial Museum. Accessed September 09, 2018. https://encyclopedia.ushmm.org/content/en/article/antisemitic-legislation-1933-1939.

4. United States Holocaust Memorial Museum. "Paragraph 175." United States Holocaust Memorial Museum. Accessed October 23, 2018. https://www.ushmm.org/learn/students/learning-materials-and-resources/homosexuals-victims-of-the-nazi-era/paragraph-175.

5. Peron, James. "The Three Trials of Hans Scholl – The Radical Center – Medium." The Radical Center. September 08, 2018. Accessed September 09, 2018. https://medium.com/the-radical-center/the-three-trials-of-hans-scholl-9bb31ea9cd65.

6. Michalczyk, John J. *Resisters, rescuers, and refugees: Historical and Ethical Issues* (Rowman & Littlefield, 1997), 53.

7. Probst, Ernst. *Superfrauen 3 – Politik* (Grin Verlag, 2008), 184.

8. Burns, Margie. "Sophie Scholl and the White Rose." The International Raoul Wallenberg Foundation. Accessed September 09, 2018. http://www.raoulwallenberg.net/holocaust/articles-20/sophie-scholl-white-rose/.

9. Prager, Stan. "Review Of: *At the Heart of the White Rose: Letters and Diaries of Hans and Sophie Scholl, Edited by Inge Jens*." Regarp Book Blog. May 06, 2018. Accessed September 09, 2018. https://regarp.com/2018/05/06/review-of-at-the-heart-of-the-white-rose-letters-and-diaries-of-hans-and-sophie-scholl-edited-by-inge-jens/.

Felice Schragenheim:

1. Fischer, Erica. *Aimée & Jaguar: A Love Story, Berlin 1943* (New York: HarperCollins, 1994), 47.

2. "American Press Comment on Nazi Riots." *The New York Times*, November 12, 1938. Accessed September 15, 2018. https://timesmachine.nytimes.com/timesmachine/1938/11/12/502448492.html?action=click&contentCollection=Archives&module=ArticleEndCTA&ion=ArchiveBody&pgtype=article&pageNumber=4.

3. Fischer, Erica. *Aimée & Jaguar: A Love Story, Berlin 1943* (New York: HarperCollins, 1994), 54.

4. Ibid., 77-78.

5. Ibid., 107.

6. Ibid., 28.

7. Ibid., 32.

8. Ibid., 112.

9. Ibid., 122.

10. Ibid., 123.

Charlotte Wolff:

1. Wolff, Charlotte. *Hindsight: An Autobiography* (London: Quartet Books, 1980), 26.

2. Ibid., 65.

3. Freidenreich, Harriet. "Charlotte Wolff." *Jewish Women: A Comprehensive Historical Encyclopedia*. 1 March 2009. Jewish Women's Archive. Accessed August 19, 2018. https://jwa.org/encyclopedia/article/wolff-charlotte.

4. United States Holocaust Memorial Museum. "Examples of Antisemitic Legislation, 1933–1939." United States Holocaust Memorial Museum. Accessed August 19, 2018. https://www.ushmm.org/wlc/en/article.php?ModuleId=10007459.

5. Brennan, Toni and Peter Hegarty. 2010. "Charlotte Wolff and Lesbian History: Reconfiguring Liminality in Exile." *Journal of Lesbian Studies* 14 (4): 338-358. doi:10.1080/10894161003677232. 348.

6. Grau, Günter. The Hidden Holocaust?: *Gay and Lesbian Persecution in Germany, 1933-4* (Chicago: Fitzroy Dearborn, 1995), 28.

7. United States Holocaust Memorial Museum. "Book Burning" United States Holocaust Memorial Museum. Accessed August 19, 2018. https://www.ushmm.org/wlc/en/article.php?ModuleId=10005852.

8. United States Holocaust Memorial Museum. "Book Burning—Historical Film Footage" United States Holocaust Memorial Museum. Accessed August 19, 2018. https://www.ushmm.org/wlc/en/media_fi.php?ModuleId=10005852&MediaId=158.

9. United States Holocaust Memorial Museum. "Book Burning" United States Holocaust Memorial Museum. Accessed August 19, 2018. https://www.ushmm.org/wlc/en/article.php?ModuleId=10005852.

Tatamkhulu Afrika:

1. "Afrika, Tatamkhulu 1920-2002." Gale Library of Daily Life: Slavery in America. 2009. Accessed September 05, 2018. https://www.encyclopedia.com/arts/educational-magazines/afrika-tatamkhulu-1920-2002.

2. Cornwell, Gareth, Dirk Klopper, and Craig MacKenzie. *The Columbia Guide to South African Literature in English since 1945* (New York: Columbia University Press, 2011), 46.

3. Dunton, Chris. "Tatamkhulu Afrika: The Testing of Masculinity." *Research in African Literatures* 35, no. 1 (2004): 148-61. http://www.jstor.org/stable/3821408.

4. Ibid.

5. "South African World War II CASUALTIES Genealogy Project." Geni_family_tree. Accessed September 08, 2018. https://www.geni.com/projects/South-African-World-War-II-CASUALTIES/38814.

6. "Afrika, Tatamkhulu 1920-2002." "Afrika, Tatamkhulu 1920-2002." Gale Library of Daily Life: Contemporary Authors. 2018. Accessed September 08, 2018. https://www.encyclopedia.com/arts/educational-magazines/afrika-tatamkhulu-1920-2002.

7. Dunton, Chris. "Tatamkhulu Afrika: The Testing of Masculinity." *Research in African Literatures* 35, no. 1 (2004): 148-61. http://www.jstor.org/stable/3821408.

8. Baderoon, Gabeba. "The Five Names of Tatamkhulu Afrika: Africanness, Europeanness, and Islam in a South African Autobiography." *World Literature Today* 83, no. 1 (2009): 56-60. http://www.jstor.org/stable/20621479.

9. Ibid.

10. Afrika, Tatamkulu. *Mr. Chameleon: An Autobiography* (Johannesburg: Jacana, 2005), 355.

11. Stobie, Cheryl. "Mother, missus, mate: bisexuality in Tatamkhulu Afrika's Mr. Chameleon and Bitter Eden (1)." *English in Africa*, vol. 32, no. 2, 2005, p. 185+. Academic OneFile, http://link.galegroup.com/apps/doc/A151844689/AONE?u=sfpl_main&sid=AONE&xid=b9d63877. Accessed 5 Sept. 2018.

12. Ibid.

13. Stobie, Cheryl. *Somewhere in the Double Rainbow: Representations of Bisexuality in Selected Post-apartheid South African Novels.* Master's thesis, 2005.

Cecil Williams:

1. Redgrave, Greta, dir. *The Man Who Drove With Mandela*. Performed by Corin Redgrave. United Kingdom: Jane Balfour Films Ltd., 1998. Film.

2. Ibid.

3. Ibid.

4. "Cecil Williams." Wikipedia. Accessed August 18, 2018. https://de.wikipedia.org/wiki/Cecil_Williams.

5. Redgrave, Greta, dir. *The Man Who Drove With Mandela*. Performed by Corin Redgrave. United Kingdom: Jane Balfour Films Ltd., 1998. Film.

6. Ibid.

7. France-Presse, Agence. "Ex-CIA Spy Admits Tip Led to Nelson Mandela's Long Imprisonment." *The Guardian*. May 15, 2016. Accessed August 18, 2018. https://www.theguardian.com/us-news/2016/may/15/cia-operative-nelson-mandela-1962-arrest.

8. Redgrave, Greta, dir. *The Man Who Drove With Mandela*. Performed by Corin Redgrave. United Kingdom: Jane Balfour Films Ltd., 1998. Film.

9. Ibid.

Elisabeth Eidenbenz:

1. "Elisabeth Eidenbenz." Memoria Del Exilio. June 03, 2008. Accessed September 16, 2018. https://memoriadelexilio.wordpress.com/recursos/assumpta-montella/elisabeth-eidenbenz/.

2. Carlos, Assumpta Montellà I. *Elisabeth Eidenbenz: Més Enllà De La Maternitat D'Elna* (Badalona: Ara Llibres, 2011).

3. Montella, Assumpta. "Elisabeth Eidenbenz, La Enfermera Que Burló a La Gestapo." *EL PAÍS*. May 26, 2011. Accessed September 17, 2018. https://elpais.com/diario/2011/05/26/necrologicas/1306360801_850215.html.

4. Caistor, Nick. "Spanish Civil War Fighters Look Back." *BBC News*. February 28, 2003. Accessed September 17, 2018. http://news.bbc.co.uk/2/hi/programmes/from_our_own_correspondent/2809025.stm.

5. Cate-Arries, Francie. *Spanish Culture behind Barbed-wire: Memory and Representation of the French Concentration Camps, 1939-1945*. Lewisburg, PA: Bucknell Univ. Press, 2007.

6. "Eidenbenz FAMILY." The Righteous Among The Nations. Accessed September 17, 2018. http://db.yadvashem.org/righteous/family.html?language=en&itemId=8909129.

7. Howitt, Basil. "The Maternité Suisse D'Elne | P-O Life." Anglophone-direct. January 19, 2013. Accessed September 17, 2018. https://anglophone-direct.com/maternite-suisse-elne/.

8. Montella, Assumpta. "Elisabeth Eidenbenz, La Enfermera Que Burló a La Gestapo." EL PAÍS. May 26, 2011. Accessed September 17, 2018. https://elpais.com/diario/2011/05/26/necrologicas/1306360801_850215.html.

9. "The Holocaust: The Holocaust in France The German Occupation." Yad Vashem: The World Holocaust Remembrance Center. Accessed September 17, 2018. http://www.yadvashem.org/yv/en/holocaust/france/occupation.asp#!prettyPhoto.

10. Crampton, Suein. "Elisabeth Eidenbenz." Sheroesofhistory.wordpress.com. April 27, 2018. Accessed September 17, 2018. https://sheroesofhistory.wordpress.com/2018/04/27/elisabeth-eidenbenz/.

11. Altuna, Pablo Esparza. "The House That Saved Refugee Mothers From the Spanish Civil War." OZY. Accessed September 17, 2018. https://www.ozy.com/flashback/the-house-that-saved-refugee-mothers-from-the-spanish-civil-war/83378.

12. Carlos, Assumpta Montellà I. *Elisabeth Eidenbenz: Més Enllà De La Maternitat D'Elna*. Badalona: Ara Llibres, 2011.

13. Huber, Brigitte. "Henriette Hierhammer Feierte Jetzt Den 103. Geburtstag." Meinbezirk.at. May 14, 2018. Accessed September 17, 2018. https://www.meinbezirk.at/purkersdorf/lokales/henriette-hierhammer-feierte-jetzt-den-103-geburtstag-d2604113.html.

Annemarie Schwarzenbach:

1. Carr, Virginia Spencer. *The Lonely Hunter: A Biography of Carson McCullers* (Garden City, NY: Doubleday, 1975), 102.

2. "Annemarie Schwarzenbach." Contemporary Authors Online, Gale, 2013. Biography In Context, http://link.galegroup.com/apps/doc/H1000302521/BIC?u=sfpl_main&sid=BIC&xid=8a8e33ca. Accessed 24 July 2018.

3. Klaus, Mann. *The Turning Point: Thirty-five Years in This Century* (New York: L. B. Fisher, 1942), 51-52.

4. Schwarzenbach, Alexis. "Schriftsteller: Dieses Bittere Jungsein." ZEIT ONLINE. May 15, 2008. Accessed July 24, 2018. https://www.zeit.de/2008/21/A-Schwarzenbach/komplettansicht.

5. "Annemarie Schwarzenbach." World Heritage Encyclopedia. Accessed July 24, 2018. http://www.worldheritage.org/article/WHEBN0008171748/Annemarie Schwarzenbach.

6. United States Holocaust Memorial Museum. "Spanish Civil War." United States Holocaust Memorial Museum. Accessed July 24, 2018. https://www.ushmm.org/wlc/en/article.php?ModuleId=10008214.

7. Leybold-Johnson, Isobel. "Swiss Writer's Life Was Stranger than Fiction." SWI Swissinfo.ch. May 23, 2008. Accessed July 25, 2018. https://www.swissinfo.ch/eng/swiss-writer-s-life-was-stranger-than-fiction/1015688.

8. Schwarzenbach, Annemarie. *Death in Persia*. Translated by Lucy Renner (Jones. London: Seagull Books, 2013), ix.

9. Lorey De Lacharrière, Barbara. "Annemarie Schwarzenbach: A Life." Swiss Institute. 1989. Accessed July 25, 2018. https://www.swissinstitute.net/2001-2006/Exhibitions/2002_Lounge_Specials/2002_Annemarie_Schwarzenbach/SchwarzenbachBIO.htm

10. Spotts, Frederic. *Cursed Legacy: The Tragic Life of Klaus Mann* (New Haven: Yale University Press, 2016), 165.

11. "Annemarie Schwarzenbach." World Heritage Encyclopedia. Accessed July 24, 2018. http://www.worldheritage.org/article/WHEBN0008171748/Annemarie Schwarzenbach.

Willem Arondeus:

1. "Arondeus FAMILY." The Righteous Among The Nations. Accessed September 29, 2018. http://db.yadvashem.org/righteous/family.html?itemId=4043044&language=en.

2. "Twenty Homosexuals in War and Resistance." Archive.li. August 23, 2006. Accessed September 29, 2018. http://www.bevrijdingintercultureel.nl/eng/homoseksuelen.html.

3. Groeneveld, E.G. "Arondeus, Willem Johan Cornelis (1894-1943)." Resources. November 12, 2013. Accessed September 28, 2018. http://resources.huygens.knaw.nl/bwn1880-2000/lemmata/bwn1/arondeus.

4. Ibid.

5. Coulthart, John. "The Art of Willem Arondeus, 1894–1943." { Feuilleton }. January 19, 2016. Accessed September 29, 2018. http://www.johncoulthart.com/feuilleton/2016/01/19/the-art-of-willem-arondeus-1894-1943/.

6. Patrick. "Rotterdam Blitz, A City on Fire – Netherlands." LandmarkScout. April 13, 2013. Accessed August 04, 2018. https://www.landmarkscout.com/rotterdam-blitz-a-city-on-fire-netherlands/.

7. Wotherspoon, Garry, and Robert Aldrich. *Who's Who in Gay and Lesbian History: From Antiquity to World War II* (London: Routledge. 2000), 35.

Sjoerd Bakker:

1. "Gays and Lesbians in War and Resistance." Gays and Lesbians in War and Resistance. Accessed August 02, 2018. http://www.bevrijdingintercultureel.nl/bi/eng/homoseksuelen.html#bakker.

2. Patrick. "Rotterdam Blitz, A City on Fire – Netherlands." LandmarkScout. April 13, 2013. Accessed August 04, 2018. https://www.landmarkscout.com/rotterdam-blitz-a-city-on-fire-netherlands/.

3. United States Holocaust Memorial Museum. "Amsterdam." Holocaust Encyclopedia. Accessed August 04, 2018. https://www.ushmm.org/wlc/en/article.php?ModuleId=10005434.

4. United States Holocaust Memorial Museum. "Amsterdam." Holocaust Encyclopedia. Accessed August 04, 2018. https://www.ushmm.org/wlc/en/article.php?ModuleId=10005434

5. "Gays and Lesbians in War and Resistance." Gays and Lesbians in War and Resistance. Accessed August 02, 2018. http://www.bevrijdingintercultureel.nl/bi/eng/homoseksuelen.html#bakker.

6. "Hollandia-Kattenburg." Joods Monument. June 16, 2004. Accessed August 04, 2018. https://www.joodsmonument.nl/nl/page/750/hollandia-kattenburg.

7. "The Righteous Among The Nations." Db.yadvashem.org. Accessed August 05, 2018. http://db.yadvashem.org/righteous/family.html?language=en&itemId=4042651.

8. "Persoonsregister." Persoonsregister | Stichting De Eerebegraafplaats Te Bloemendaal. Accessed October 22, 2018. https://www.eerebegraafplaatsbloemendaal.eu/persoonsregister.

9. "Sjoerd Bakker." Oorlogs Graven Stichting. Accessed August 04, 2018. https://oorlogsgravenstichting.nl/persoon/5829/sjoerd-bakker.

Frieda Belinfante:

1. Hogstad, Emily E. "Frieda Belinfante: Cellist, Conductor, Outwitter of Nazis." Song of the Lark. August 15, 2017. Accessed September 05, 2018. https://songofthelarkblog.com/2017/08/14/frieda-belinfante-cellist-conductor-outwitter-of-nazis/.

2. "Oral History Interview with Frieda Belinfante." Interview by Frieda Belinfante. United States Holocaust Memorial Museum. May 31, 1994. Accessed July 29, 2018. https://collections.ushmm.org/search/catalog/irn504443. 28.

3. Verzet, Ben. "Heroine, Who Was Also Denied by Loe De Jong." Concentratiekampen. 2011. Accessed July 29, 2018. http://www.dedokwerker.nl/bet_van_beeren.html.

4. "Oral History Interview with Frieda Belinfante." Interview by Frieda Belinfante. United States Holocaust Memorial Museum. May 31, 1994. Accessed July 29, 2018. https://collections.ushmm.org/search/catalog/irn504443. 33.

5. Hogstad, Emily E. "Frieda Belinfante: Cellist, Conductor, Outwitter of Nazis." Song of the Lark. August 15, 2017. Accessed September 05, 2018. https://songofthelarkblog.com/2017/08/14/frieda-belinfante-cellist-conductor-outwitter-of-nazis/.

6. "Welkom | Stichting De Eerebegraafplaats Te Bloemendaal." Gideon Willem BOISSEVAIN | Stichting De Eerebegraafplaats Te Bloemendaal. Accessed July 30, 2018. https://www.eerebegraafplaatsbloemendaal.eu/welkom.

7. "Oral History Interview with Frieda Belinfante." Interview by Frieda Belinfante. United States Holocaust Memorial Museum. May 31, 1994. Accessed July 29, 2018. https://collections.ushmm.org/search/catalog/irn504443. 30.

Bet Van Beeren:

1. Beere, Hilde Brand. "Beeren, Elisabeth Maria Van (1902-1967)." Resources. January 18, 2018. Accessed July 25, 2018. http://resources.huygens.knaw.nl/vrouwenlexicon/lemmata/data/Beeren.

2. United States Holocaust Memorial Museum. "The Netherlands."" United States Holocaust Memorial Museum. Accessed July 28, 2018. https://www.ushmm.org/wlc/en/article.php?ModuleId=10005436.

3. Baker, Andy. "Café 't Manje (The Basket)." Lost Womyn's Space. January 01, 1970. Accessed July 28, 2018. http://lostwomynsspace.blogspot.com/2011/05/cafe-t-manje-basket.html.

4. "Wilhelmina of the Netherlands." New World Encyclopedia. Accessed October 21, 2018. http://www.newworldencyclopedia.org/entry/Wilhelmina_of_the_Netherlands#cite_note-5. Berzet, Ben. "Wapens Op Zolder, Joden in De Kelder, Duitsers Aan De Bar." Concentratiekampen. Accessed July 28, 2018. http://www.dedokwerker.nl/bet_van_beeren.html.

5. Lakeman, Karin. "Bet Van Beeren: Bijna-mythische Kroegbazin." Ons Amsterdam. January 2008. Accessed October 21, 2018. https://web.archive.org/web/20160817002534/http://www.onsamsterdam.nl/component/content/article/26-tijdschrift/tijdschrift-jaargang-2008/179-nummer-1-januari-2008?showall=&start=1.

6. Ruppenstein, Andrew. "Bet Van Beeren Historical Marker." HMdb.org. July 07, 2017. Accessed July 28, 2018. https://www.hmdb.org/marker.asp?marker=105163.

Valentine Ackland:

1. Ackland, Valentine. *For Sylvia: An Honest Account* (London: Chatto and Windus, 1985), 68.

2. Ibid., 62.

3. Mulford, Wendy. *This Narrow Place: Sylvia Townsend Warner and Valentine Ackland: Life, Letters and Politics, 1930-1951* (London: Pandora, 1988), 18-21.

4. Ackland, Valentine. *For Sylvia: An Honest Account* (London: Chatto and Windus, 1985), 94.

5. Ibid., 32.

6. Ibid., 98.

7. Warner, Sylvia Townsend., Valentine Ackland, and Susanna Pinney. *I'll Stand by You: Selected Letters of Sylvia Townsend Warner and Valentine Ackland, with Narrative by Sylvia Townsend Warner* (London: Pimlico, 1998), 43.

8. Simkin, John. "Valentine Ackland." Spartacus Educational. November 2015. Accessed September 02, 2018. http://spartacus-educational.com/Wackland.htm.

9. Brown, Susan, Patricia Clements, and Isobel Grundy. "Valentine Ackland." Orlando Project: Women's Writing in the British Isles from the Beginnings to the Present. Accessed September 02, 2018. http://orlando.cambridge.org/protected/svPeople?formname=r&people_tab=3&person_id=acklva&heading=h.

Joe Carstairs:

1. Summerscale, Kate. *The Queen of Whale Cay* (London: Bloomsbury, 2012), 11.

2. Ibid., 18.

3. Ibid., 25.

4. Ibid., 27

5. Ibid., 27

6. Cheshire, Tom. "Boss of the Bahamas: JOE CARSTAIRS." The Rake. June 2016. Accessed August 09, 2018. https://therake.com/stories/icons/joe-carstairs/.

7. Hamer, Emily. "May Toupie Lowther." Lives of the First World War. Accessed August 12, 2018. https://livesofthefirstworldwar.org/lifestory/5145722.

8. Mavroudi, Nancy. "Behind the Wheel and on the Front Line: Women Ambulance Drivers in WWII." Museum of the Order of St John. March 07, 2017. Accessed August 12, 2018. http://museumstjohn.org.uk/behind-wheel-front-line-women-ambulance-drivers-wwii/

9. "Hackett-Lowther Ambulance Unit." Hackett-Lowther Ambulance Unit. Accessed August 12, 2018. https://livesofthefirstworldwar.org/community/5196.

10. Summerscale, Kate. *The Queen of Whale Cay* (London: Bloomsbury, 2012), 163.

11. "Marion Barbara Aka Joe Carstairs." Lives of the First World War. Accessed August 13, 2018. https://livesofthefirstworldwar.org/lifestory/7673258.

12. Summerscale, Kate. *The Queen of Whale Cay* (London: Bloomsbury, 2012), 218.

13. Ibid., 113-114.

14. Ibid., 106-107.

Ian Gleed:

1. Markus, DH. "Wing Commander Ian Richard Gleed." Wing Commander Ian Richard Gleed. Accessed September 10, 2018. http://www.hatfield-herts.co.uk/aviation/gleed.html.

2. Ibid.

3. Maugham, W. Somerset. *Strictly Personal* (New York: Arno Press, 1977). https://archive.org/stream/in.ernet.dli.2015.523919/2015.523919.Strictly-Personal1942_djvu.txt.

4. "The Airmen's Stories - F/Lt. I R Gleed." Battle of Britain London Monument - Sgt. J FRANTISEK. Accessed September 12, 2018. http://www.bbm.org.uk/airmen/Gleed.htm.

5. Bourne, Stephen. *Fighting Proud: The Untold Story of the Gay Men Who Served in Two World Wars* (S.l.: I B TAURIS, 2018). LOC 1554.

6. Bourne, Stephen. *Fighting Proud: The Untold Story of the Gay Men Who Served in Two World Wars* (S.l.: I B TAURIS, 2018). LOC 1467.

7. *It's Not Unusual: Age of Innocence* (YouTube. March 5, 2015. Accessed September 10, 2018), https://www.youtube.com/watch?time_continue=1929&v=Z9NQbZlKfY4.

8. Bourne, Stephen. *Fighting Proud: The Untold Story of the Gay Men Who Served in Two World Wars* (S.l.: I B TAURIS, 2018). LOC 1525.

Evelyn Irons:

1. McCrystal, Cal. "Evelyn Irons—woman of distinction." (*British Journalism Review* 11.3, 2000), 48.

2. Jagose, Annamarie. "The Evolution of a Lesbian Icon: Annamarie Jagose Interviews Laura Doan about Her New Book, *Fashioning Sapphism: The Origins of a Modern English Lesbian Culture*." Genders 1998-2013. July 02, 2001. Accessed September 25, 2018. https://www.colorado.edu/gendersarchive1998-2013/2001/07/02/evolution-lesbian-icon-annamarie-jagose-interviews-laura-doan-about-her-new-book.

3. Dennison, Matthew. *Behind the Mask: The Life of Vita Sackville-West* (New York: Griffin, 2016), 231.

4. Ibid., 233-234.

5. Dowson, Jane. *Women's Poetry of the 1930s: A Critical Anthology* (London: Routledge, 1996), 119.

6. Dennison, Matthew. *Behind the Mask: The Life of Vita Sackville-West* (New York: Griffin, 2016), 239.

7. Irons, Evelyn. "An Evening With Virginia Wolfe." *The New Yorker*, March 30, 1963, 118. Accessed September 24, 2018. http://archives.newyorker.com/?i=1963-03-30#folio=114.

8. Wilkes, Roger. "Inside Story: a woman of no little importance." *The Telegraph*. June 27, 2001. Accessed September 25, 2018. https://www.telegraph.co.uk/finance/property/advice/propertymarket/3290232/Inside-story-a-woman-of-no-little-importance.html.

9. McCrystal, Cal. "Evelyn Irons—woman of distinction." (*British Journalism Review* 11.3, 2000), 53.

10. Ibid., 53.

11. Ibid., 54.

ENDNOTES *continued*

12. Wilkes, Roger. "Inside Story: a woman of no little importance." *The Telegraph*. June 27, 2001. Accessed September 25, 2018. https://www.telegraph.co.uk/finance/property/advice/propertymarket/3290232/Inside-story-a-woman-of-no-little-importance.html.

13. Ibid.

14. McCrystal, Cal. "Evelyn Irons—woman of distinction." (*British Journalism Review* 11.3, 2000), 47.

15. Ibid., 48.

16. Wilkes, Roger. "Inside Story: a woman of no little importance." *The Telegraph*. June 27, 2001. Accessed September 25, 2018. https://www.telegraph.co.uk/finance/property/advice/propertymarket/3290232/Inside-story-a-woman-of-no-little-importance.html.

17. Horowitz, Glenn. "Irons, Evelyn." The Dobkin Family Collection of Feminism. Accessed September 25, 2018. http://www.glennhorowitz.com/dobkin/archive_evelyn_irons_archive._5_large_slipcases.

Alan Turing:

1. Jacobson, Rebecca. "8 Things You Didn't Know about Alan Turing." PBS. November 28, 2014. Accessed July 16, 2018. https://www.pbs.org/newshour/science/8-things-didnt-know-alan-turing.

2. Popova, Maria. "Alan Turing's Little-Known Contributions to Biology and His Mesmerizing Hand-Drawn Diagrams of Dappling Patterns." Brain Pickings. March 01, 2016. Accessed July 17, 2018. https://www.brainpickings.org/2016/03/01/alan-turing-morphogenesis-diagrams/.

3. Hodges, Andrew. *Alan Turing, the Enigma* (London: Burnett Books, 1983), 26.

4. Ibid., 35.

5. Ibid., 43.

6. Ibid., 87.

7. Ibid., 150-151.

8. O'Hanlon, G. "A.M. Turing (h 1926-1931)." *The Shirburnian*, Summer 1954, 54-55.

9. "World War II Casualties." Wikipedia. July 21, 2018. Accessed July 22, 2018. https://en.wikipedia.org/wiki/World_War_II_casualties.

10. Copeland, Prof Jack. "Alan Turing: The codebreaker who saved 'millions of lives'." BBC News. June 19, 2012. Accessed July 22, 2018. https://www.bbc.com/news/technology-18419691.

11. Hodges, Andrew. "Alan Turing - a Short Biography." Alan Turing Internet Scrapbook. 1995. Accessed July 22, 2018. http://www.turing.org.uk/publications/dnb.html.

12. Hodges, Andrew. *Alan Turing, the Enigma* (London: Burnett Books, 1983), 449-457.

13. Ibid., 473-476.

14. Ibid., 486.

15. Blanchard, Jack. "Pardon for Thousands of Gay Sex Criminals Turing Law Gives Posthumous Justice." *The Mirror* (London, England), October 20, 2016. Accessed October 19, 2018. http://www.highbeam.com/doc/1G1-467144496.html?refid=easy_hf

Dolly Wilde:

1. Schenkar, Joan. *Truly Wilde: The Unsettling Story of Dolly Wilde, Oscar's Unusual Niece* (New York: Basic Books, 2000), 59.

2. Ibid., 6.

3. "Dolly Wilde: An Impossible Burden." Beside Every Man. October 13, 2016. Accessed August 09, 2018. https://eafitzsimons.wordpress.com/2016/07/11/dolly-wilde-an-impossible-burden/.

4. Schenkar, Joan. *Truly Wilde: The Unsettling Story of Dolly Wilde, Oscar's Unusual Niece* (New York: Basic Books, 2000), 88.

5. Cheshire, Tom. "Boss of the Bahamas: JOE CARSTAIRS." The Rake. June 2016. Accessed August 09, 2018. https://therake.com/stories/icons/joe-carstairs/.

6. Hamer, Emily. "May Toupie Lowther." Lives of the First World War. Accessed August 12, 2018. https://livesofthefirstworldwar.org/lifestory/5145722.

7. Mavroudi, Nancy. "Behind the Wheel and on the Front Line: Women Ambulance Drivers in WWII." Museum of the Order of St John. March 07, 2017. Accessed August 12, 2018. http://museumstjohn.org.uk/behind-wheel-front-line-women-ambulance-drivers-wwii/.

8. "Hackett-Lowther Ambulance Unit." Hackett-Lowther Ambulance Unit. Accessed August 12, 2018. https://livesofthefirstworldwar.org/community/5196.

9. Schenkar, Joan. *Truly Wilde: The Unsettling Story of Dolly Wilde, Oscar's Unusual Niece* (New York: Basic Books, 2000), 78.

10. Ibid., 89.

11. Luscher, Adam. "The Mystery of Shellshock Solved: Scientists Identify the Unique Brain Injury Caused by War." *The Independent*, January 15, 2015. Accessed October 19, 2018. https://www.independent.co.uk/news/the-mystery-of-shellshock-solved-scientists-identify-the-unique-brain-injury-caused-by-war-9981443.html.

12. "Dolly Wilde: An Impossible Burden." Beside Every Man. October 13, 2016. Accessed August 09, 2018. https://eafitzsimons.wordpress.com/2016/07/11/dolly-wilde-an-impossible-burden/.

13. Harris, John. "Tancred Borenius—Forgotten Intelligence Hero or Messenger for Wartime Churchillian Coup?" Military History Online—Was Britain's Participation in WWI Justified? June 26, 2017. Accessed August 12, 2018. https://www.militaryhistoryonline.com/wwii/articles/tancredborenius.aspx.

Tiny Davis:

1. Smith, Patricia. "'Tiny & Ruby' Relives Era of Hot Jazz and Fast Living." *Chicago Sun-Times*, October 2, 1988. Accessed September 26, 2018. http://www.highbeam.com/doc/1P2-3907371.html?refid=easy_hf.Ibid.

2. De La Croix, St. Sukie. *Chicago Whispers: A History of LGBT Chicago Before Stonewall* (Madison, WI: University of Wisconsin Press, 2012), 154.

3. Ibid., 154.

4. Smith, Patricia. "'Tiny & Ruby' Relives Era of Hot Jazz and Fast Living." *Chicago Sun-Times*, October 2, 1988. Accessed September 26, 2018. http://www.highbeam.com/doc/1P2-3907371.html?refid=easy_hf.Ibid.

5. Tucker, Sherrie. *Swing Shift: "All-Girl" Bands of the 1940s* (Durham, NC: Duke University Press, 2001), 49.

6. Ibid. 49.

7. The Ratgirl, Paghat. "INTERNATIONAL SWEETHEARTS OF RHYTHM. 1947." Wild Realm Reviews: International Sweethearts of Rhythm. Accessed September 26, 2018. http://www.weirdwildrealm.com/f-internationalsweethearts.html.

8. Schiller, Greta and Andrea Weiss, dir. *Tiny and Ruby: Hell Divin' Women*. Jezebel Productions: Channel 4 (UK). 1996. Accessed September 26, 2018. https://www.kanopy.com/product/tiny-and-ruby-hell-divin-women.

9. Fleet, Susan. "The International Sweethearts of Rhythm." Sweethearts of Rhythm. February 03, 2017. Accessed September 27, 2018. http://archives.susanfleet.com/documents/international_sweethearts_of_rhythm.html.

10. Smith, Patricia. "'Tiny & Ruby' Relives Era of Hot Jazz and Fast Living." *Chicago Sun-Times*, October 2, 1988. Accessed September 26, 2018. http://www.highbeam.com/doc/1P2-3907371.html?refid=easy_hf.Ibid.

11. Eaklor, Vicki Lynn. *Queer America: A Peoples GLBT History of the United States*. (New York: New Press, 2011), 43.

Marlene Dietrich:

1. Brendan. "Wenn Die Beste Freundin." Cabaret Berlin. May 17, 2010. Accessed September 27, 2018. http://www.cabaret-berlin.com/?p=58.

2. Gammel, Irene. "Lacing up the Gloves: Women, Boxing and Modernity." Cultural and Social History 9.3 (2012), 372.

3. Riva, J. David, and Guy Stern. *A Woman at War: Marlene Dietrich Remembered* (Detroit, MI: Wayne State University Press, 2006), 6.

4. Ibid. 6.

5. Brendan. "The Silhouette." Cabaret Berlin. October 31, 20120. Accessed September 27, 2018. http://www.cabaret-berlin.com/?p=834

6. Baxter, John. "Berlin Year Zero: The Making of 'The Blue Angel'." *Framework: The Journal of Cinema and Media 51*, no. 1 (2010): 164-89. http://www.jstor.org/stable/41552573. http://www.cabaret-berlin.com/?p=58.

7. Cheshire, Tom. "Boss of the Bahamas: JOE CARSTAIRS." The Rake. June 2016. Accessed September 27, 2018. https://therake.com/stories/icons/joe-carstairs/.

8. Helm, Toby. "Film Star Felt Ashamed of Belsen Link." *The Telegraph*. June 24, 2000. Accessed September 27, 2018. https://www.telegraph.co.uk/news/worldnews/europe/1344765/Film-star-felt-ashamed-of-Belsen-link.html.

9. "Thanks Soldier." Marlene Plus. https://web.archive.org/web/20110925155636/http://www.marlenedietrich.org/plusMuseum6.htm.

Janet Flanner Endnotes

1. Zox-Weaver, Annalisa. "At Home with Hitler: Janet Flanner's Führer Profiles for the 'New Yorker'." *New German Critique*, no. 102 (2007): 101-25. http://www.jstor.org/stable/27669212.

2. Wineapple, Brenda. *Genêt, A Biography of Janet Flanner* (London: Pandora, 1994), 54.

3. Norris, Sian. "WOMEN OF 1920s PARIS: Janet Flanner - Journalist." The Heroine Collective. June 16, 2016. Accessed August 05, 2018. http://www.theheroinecollective.com/janet-flanner/.

4. Murray, William. *Janet, My Mother, and Me: A Memoir of Growing up with Janet Flanner and Natalia Danesi Murray* (New York: Simon & Schuster, 2000), 45.

5. Gellately, Robert. *Backing Hitler: Consent and Coercion in Nazi Germany* (Oxford University Press), 18.

6. Overbey, Erin. "Eighty-Five from the Archive: Janet Flanner." *The New Yorker*, March 1, 2010. March 1, 2010. Accessed August 5, 2018. https://www.newyorker.com/books/double-take/eighty-five-from-the-archive-janet-flanner.

7. Janet, Flanner. "Profiles: Führer II." *The New Yorker* Digital Edition : Jul 14, 1956. Accessed September 04, 2018. http://archives.newyorker.com/?i=1936-03-07#folio=028. 29-30.

8. Ibid. 30.

9. Janet, Flanner. "Profiles: Führer III." *The New Yorker* Digital Edition : Jul 14, 1956. Accessed September 04, 2018. http://archives.newyorker.com/?i=1936-03-14#folio=022. 22.

10. Flanner, Janet. *An American in Paris: Profile of an Interlude between Two Wars* (New York: Simon and Schuster), 374.

11. Zox-Weaver, Annalisa. "At Home with Hitler: Janet Flanner's Führer Profiles for the 'New Yorker'." *New German Critique*, no. 102 (2007): 101-25.

12. Murray, William. *Janet, My Mother, and Me: A Memoir of Growing up with Janet Flanner and Natalia Danesi Murray* (New York: Simon & Schuster, 2000), 182.

Alberta Hunter:

1. Taylor, Frank C. *Alberta Hunter: a Celebration in Blues* (McGraw-Hill Book Company, 1988), 34

2. Washington, Ellery. "James Baldwin's Paris." *The New York Times*, January 07, 1914. Accessed October 29, 2018. https://www.nytimes.com/2014/01/19/travel/james-baldwins-paris.html.

3. Ibid. 88.

4. Ibid. 91

5. Ibid. 90

6. Ibid. 128

7. Ibid. 157

8. Ibid. 132

9. Ibid. 139

10. Ibid. 152

11. Monahan, Patrick. "Alberta Sings the Blues." *The Paris Review*, March 01, 1912. Accessed October 29, 2018. https://www.theparisreview.org/blog/2012/03/01/alberta-sings-the-blues/.

12. Ibid. 165

13. Monahan, Patrick. "Alberta Sings the Blues." *The Paris Review*, March 01, 1912. Accessed October 29, 2018. https://www.theparisreview.org/blog/2012/03/01/alberta-sings-the-blues/.

Vincent Miles:

1. Bérubé, Allan, John DEmilio, and Estelle B. Freedman. *Coming Out Under Fire: The History of Gay Men and Women in World War II* (Chapel Hill: University of North Carolina Press, 2010), 199.

2. Ibid., 183.

3. Lehmann, Herman. *9 Years Among the Indians, 1870-1879* (Von Boeckmann-Jones Company, 1927), 121.

4. Redish, Laura, and Orrin Lewis. "Native American Buffalo Mythology." Native American Indian Buffalo Legends, Meaning and Symbolism from the Myths of Many Tribes. 1998. Accessed October 13, 2018. http://www.native-languages.org/legends-buffalo.htm.

5. Callard, Abby. "Memoirs of a World War II Buffalo Soldier." Smithsonian.com. November 06, 2009. Accessed October 13, 2018. https://www.smithsonianmag.com/history/memoirs-of-a-world-war-ii-buffalo-soldier-149170923/.

6. Ibid.

7. Aizenman, Nurith C. "Black Soldiers Battled Fascism and Racism; Veterans Remember Bitterness of Bias-Tainted Homecomings." *The Washington Post*, May 26, 2004. Accessed October 13, 2018. http://www.highbeam.com/doc/1P2-182231.html?refid=easy_hf.

8. Hodges, Robert. "How the 'Buffalo Soldiers' Helped Turn the Tide in Italy during World War II." HistoryNet. February 1999. Accessed October 13, 2018. http://www.historynet.com/how-the-buffalo-soldiers-helped-turn-the-tide-in-italy-during-world-war-ii.htm.

9. Ibid.

Reed Peggram:

1. Whitmire, Ethelene, and Katherine Lam. "The Gay Black American Who Stared Down Nazis in the Name of Love." *Narratively*. September 05, 2018. Accessed September 26, 2018. http://narrative.ly/the-gay-black-american-who-stared-down-nazis-in-the-name-of-love/.

2. Goggin, Jacqueline Anne. *Carter G. Woodson: A Life in Black History* (Baton Rouge: Louisiana State University Press, 1997), 154.

3. Painter, Nell. "Jim Crow at Harvard: 1923." *The New England Quarterly* 44, no. 4 (1971): 627-34. doi:10.2307/364477.

4. Whitmire, Ethelene, and Katherine Lam. "The Gay Black American Who Stared Down Nazis in the Name of Love." *Narratively*. September 05, 2018. Accessed September 26, 2018. http://narrative.ly/the-gay-black-american-who-stared-down-nazis-in-the-name-of-love/.

5. Ibid.

6. Taylor, Frank C. *Alberta Hunter: a Celebration in Blues* (McGraw-Hill Book Company, 1988), 139.

ENDNOTES *continued*

7. Gross, Daniel A. "The U.S. Government Turned Away Thousands of Jewish Refugees, Fearing That They Were Nazi Spies." *Smithsonian.com*. November 18, 2015. Accessed September 26, 2018. https://www.smithsonianmag.com/history/us-government-turned-away-thousands-jewish-refugees-fearing-they-were-nazi-spies-180957324/.

8. Delmont, Matthew. "African-Americans Fighting Fascism and Racism, from WWII to Charlottesville." *The Conversation*. August 21, 2017. Accessed September 25, 2018. https://theconversation.com/african-americans-fighting-fascism-and-racism-from-wwii-to-charlottesville-82551.

9. Whitmire, Ethelene, and Katherine Lam. "The Gay Black American Who Stared Down Nazis in the Name of Love." *Narratively*. September 05, 2018. Accessed September 26, 2018. http://narrative.ly/the-gay-black-american-who-stared-down-nazis-in-the-name-of-love/.

10. Ibid.

11. Ibid.

12. Ibid.

Claire De Forbin and Isabel Townsend Pell:

1. Pell, Eve. "La Femme à la Mèche Blonde." *Ms Magazine*, (New York), Spring 2005. http://www.msmagazine.com/spring2005/isabelpell.asp (accessed March 11, 2018).

2. "Freighter Rescues Two New York Women Adrift In A Disabled Seaplane Off Sweden." (1933, Aug 27). *New York Times* (1923-Current File) Retrieved from http://ezproxy.sfpl.org/login?url=https://search-proquest-com.ezproxy.sfpl.org/docview/100910057?accountid=35117

3. Emerson, Maureen. *Riviera Dreaming: Love and War on the Côte D'Azur*. (London: I.B. Tauris &, 2018)

4. Ibid.

5. McIntosh, Elizabeth P. "The Role of Women in Intelligence." *Association of Former Intelligence Officers*. 1989. Accessed October 6, 2018. https://www.afio.com/publications/monographs/McIntosh Elizabeth Role of Women in Intelligence AFIO Monograph 5.pdf.

6. Ibid.

7. Emerson, Maureen. *Riviera Dreaming: Love and War on the Côte D'Azur*. (London: I.B. Tauris &, 2018)

8. Acosta, Mercedes De. *Here Lies the Heart: A Tale of My Life* (Mansfield Centre, CT: Martino Publishing, 2016)

9. Ibid.

GLOSSARY OF SELECTED TERMS

Blut und Boden (Blood and Soil)

Blut und Boden was one of Nazi Germany's cornerstone ideologies, combining reverence of rural life (soil) with racism and anti-Semitism (blood). *Blut und Boden* was a popular unifying propaganda tool during the rise of Nazi Germany. *Neuadel aus Blut und Boden* (*A New Nobility Based On Blood And Soil*, published in 1930) was written by Richard Walther Darré, a race theorist who advocated for a Nazi systematic eugenics program. Darré was the Reich Minister of Food and Agriculture from 1933 to 1942 and a high ranking Nazi SS member.

Entartete Kunst (Degenerate Art)

Entartete Kunst was a term used by the Nazi regime to describe modernist art. Modern art was banned because it was considered by the government to be un-German, Jewish, or Communist in nature. If an artist created *entartete kunst*, they would be forbidden from teaching, and showing or selling artwork, and sometimes even sent to concentration camps or killed. This ban on modernism applied to all forms of art expression. This meant that the government controlled art, using it as a propaganda tool to promote racism, anti-Semitism, and other nationalist beliefs. In 1933, the *Reichskulturkammer* (Reich Culture Chamber) was formed. Joseph Goebbels, Hitler's *Reichminister für Volksaufklärung und Propaganda* (Reich Minister for Public Enlightenment and Propaganda), was in charge.

Gesetz zur Behebung der Not von Volk und Reich (Law to Remedy the Distress of People and Reich, or the Enabling Act of 1933)

This law was passed by the Reichstag and the Reichsrat on March 24, 1933, and was the foundation for Hitler's ascendance to absolute power in Germany. It granted him the ability to enact laws without the approval of Parliament. The law was passed because Hitler cheated by stopping dissenting members of the Reichstag from voting against it by holding 107 house members in protective custody and using police intimidation on the rest.

Gesetz zur Wiederherstellung des Berufsbeamtentums (The Reich Law for the Restoration of the Civil Service, Civil Service Law, or the Civil Service Restoration Act)

This anti-Semitic law was passed in 1933, just a couple of months after Hitler was declared Chancellor. Under the Civil Service Restoration Act, Jewish people, non-Aryans, and political opponents, such as Communists of the Nazi regime, were fired from their jobs. Forbidden occupations for Jewish people, non-Aryans, and political opponents included school teachers, professors, judges, government positions, lawyers, doctors, tax consultants, musicians, and notaries.

Gesetz zum Schutze des Deutschen Blutes und der Deutschen Ehre or Blutschutzgesetz (Blood Protection Law, or the Law for the Protection of German Blood and German Honor)

The Blood Protection Law is one of two Nuremberg Laws. This 1935 law governed marriage and sexual relations between Jewish Germans and non-Jewish Germans. It banned non-Jewish women under the age of 45 from working for Jewish people in order to prevent pregnancies between non-Jewish female employees and Jewish male employers. The Blood Protection Law also banned Jewish people from displaying the German flag and colors. The sentence for breaking the Blood Protection Law was up to one year in prison and a fine, and many times a person was immediately sent to a concentration camp after release from prison.

Gleichschaltung (Nazification)

Gleichschaltung was the process that the Nazi regime used to control its citizens by heavy-handed involvement in German daily life, from economy and trade associations to the media, culture, and schools. The passage of the Enabling Act of 1933 and the Civil Service Restoration Act gave Hitler full reign to control his country through coordinated propaganda and the denial of civil liberties. Within weeks, the *Erstes Gleichschaltungsgesetz* (First *Gleichschaltung* Law) was passed, then the *Zweites Gleichschaltungsgesetz* (Second *Gleichschaltung* Law). In a 1933 speech, chief Nazi propagandist Joseph Goebbels said, "The secret of propaganda [is to] permeate the person it aims to grasp, without his even noticing that he is being permeated. Of course propaganda has a purpose, but the purpose must be concealed with such cleverness and virtuosity that the person on whom this purpose is to be carried out doesn't notice it at all," (from *The Coming of the Third Reich* by Richard Evans).

Hitlerjugend (Hitler Youth, or HJ) and *Bund Deutscher Mädel* (Band of German Maidens, or BDM)

The *Hitlerjugend* and *Bund Deutscher Mädel* were the only official and legal youth groups for 10–18 year old boys and 10–21 year old girls in Germany between 1933 until 1945. There were several subgroups by age. In order to join these groups, the youth needed to be ethnic Germans citizens and free of hereditary diseases. Membership was mandatory, making the group a powerful propaganda and policing tool.

Institut für Sexualwissenschaft (Institute for Sexual Science)

The *Institut für Sexualwissenschaft* was a sexuality studies research institute located in Berlin that was headed by the acclaimed gay scholar, Magnus Hirschfeld. Founded in 1919 by Magnus and Arthur Kronfeld, the *Institut für Sexualwissenschaft* was a cornerstone of sexuality studies during the Weimar Republic. Magnus coined the word *transvestit* (transvestite) and was a tireless ally for sexual minorities. The *Institut für Sexualwissenschaft*'s immense sexology library and archives was torched by conservative German students in May of 1933, in a *feuersprüche* (a fire decree). Approximately 20,000 books and journals, and 5,000 images on sex and gender, were destroyed.

Kristallnacht (Crystal Night, or Night of Broken Glass)

Kristallnacht was a two-day riot or pogrom that took place in the German Reich on November 9–10, 1938. The impetus of *Kristallnacht* was the assassination of a Nazi German diplomat by a Jewish teenager. It was led by the Nazi paramilitary force *Sturmabteilung* (Storm Detachment) along with angry German citizens. There was massive looting and destruction of Jewish-owned stores, buildings, cemeteries, hospitals, schools, and synagogues. Over 200 synagogues and 7,000 Jewish businesses were damaged during this two-day Nazi crime spree. Over 50 Jewish people were killed, and over 30,000 Jewish men were arrested and taken to concentration camps during *Kristallnacht*. *Kristallnacht* marks the beginning of the Holocaust.

Mischling Test (mixed-blood test)

The Mischling test was a method of determining whether a citizen was Jewish. *Die Nurnberger Gesetze* (Nuremberg Race Laws) were developed during the formation of the Nazi Germany's Nuremberg Laws. *Mischling* means mixed blood, and refers to people with both Aryan and Jewish ancestry. The test divided *Mischlinge* into degrees, depending upon how many Jewish grandparents a person had. The Nuremberg Race Laws' racial or Jewish categories were *Deutsche-blutige* (German blood or Aryan), two degrees of *Mischlinge*, and two degrees of *Jude* (Jewish). For instance, a Jude was defined as a person with three Jewish grandparents, and a *Mischlinge* had between one and two Jewish grandparents. Conversion to Christianity usually had no bearing upon determination of Jewish blood. Jews were no longer considered German citizens and had many civil rights removed. *Die Nürnberger Gesetze* is a well-documented Nazi racial classification chart.

Nürnberger Gesetze (The Nuremberg Laws)

These were two anti-Semitic and racial laws passed in the Reichstag on September 15, 1935. The laws were the Blood Protection Law and the Reich Citizenship Law. These laws reversed the process of emancipation for Jewish citizens. It declared that Jewish people were no longer equal German citizens, and made it possible to enact further anti-Semitic measures by legally distinguishing between Germans and Jews. The Nuremberg laws were amended later on that year to apply to black and Romani people too (see Paragraph 175 for the legal persecution of gay men).

Paragraph 175

Paragraph 175 was the law forbidding gay male homosexuality and did not apply to lesbians. Although Paragraph 175 had been a law since 1871, in 1935 the Nazis expanded the definition of homosexual behavior to include such nebulous actions as any contact between men with sexual intent, even "simple looking" or "simple touching," and made homosexual behavior between men into a felony, thereby increasing the maximum imprisonment penalty to five years. Between 1933 and 1945, approximately 100,000 men were arrested as homosexuals and between 5,000 and 50,000 of these men were sent to concentration camps where up to 60% of them died.

Reich Citizenship Law

The Reich Citizenship Law is one of two Nuremberg Laws. This law defined who had civil rights as a German citizen. Under the law, Jewish people were stripped of their German citizenship, reviled, and removed from society. Jewish people were then legally fired from their jobs, shunned, forbidden from attending schools, harassed, and more. The law applied to all Jewish people, including non-practicing ones. Racial and Jewish status was determined with the Mischling Test.

Reichsarbeitsdienst (Reich Labor Service, or RAD)

Reich Labor Service was a government-run organization that was formed to fight unemployment and indoctrinate German citizens between ages 18-25 with Nazi propaganda or doctrine. During WWII, all men were mandated to serve in RAD for six months before they joined the army, Women were also mandated to serve in RAD, but were not drafted into the army. The work week in RAD could be up to 75 hours per week, working for military or civic and agricultural construction projects.

Reichstagsbrand (Reichstag fire)

The *Reichstagsbrand* was an arson attack on the Reichstag building in Berlin, home of the German parliament. This occurred on February 27, 1933, one month after Hitler was sworn in as Chancellor. It's widely believed that the Reichstagsbrand was a false flag operation that deflected the public from Hitler's subsequent power grab. The day after the fire, the *Reichstagsbrandverordnung* (Reichstag Fire Decree) was enacted. The Reichstag Fire Decree suspended many civil liberties in Germany, including habeas corpus, freedom of expression, freedom of the press, the right of public assembly, and the privacy of the mail and telephone.

Reichstagsbrandverordnung (Reichstag Fire Decree, or the Decree of the Reich President for the Protection of People and State)

The Reichstag Fire Decree was made into law immediately after the German parliament was burnt down by arson in February of 1933. The fire acted as a cover for the Nazi government to suspend the Constitution, and pass laws restricting civil liberties under the guise of protecting the people. It outlawed opposition to the Nazi government and removed many of the German citizens' civil liberties. Parts of the law read, "It is therefore permissible to restrict the rights of personal freedom [*habeas corpus*], freedom of (opinion) expression, including the freedom of the press, the freedom to organize and assemble, the privacy of postal, telegraphic and telephonic communications. Warrants for House searches, orders for confiscations as well as restrictions on property, are also permissible beyond the legal limits otherwise prescribed."

Reichsrat and the Reichstag legislative bodies

The Reichsrat and the Reichstag were the two German legislative bodies of Parliament. The Reichsrat members were appointed and the Reichstag members were elected.

Service de Travail Obligatoire (Compulsory Work Service, or STO)

The Compulsory Work Service was a law enacted in several stages between 1942 and 1944 that forced French citizens under the Nazi Occupation of France to labor in work camps in Nazi Germany in exchange for the release of French prisoners of war. One French prisoner of war was freed for every three French workers sent to labor in Germany. 600,000 to 650,000 French citizens were sent to work in Nazi Germany between 1942 and 1944. Resentment against this law contributed to the strength of the French Resistance.

Vorbeugehaft (police detention/protective custody)

Vorbeugehaft was a police order whereby a person could be held in jail or prison indefinitely without being charged or appearing in court. There were no appeals and, often, people would be transferred to a concentration camp upon release from detention. The *polizeiliche Vorbeugehaft* or basic decree was signed in December of 1937. Although *Vorbeugehaft* was instituted as a public safety and crime-fighting measure, it was apparent that *Vorbeugehaft* was a blank slate to remove undesirables from the public sphere without consequences. Reasons for being taken into protective custody included being Jewish, gay or lesbian, Roma, homeless, unemployed, a sex worker, or the nebulous term "anti-social."

Additional Holocaust Resources:

The United States Holocaust Memorial Museum Holocaust Encyclopedia, https://encyclopedia.ushmm.org/

Cybrary of the Holocaust, http://remember.org

Facing History and Ourselves, https://www.facinghistory.org

THE ARTISTS

Ajuan Mance is a Professor of African American literature at Mills College and a lifelong artist and writer. Ajuan's comics and zines include *Gender Studies*, an autobiographical comic series; *A Blues for Black Santa*, the 1001 Black Men series, the web-based comic strip *Check All that Apply*, and others. Her drawings and comics have appeared in a number of publications including, most recently, the *San Francisco Chronicle*, *The New York Times*, *Brown Alumni Monthly*, the *Mills Quarterly*, and the *Women's Review of Books*. Both her scholarly writings and her comics and zines explore the relationship between race, gender, and representation, specifically as it applies to people of African descent in the U.S. Ajuan is the author of two books on the history of African-American writers, *Inventing Black Women* and *Before Harlem*.

Anne Williams is a San Francisco-based artist, mom, yogi, feminist, knitter and tattooist. She is the proud owner of Mermaids Tattoo Studio, the woman artist owned and operated tattoo studio and gallery in San Francisco's Mission district. You can follow her on Facebook or Instagram at @mermaidstattoo or reach her through MermaidsTattoo.com. It thrills her to be included in this notable community of artists!

Ashley R. Guillory works as a storyboard artist for live-action film. She lives with her cat in Burbank, CA where she spends most of her time drawing. In her spare time, she creates comics to promote conversation about health issues such as endometriosis and interstitial cystitis. Her comics and other art can be found on Twitter, Instagram, and Tumblr @ashleyrguillory, or on her website: ashleyrguillory.com

Avery Cassell is a writer, artist, historian, queer, ex-punk, butch, editor, and documentarian. Their childhood was spent in Iran. In their spare time, they like to feed the squirrels at the San Francisco Botanical Garden in Golden Gate Park, read mysteries, and sew. Their books include the *Butch Lesbians of the 20s, 30s, and 40s Coloring Book*, the *Butch Lesbians of the 50s, 60s, and 70s Coloring Book*, and the queer erotic romance, *Behrouz Gets Lucky*. See more of their work at averycassell.com and on Instagram at avery_g_cassell.

Burton Clarke is an illustrator, cartoonist, and creator of a series of year-end, black-and-white art cards begun in 1986. Initially, that series paid tribute to friends lost to the AIDS epidemic, but gradually the annual themes became more pointedly political (the Iraq War, Katrina, 9/11, same-sex marriage). He is perhaps best known for stories that appeared in *Gay Comix* ("Cy Ross and the Snow Queen Syndrome," "Satyr," and "Some Day My Prints Will Come"), and his cartoon work is listed in the archive of the Alexander Street Press Digital Library. He lives in San Francisco and enjoys contributing to selected art projects like this book. E-mail: blutherclarke@gmail.com

Diane Kanzler is a queer butch writer, book designer, and illustrator. She lives in beautiful, rural western Massachusetts and is a *cum laude* graduate of Moore College of Art and Design in Philadelphia. Her grandparents and their three sons fled Nazi Germany before World War II broke out and settled in the northeastern United States. The eldest son—her uncle—proudly served in the U.S. Army as a German language translator and interpreter during the North African Campaign, the surrender of Italy to the Allies, and the defeat of Nazi Germany.

THE ARTISTS *continued*

Diego Gomez, a.k.a. Trangela Lansbury, is a San Francisco native, graphic design graduate of the Art Institute, *SF WEEKLY*'s Best Bearded Lady, granddaughter of the Cockettes, lipstick thespian, and snatching gigs! They are the queer book creator of *The Hard-Femme Ex-Men, 1963 Is Not an End But A Beginning: A Graphic History*, and *Daddy Issues* magazine. They've taught Fashion Illustration at City College San Francisco, computer application outreach to kids, and makeup classes to creeps.
Follow their arts: http://www.instagram.com/designnurd
Follow their farts: http://www.instagram.com/trangelalansbury

Dorian Katz is a visual artist and curator based in Oakland, California. For over 10 years, the majority of her art projects are conceived and executed by her alter ego, Poppers the Pony. She began drawing animals by imagining a queer sex utopia and wondering what it would be like if humans were socialized like other species, such as the bonobo monkey, and what would it look like if historically vilified animals, such as the spotted hyena, received heroically queer narratives. Whether drawing as Poppers or Dorian, they strive to present inclusive views of sexuality with beauty and humor.

Jennifer Camper's books include *Rude Girls and Dangerous Women* and *subGURLZ*, and she edited two *Juicy Mother* comics anthologies. She's the founding director of the Queers & Comics Conference. jennifercamper.com

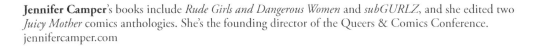

Jessica Bogac-Moore is a queer, Black Native Hawaiian illustrator based in Oakland, CA. Jessica is highly influenced by queer Leather culture and portrays aspects of this subject matter in picture books for young adult to mature audiences involving navigation of teen years growing up a queer black native person in the Pacific, discovering racial and sexual identity, sharing personal narratives of diaspora and cultural awareness within editorial, fine art, and comics.

Jon Macy is the author of Lambda Literary Award winner *Teleny and Camille*. Look for more of his work at stackeddeckpress.com and northwestpress.com.

Justin Hall created the comics series *True Travel Tales*, *Hard to Swallow*, and *Glamazonia*, as well as the Lambda Literary Award-winning collection *No Straight Lines: Four Decades of Queer Comics*, which is now being turned into a feature length documentary film. He is an Associate Professor of Comics at California College for the Arts and a Fulbright Scholar.

172

THE ARTISTS *continued*

M Rocket is an artist, instigator, and community organizer, living in San Francisco with as many dogs as possible. You can see more work at their website, www.mrocket.squarespace.com

Maia Kobabe is a nonbinary, queer author and illustrator with an MFA in Comics from California College of the Arts. Eir first full length book, *GENDER QUEER: A MEMOIR* is forthcoming from Lion Forge in May 2019. Eir work focuses on themes of identity, sexuality, anti-fascism, fairy tales, and homesickness. Find eir work here: @redgoldsparks on tumblr and instagram.

Margo Rivera-Weiss, an artist/illustrator, lives in Oakland, CA with their wife Hadas and their pit bull Rosie. margoriveraweiss.com.

Pat Tong is a cartoonist living in Oakland with her wife Jenifer, four dogs, and several chickens. Contact her at camisado@aol.com; website at houseoftong.com.

Phoebe Kobabe is is a digital witch, gif magician, and painting conjuror. In 2013 she moved to L.A., the sparkle smog city, from the Bay Area and spends as much time as possible in nature. Find her work here: phoebekobabe.com and here: @phoroko

Rachael House is an artist who makes events, objects, performances, drawings, and zines. She exhibits inside and away from gallery spaces, locally and internationally. In the 1990s, her autobiographical comic zine *Red Hanky Panky* was part of a thriving UK queerzine scene. She enjoys smashing the patriarchy and making zines about her punk rock menopause. Rachael lives with her lover and a very splendid cat. www.rachaelhouse.com
Instagram @rachaellhouse

Soizick Jaffre is a teacher and comic artist based in France. She can be found on social networking sites. soizickjaffrecomics.com

Tara Madison Avery is a cartoonist, illustrator, editor, and the publisher of Stacked Deck Press. Her current projects are the trans/bi/poly romantic satire *Merrier*, and *Agents of A.S.C.E.N.D.*, a politically explicit take on superheroes in the age of Trump. Avery lives in southern California.

Tyler Cohen is a cartoonist who uses autobiography and surrealism to explore gender, parenthood, race, and female experience. Her book *Primahood: Magenta* won the 2017 Bisexual Book Award for Graphic Memoir. Her work has appeared online at *PEN Illustrated* and MuthaMagazine.com and in print in numerous anthologies. See more of her work at www.primazonia.com

INDEX

Made in the USA
Monee, IL
04 October 2022

15244296R00103